Memphis
Going Down

A Century of Blues, Soul and Rock 'n' Roll

History as Memoir

JAMES L. DICKERSON

SARTORIS
LITERARY
GROUP

A traditional publisher with a non-traditional approach to publishing

Sartoris Literary Group, Inc.
Jackson, Mississippi
www.sartorisliterary.com

To my mother,

Miss Juanita

OTHER BOOKS BY JAMES L. DICKERSON

Faith Hill
The Long Road Back

That's Alright, Elvis
The Untold Story of Elvis's First Guitarist
 and Manager, Scotty Moore

Just for a Thrill
Lil Hardin Armstrong, First Lady of Jazz

Go, Girl, Go!
The Women's Revolution in Music

Ashley Judd
Crying on the Inside

Mojo Triangle
Birthplace of Country, Blues, Jazz and Rock 'n' Roll

The Fabulous Vaughan Brothers
Jimmie & Stevie Ray

Trader Jon's
Cradle of U.S. Naval Aviation

Legend of the Soul Eater (novel)

Love on the Rocks: Romance to the Rescue (novel)

Two Women, One Man: A Memphis Love Story (novel)

Someone is Trying to Kill Me (novel)

CONTENTS

3

W.C. Handy, right, with trumpet
Photo courtesy of Memphis/Shelby County Public Library

4

CHAPTER 1

Let There Be Blues

In 1905 Memphis, Tennessee, had a national reputation, but not for music. It was the murder capital of the United States. Cocaine addiction was at epidemic proportions. And the city's booming sex industry was attracting ambitious, wild-eyed young girls from all over the Mid-South. With a population of 150,000, the city had over five hundred saloons, most of which had back rooms used for gambling and prostitution. Not surprisingly, the city was governed by underworld figures that forged an underground economy that entrenched them in the social fabric of the city for nearly a century.

For Memphis residents, 1905 began with a gruesome New Year's Eve murder. Readers of the city's morning newspaper, *The Commercial Appeal*, celebrated the New Year with the following headline:

**NEGRO DEMON BEATS THE HEAD OF HIS VICTIM
INTO UNRECOGNIZABLE MASS**

The story said that a black woman, Mattie Maben, had been bludgeoned to death while her husband was attending midnight church services. The killer, a black man, was quickly apprehended by neighbors and turned over to authorities. As horrible as the murder was, it was just one of many that month. On January 28 *The Commercial Appeal* ran a story bemoaning the fact that there were five black women in jail charged with killing their husbands. What was the city coming to if a man could no longer trust his wife?

It was the question on everyone's mind. A study done by the Prudential Insurance Company of America found that for the decade ending in 1910 Memphis had the highest homicide rate of 31 major cities surveyed. The author of the study called Memphis the "murder town" of the nation. It was a distinction the city would have for over three decades. Of course, murder was not the only problem facing the city.

Judge Moss, a county judge who enjoyed the support of the newspaper, declared war on gambling. NO MERCY ON CRAP SHOOTERS, read one headline. JUDGE MOSS LAYS DOWN THE LAW, DECLARES CRAP SHOOTING MUST CEASE AND NEGROES WORK.

"It seems to me the Negroes of Memphis have gone crazy on the subject of crap shooting," said Judge Moss from the bench. "You Negroes are needed in the cotton fields and should be there at work instead of gambling and shooting each other to pieces."

Into this social maelstrom walked W.C. Handy. The son of slaves, he was born in Florence, Alabama, in 1873, only eight years after the end of the Civil War. As a child it became clear to his family that he had a knack for music. His father, a God-fearing Methodist minister, let Handy know in no uncertain terms that he would prefer to have no son at all as to one who pursued a career in music.

But Handy could not suppress his love of music. While attending the Florence District School for Negroes, he sang in the school's choral group. One day, toward the end of his tenure at the school, an alcoholic fiddle player from Memphis, a man fleeing a love affair gone sour, stopped off long enough in Florence to organize an orchestra. The man befriended Handy and filled his head with colorful stories about Beale Street.

Without letting his father know, Handy got a cornet. As luck would have it, a circus became stranded in Florence at that time. To make a living, the white bandleader gave music lessons in the barber shop. Handy stopped by the barber shop every day after school. He peered through the windows and memorized the blackboard charts the bandleader made for his students. He applied that knowledge to the musical training he received in the choral group. By the time he left school, he was good enough as a musician to join a traveling minstrel show.

After several years of traveling the back roads of the South, Handy got his first big break. He was booked to play at a society barbecue in Henderson, Kentucky. There he met Carl Lindstrom, cornet soloist in the Gilmore Band, a famous group that had once counted John Philip Sousa among its members. Lindstrom urged

Handy to stick with his music career.

Encouraged by his experiences in Henderson, Handy decided to stay a while longer. He joined a band and met Elizabeth Price, the woman he later would marry. He discovered Henderson had a German choir of several hundred members. He was so impressed by the quality of the music he took a job as a janitor in their rehearsal hall so that he could learn their techniques.

After several more years of performing around the South, Handy got a job with a minstrel show based in Chicago. That didn't please Elizabeth's parents, who felt such work was only for lower class blacks. But the job paid well and Handy soon was able to afford a new Conn gold-plated trumpet. More years on the road followed.

In 1903 Handy settled in the Delta town of Clarksdale, Mississippi, where he formed a band. By that time he was a seasoned musician. His band performed for the usual functions—weddings, funerals, plantation events—and on occasion found work as a warm-up act for white politicians during election year campaigns. Typically, Handy would play the music of the day, and then sit quietly while the politicians baited his white audiences with promises to keep "the nigger" in his place. Handy pocketed the money, tolerated the racist talk and continued to grow as a musician.

It was during this time that he was influenced by the folk blues he heard in and around Clarksdale. It was not so much a musical form as it was a raw expression of poetic sentiment by black field hands who had been exposed to the counter-beat rhythms of the Choctaw and Chickasaw. It was expressed in hollers in the fields during the day and on the porches of shanties at day's end. Handy was moved by the emotionalism of the music and he felt a strange subterranean attraction to the rhythmic chants. But he was a classically trained musician, a trumpet player who felt an equal attraction to the European based music he had enjoyed since childhood. What on earth could he do with field hollers and obscure tribal chants? The question gnawed at him.

In 1905, at the age of 32, Handy relocated in Memphis. His impressions of the city, as expressed in his autobiography, indicate he was dazzled, if not overwhelmed, by the bright lights and excitement that greeted him on Beale Street. He set up shop at Pee Wee's Saloon, as did many other musicians.

"Through Pee Wee's swinging doors passed the heroic darktown figures of an age that is now becoming fabulous," wrote Handy. "They ranged from cooks and waiters to professional gamblers, jockeys and racetrack men of the period. Glittering young devils in silk toppers and Prince Alberts drifted in and out with insolent self-assurance. Chocolate dandies with red roses embroidered on cream waistcoats loitered at the bar. Now and again a fancy gal with shadowed eyes and a wedding-ring waist glanced through the doorway or ventured inside to ask if anybody had set eyes on the sweet good man who had temporarily strayed away."

At this time, Beale Street was the most prominent gathering place for blacks in the nation. But, unlike other entertainment districts of that era, Beale Street was not racially segregated. White-owned and black-owned businesses thrived side by side, as both white and black customers gathered to gamble, drink, whore, pawn valuables, shop, snort cocaine and dance the night away. The street itself was several blocks in length and ended at the Mississippi River on a bluff that served as a natural levee that protected the city during times of high water.

Pee Wee's Saloon was popular with musicians because Pee Wee, whose real name was Vigello Maffei, would allow them to congregate there. Pee Wee, a diminutive Italian, and his son-in-law, Lorenzo Pacini, further endeared themselves to musicians by taking phone messages for them.

One of the street's oldest bars was Hammitt Ashford's saloon at Beale and Fourth. Ashford, a light-skinned black who dressed fashionably and wore a diamond stick-pen in his tie, presided over what was probably the most popular joint on the street. With an elegant mahogany bar and marble table tops, it had an air of decency about it. The classiest nightspot was probably the Monarch Club. It boasted mirrored walls, cushioned seats and a brass-railed mahogany bar.

Also setting his sights on Beale Street was a transplanted Mississippian named E.H. Crump. A tall, gangly, red-headed man with the gift of gab, Crump married a Memphis socialite and invested in a buggy business. Before long, he got involved in politics and it is said that he was not opposed to using his fists to settle political differences of opinion. In 1905, at the age of 31, he won a seat on the city's lower legislative council. It was the chance intersection of the lives of those two men—Crump and Handy— that would forever change American music history.

As Handy settled into the music scene, Crump settled into the backwater politics of the era. For Handy that meant, playing the music of the era: polkas, waltzes, one-steps. For Crump, it meant pursuing the black vote. He had seen the future and the future was black with promise. As Handy and Crump cemented their separate destinies, Beale Street flaunted its bare-assed wildness for all to see.

The Commercial Appeal pleaded for someone to do something about the crime problem. A murder was being committed almost every day. Armed robberies were occurring with even greater frequency. A black community leader, Professor Willie Councill, let it be known that he had found the solution, and before an audience of 1200 at the Church Park auditorium, he summoned all the oratorical splendor at his command to denounce the influence of "coon songs."

"Make the young negroes [sic] turn from coon songs and go to the songs of our mothers and fathers," the professor pleaded. "The coon songs. . . make sentiment against us."

Ever the romantic, Handy, who had played his share of so-called "coon" music as a minstrel musician, saw only good things in the city. On the surface Beale was a thriving entertainment district that attracted whites as well as blacks. Women often were well dressed. Skirts were worn angle length at that time and hats were gaudy and adorned with handsome plumes. Furs were a common sight. A catalog of the day for Ell Jay Garments advertises blue-gray Russian wolf wraps for $6.95 and tailored "imported Persian lamb cloth" coats for $22.75. Unlike nightclubs in other cities, the Beale Street clubs had an open door policy for women performers.

Unhappy with the way city politics was structured, Crump led a campaign to re-shape the government. He successfully lobbied the General Assembly in Nashville for the creation of a commission form of government. The new form combined the functions of the

9

legislative and executive branches, creating a five-member commission that would be presided over by the mayor. In 1909 Crump decided to run for the office of mayor. The commission form of government went into effect in 1910. If he won, Crump would become the first mayor to serve as head of the commission.

Crump ran against a political machine that was engrained in the white power structure of the city. His only hope of victory lay with a combination of white and black votes. He ran on a reform ticket, which endeared him to many white voters, but his promises to clean up the gambling dens were not popular among black voters. For them, anti-gaming rhetoric was code talk for punishing blacks. To boast his popularity among blacks, one of Crump's political committees hired Handy to compose a campaign song for Crump.

Handy needed a song that would appeal to black voters, yet not alienate white voters. A song that could be played on both sides of the tracks. Handy racked his brains. What kept coming to him was the music he had heard in Clarksdale. Once, at one of those Delta dances that had become a staple for his nine-piece band, he was asked if some local boys could perform a few songs. Handy was apprehensive when three raggedly dressed black men took the spotlight, but when the men performed "a rain of silver dollars began to fall." Handy wrote in his autobiography: "The boys lay more money than my nine musicians were being paid for the entire engagement. Then I saw the beauty of primitive music."

Handy decided to write a campaign song for Crump that would combine the emotional appeal of the "primitive music" from the Delta with the classical familiarity of orchestra music. Up until that point, the blues had been confined to cheap guitars, washboards, and empty jugs. At that time, the standard measure for popular American music was the sixteen-bar strain. Handy based his campaign song, titled "Mister Crump," on the twelve-bar, three-line structure of the folk blues. He added a tango rhythm bass line and a three-cord harmonic structure. Then he wrote parts for the instruments in his band. When he finished, he had a song with African rhythms and European harmonies.

Handy later wrote lyrics for the song to give to visiting bands. The lyrics poked fun at Crump and his promises of reform. "Luckily for us, Mr. Crump himself didn't hear us sing these words. But we were hired to help out over his campaign, and since I knew that reform was about as palatable to Beale Street voters as castor oil, I was sure those reassuring words would do him more good than harm," Handy later wrote. Crump won the election by a mere 79 votes and went on to establish a political dynasty that lasted more than four decades. Encouraged by the positive reaction to "Mr. Crump," Handy re-wrote the lyrics and changed the name of the song to "The Memphis Blues." He offered it to the major music publishers in New York. All turned him down.

Three years later, dejected but confident of the song's worth, he turned to a local music store for help. The white store manager told him that if he would get the song sheets printed, he would sell them there in the store. That sounded like a good deal to Handy. In 1912, Handy's self-published version of "The Memphis Blues" went on sale. Unfortunately, Handy was unable to get the other stores in town to sell the music. After a while, his partner told him the music had stopped selling. He offered to reimburse him for the printing costs in exchange for the copyright to the song. Thinking he had hit a dead-end with the song, Handy agreed. As a result, the "Father of the Blues" was shut out of receiving any royalties from "The Memphis Blues" until the copyright expired and reverted back to Handy. That took 28 years.

"The Memphis Blues" spread like wildfire, south to New Orleans and north to Chicago. Soon it was all the rage in New York. Handy went on to write a number of hit songs: "The St. Louis Blues," "The Beale Street Blues," and "Joe Turner Blues," to name a few. Handy moved to Chicago in 1918 and then to New York, where he established a publishing house. He died in 1958 at the age of 85. He lived to see Memphis honor his achievement, when in 1931 the city named a park on Beale Street after him.

W.C. Handy didn't invent the blues. His accomplishment was to merge black folk blues with European instrumentation and harmonic structure. That union created a new musical form, one that combined the raw energy of his African heritage with the stoic discipline of his European-influenced education. He defined blues as we know it today. Along the way, he launched a revolution in American music.

*   *   *

11

Apart from being the home of the blues, Memphis had another distinction at the turn of the century. Beale Street was the only entertainment district in the nation openly hospitable to women entertainers. They were provided a safe environment in which to perform and afforded equal status with men.

Unfortunately, that enlightened attitude was not the result of a premature flowering of feminism in the musky, bare-knuckled river town, but due to the fact that black women, along with cocaine and whisky, were the currency of choice in a man's world. Since their economic value was so high, black women were protected from the rowdiness of male patrons and encouraged to work on the street as entertainers. By the 1980s, the equation would change—white women would become the currency of choice—but the formula itself has not changed since the turn of the century.

Three of the best known blues women of that era associated with Beale Street are Alberta Hunter, Memphis Minnie and Lil Hardin, the second wife of Louis Armstrong. Of the three, Alberta and Lil fled Beale to escape what record producer Jim Dickinson, paraphrasing bluesman Sleepy John Estes, once called "the center of all evil in the known universe." Only Memphis Minnie, perhaps the most accomplished female guitarist who ever lived, succumbed to the temptations of the street and supplemented her earnings as a performer by working as a prostitute. But who can fault her for that? The times were tough. She did what it took to survive. Beside, by all accounts, she was addicted to the pleasures associated with sex.

Alberta Hunter was actually born on Beale Street. Her father, Charles Hunter, worked as a Pullman porter, a job that gave him high social status in the black community. Her mother, Laura Peterson Hunter, worked as a chambermaid in one of the street's more elegant whorehouses. In those days prostitution carried a much higher social status than it does today. For a black woman of that era, becoming a prostitute was seen as a way to advance herself socially, comparable, by today's standards, to becoming a corporate lawyer or physician. Alberta's father abandoned the family before she was old enough to remember him and, after living with her grandmother for a number of years, Alberta and her mother rented a room at 170 Beale, where she grew up in the heart of the district. It was there that she developed her passion for music. In particular, the Handy Band, with its bright uniforms and glitzy instruments, grabbed her attention as they marched and strutted up and down the street outside her apartment. "We'd hear that ta-da, ta-da of the band, and Lord, we'd be out the door so fast," she told Frank Taylor, co-author of *Alberta: A Celebration in Blues.*

Alberta began singing at an early age and there is evidence she performed as a teenager at the famous Palace Theater, which featured the top black entertainers of the day. In later years, Duke Ellington, Count Basie and Ella Fitzgerald would be frequent headliners at the theater. Special shows for whites would be offered once a week and they usually featured girlie shows for a predominately male audience. Sometimes there were problems. Men often rushed the stage to get at the dark-skinned women and a great deal of diplomacy was required of the management to maintain order. Because of the reputation of the street, Alberta in later years always denied performing there. "I always wanted to stay away from anything that had a reputation of being bad," she told Taylor. Any woman who sang on Beale, she reasoned, would have a reputation for being bad. If singing on Beale had been her only chance for success, she said, she would "rather not have the chance." But, despite her denials, there is evidence she did succumb to the bright, naughty lights of Beale. In 1948, while visiting Memphis for a performance, she expressed regret to a newspaper reporter that she would not be able to visit Anselmo Barrasso, owner of the Palace Theater. The newspaper credited Barasso with discovering Alberta as a teenager and giving her the opportunity to appear on his stage.

In 1911, at the age of 16, Alberta boarded a train for Chicago. She landed her first real job at Dago Frank's, a well known hangout for prostitutes and pimps. Alberta sang for the johns who waited their turns with the prostitutes. Of course, Alberta's criticisms of the wicked lifestyle of Beale may have deeper psychological roots than would appear on the surface. Alberta was a lesbian and those complex, socially unacceptable feelings, when mixed with the normal surging hormones of a teenager, may have led her to project the "wickedness" of her own feelings onto the prostitutes.

It also could explain why she fled Memphis at such an early age. If prostitutes were wicked for selling themselves to men, how much more wicked must she be, in her mind, for wanting to be with the prostitutes herself? Even so, as her job at Dago Frank's indicates, she could run but she couldn't hide from herself.

Alberta thrived in Chicago. Her soulful, soprano voice made her a favorite in nightclubs, where cash-heavy mobsters often sent her home with tips of $400-$500 a night. In 1921 she went to New York to record at a small studio named Black Swan. The following year Paramount kicked off its "race" series with her recordings, making Alberta one of the first women to record the blues. As composer of "Downhearted Blues," Bessie Smith's first big hit, she attracted attention from other singers and composers, including her childhood idol W.C. Handy, who selected her to introduce his new work. By 1923 she had replaced Bessie Smith in the Broadway musical *How Come?* She continued to record for Paramount throughout the 1920s. In 1927, following an abortive marriage, she went to London on vacation. While there Oscar Hammerstein and Jerome Kern asked her to audition for *Showboat*. Competing against a white woman, she got the role and by the end of the decade her version of "Can't Help Lovin' Dat Man" made her an international star.

After two decades of success, she retired in the early Fifties to care for her ailing mother. When her mother died in 1954, she decided to quit singing. The day after her mother died, she enrolled in nursing school and worked as a hospital nurse for the next 20 years. "I've always been liberated," she told author Sally Placksin, "because I've always made my own, and you know, I've always been independent and never asked anybody for anything, and never wanted anybody to give me anything."

Alberta Hunter died in 1984, but not before staging a spectacular comeback in the 1970s. She appeared on television's Today Show on a regular basis and wrote the musical score for Robert Altman's movie, *Remember My Name*. The greatest moment of her life occurred in the 1970s, she frequently told interviewers, when she sang for President Jimmy Carter at the White House.

14

It was while performing at the Dreamland in Chicago in the early 1920s that Alberta first met fellow Memphian Lil Hardin and her husband Louis Armstrong, who also were booked at the popular nightspot. Like Alberta, Lil had fled the wickedness of Memphis to find a better life. Unlike Alberta, Lil had enjoyed a black middle-class upbringing. Born in 1902 or 1898 (she gave conflicting dates) her father died when she was two years of age. Raised by her mother and grandmother, both of whom hated the blues and banned it from their house, Lil was enrolled for piano lessons in the first grade. From the beginning she was nudged toward a career as a church organist. But Lil had other ideas. Once she was beaten with a broomstick by her mother after a copy of "The St. Louis Blues" was found in her possession.

The attitude of Lil's mother was not unusual in those days. Sex was inextricably linked with blues and jazz. It was not a prejudice. It was a fact of life. Once, in conversation with jazz legend Miles Davis, I made the mistake (in his eyes) of referring to his music as jazz. "Don't say that, man," he growled, his raspy voice scraping against his diaphragm. "It means Uncle Tom and stuff like that. To me it does. Know what I'm saying? What you call jazz is an old Negro thing. If the white man heard jazz, he didn't want his daughter to listen to it because it might want to make her fuck black men . . . and shit like that—and smoke marijuana. You understand what I'm saying? If a girl goes out with a man, and the father asks what he does, and she says he plays jazz, that girl will get locked up." In Davis' eyes, jazz was linked with white prejudice. If so, it was a two-way street. Often it was black parents who first pulled out the broomstick when their daughters talked about blues and jazz.

Lil may have been rebellious, but she was no fool. To placate her mother, she became the organist for her Sunday school. Years later, on a record titled *Satchmo and Me*, she talked about those tug-o-war days with her musical self: "I was supposed to be the organist for the Sunday school, and one piece especially I remembered was 'Onward Christian Soldiers.' I might have known I was gonna end up in jazz, because I played 'Onward Christian Soldier' with a definite beat . . . and the pastor used to look at me over his glasses, you know, but I didn't know I had that beat. I had it, but I didn't know it was gonna be jazz."

Determined to shield her from the evils of Beale—and ever hopeful of making a lady out of her jazz-crazed offspring—her mother enrolled her in the music program at Fisk University in Nashville. While Lil was at Fisk her mother moved to Chicago. After completing two years at the college, she returned to Memphis for a year or so, and then joined her mother in Chicago sometime between the summer of 1916 and 1918.

What happened to Lil upon her return to Memphis? What made her suddenly run to the domineering mother she had so desperately tried to escape since she was a young teen? Lil never said, but history shows that the summer of 1916 was a particularly violent one on Beale Street. Mayor Crump had consolidated his power with the help of Beale Street businessmen and black political ward chiefs. In an effort to tighten his grip on the city, Crump announced in 1914 that he was running for sheriff and planned to hold both offices.   C.P.J. Mooney, editor of *The Commercial Appeal*, was outraged. He put the full force of the newspaper behind efforts to stop Crump, who eventually backed down and ran his own man for sheriff. Crump's man won and Mooney grew more determined to break the Crump machine, which by that point had become not so much a political machine as a crime syndicate operating under the cover of a political machine.

The opportunity to put Crump away came in 1915, when the mayor refused to enforce newly enacted state Prohibition laws. The liquor and cocaine trade was the basis of his political machine. Crump couldn't shut it down without shutting himself down. Mooney stepped up his attacks. The state attorney brought suit against Crump to oust him from office.

Since Crump publicly vowed not to shut down the liquor and drug trade, the state easily won its case. But Crump had a loophole. Before the lawsuit had been brought, he had been elected to a second 4-year term that was to begin in January 1916. When Crump let it be known he would be returning as mayor on that date, *The Commercial Appeal* made it clear it would oppose him every step of the way. Rather than fight the newspaper, he waited six weeks after the date he was supposed to take office, then arranged to be sworn in on a holiday when the courts were closed. He handpicked his successor, then promptly resigned, but not before collecting six weeks backpay.

Crump learned a valuable lesson that was adhered to by organized crime interests in Memphis for decades: *The Commercial Appeal* was the only institution in the city powerful enough to challenge their interests.

The following year, in 1916, William Latura, who owned one of the city's well-known gambling establishments, began making threats against law enforcement officials. The threats were taken seriously. In 1908 Latura, who went by the nickname of Wild Bill, strolled into Hammett Ashford's Saloon at Beale and Fourth and gunned down seven black patrons. Joe Mack, who was in the club but escaped, told police what happened: "I was standing at the pool table furtherest from the door when a white man whom I recognized as Latura entered the door. He came through the door slowly, looked around and began to shoot. I hid under a table or I think he would have shot me. I don't know how many times he fired. One of the boys whom he shot begged him, as he fell, not to shoot him again. Soon after Latura came in another man walked in and stayed about five minutes and then went out. Then I called the police."

Latura was charged with the murders, but never convicted. Over the next several years he was arrested thirty-five times for liquor law violations. Finally, he was brought in on gambling charges, convicted, and sentenced to three years in prison. It was while his case was on appeal and he was out on bond that he made threats against the police chief. With Crump out of office, he, along with most of the city's five hundred or so club owners felt desperate. Police Chief Oliver Perry's response to the threats was short and to the point: "Get Latura."

Two police officers, Sandy Lyons and Charlie Davis, recently docked 10 days pay by the chief for looking the other way during Latura's criminal activities, confronted Latura outside his club. Latura cursed the police officers. "I said, 'Bill don't curse me that way,'" Officer Lyons said in his report. "He had used some hard names to me. He said, 'Aw, I'll kill you, you . . .' I said, Bill, you are under arrest.' He said, 'Aw, you can't arrest me. I'll kill you sure

17

enough.' Then he started to draw and I beat him to it."

Lyons and Davis pumped four shots into Latura. Then, fearing retaliation by Lutura's friends, they left him dying on the street and returned to headquarters. But they took their time—about 45 minutes. When they arrived and made their report, the acting captain dispatched an emergency car to the scene. They found Latura lying in the street surrounded by curious onlookers. Latura's young daughter and his chauffeur were comforting the still conscious man. The police officers loaded him into the car, but he died before they reached the hospital.

* * *

A wild night life was one thing, but the unrelenting violence common on Beale Street must have had an impact on Lil's tender sensibilities. Beale was not a huge district. Basically, the clubs, brothels and gambling dives that supported the night life were located in a two-block area. Whether Lillian was influenced by the Wild Bill Latura incident or not, we may never know. We know that shortly after the shooting occurred she left for Chicago. To her mother's horror, she took a $3-a-week job as a demonstrator at a local music store. Sheet music, not records, was the big ticket item in those days. Stores hired musicians to entice customers into purchasing sheet music.

A slender, very attractive young woman, Lil quickly became a popular attraction at the store, a favorite hangout for jazz musicians. She was more comfortable playing Bach and Chopin than jamming with the jazzmen that came in the store, but when she was asked to audition for the New Orleans Creole Jazz Band, she jumped at the chance. She was hired and her income jumped to $27.50 a week. She was afraid to tell her mother she had joined a jazz band, so she told her she was working at a dance studio. When her mother found out the truth, she blew her top. Lil talked her into meeting the guys in the band. One can only guess at the level of skepticism with which she greeted them, but they obviously were on their good behavior because she gave her consent for Lil to play in the band on condition someone walk her little girl home at night.

That gig lasted only a few months, but by that time Lil was hooked—not so much on the music, but on the money (in later years she recalled seeing someone tip Alberta Hunter $300)—and she did what jazz musicians have always done when a gig comes to an end: She joined another group. Poor Mama Hardin! She must have been praying 24 hours a day at that point for the deliverance of her daughter from the clutches of the jazz demon. By 1920 or so Lil had joined King Oliver's Creole Jazz Band, one of the best known groups of that era. They performed at Dreamland, Chicago's most elegant nightclub, and occasionally at an after-hours club frequented by mobsters. There are reports Mama Hardin herself sometimes showed up early in the morning to escort her daughter home. In search of a broader horizon, King Oliver took the band to California, but Lil was unhappy there and returned to Chicago, where she took a job as the house pianist at Dreamland.

After a while King Oliver made his way back to Chicago and restructured his band. In 1922 he hired a hot, young cornet player out of New Orleans named Louis Armstrong. That in itself is a mystery since he hired Louis to play second cornet behind himself. Bands then generally did not contain two instruments of the same type, so his addition of Louis was viewed with suspicion by other musicians. Pleased with his new acquisition, he took Louis by Dreamland to meet Lil. Louis was 5-feet-four, weighed over 200 pounds and had an awkward appearance.

Lil was not impressed. "Everything he had on was too small for him," she later recalled. "His atrocious tie was dangling down over his protruding stomach and to top it off, he had a hairdo that called for bangs, and I do mean bangs. Bangs that jutted over his forehead like a frayed canopy."

Sparks flew, like King Oliver hoped, but they were the wrong sparks. Lil recently had married an aspiring singer named Jimmy Johnson, and she simply wasn't interested in Louis. It seems obvious King Oliver was trying to impress Louis. By that time, Lil had grown into a beautiful woman. She was slender at a time when black women tended toward corpulence and she represented the epitome of elegance. If leggy, supermodels had been in existence then, Lil could have qualified for membership in that exclusive club. More important, she was educated and could do what none of the other musicians could do, including King Oliver and Louis Armstrong: she could read music. Mama Hardin had done her job well. Lil was a class act.

Enter Louis Armstrong. For the past several years he had been working on the Dixie Bell, a riverboat that plowed the Mississippi River between New Orleans and St. Louis with a 12-piece band. The boat would have made regular stops at Memphis, but by then Lil had already moved to Chicago. In 1918 Louis married Daisy Parker, a hot tempered prostitute who liked to work the dance halls frequented by black roustabouts. They fought like dogs and cats, frequently with knives, fists, whatever they could find, and either or both were arrested on numerous occasions. Daisy was pretty, but she was illiterate and Louis' associates felt it was beneath him to marry a prostitute, especially one who couldn't read. But Louis was in love and wouldn't listen to his friends.

Eventually, King Oliver persuaded Lil to return to the band. More out of sympathy than anything else, Lil befriended Louis and showed him around town and introduced him to her friends. Then she began to notice his music. King Oliver whispered into her ear that Louis was someone she should keep her eye on, and she did, even more so as her marriage began to deteriorate. When the group made its first recording in 1923, Lil noticed that King Oliver had Louis stand far away from the microphone, to reduce his presence on the record, and her heart went out to him.

Before she knew it, she had fallen in love. Louis was stunned to discover she was interested in him. By Louis' standards, Lil was an absolute goddess, not only in appearance, but by breeding. He wasn't in her social class, and he knew it. With the same determination she had shown in making a place for herself in a man's world, Lil set out to rehabilitate Louis. She taught him how to dress (he preferred second hand clothing), she persuaded him to lose about 50 pounds (he had a voracious appetite) and she urged him to stand up for himself with King Oliver. Most important, she gave him confidence in himself as a musician. Then, having accomplished all that, she arranged for divorces for the two of them. Lil and Louis were married on February 5, 1924.

Lil's devotion to Louis' career did not go unnoticed by King Oliver, who tried to drive a wedge between them. He spoke badly of Lil. The disharmony spread to other band members.

Baby Dodds, the drummer, once punched Louis off the stage. King Oliver started carrying a pistol. Lil knew what she had to do. "I thought the main thing was to get him away from Joe (King Oliver) . . . He's a fellow who didn't have much confidence in himself to begin with. He didn't believe in himself."

Lil pushed him, then pushed him some more. Finally, he quit the band, though he didn't have the courage to tell King Oliver to his face. He sent a friend with the message. Afterward, he asked Lil, "Now what do I do?"

"Get a job," she said.

Louis went to Sammy Stewart, the leader of a popular dance band. Stewart turned him down. All the band members had light skins, and Louis was dark. Louis then tried Ollie Powers, who was putting together a new group for Dreamland. To Lil's delight, Louis got a job as first trumpet. Lil stayed on with King Oliver for a while, then she and Louis went to New York to join Fletcher Henderson's big band. Dissatisfied with New York, Lil contacted the manager at Dreamland and urged him to hire Louis as a headliner. The manager said no one knew who Louis was. Well, they know me, Lil reportedly told him. The manager agreed and allowed her to form her own group. She called it the Dreamland Syncopators. Louis played first trumpet.

Once they returned to Chicago, Lil was unrelenting in her efforts on Louis' behalf. Feeling the pressure, Louis sought out an agent, white Chicago nightclub owner Papa Joe Glaser.

"I told him I was tired of being cheated and set upon by scamps and told how my head was jumping from all of that business mess," Louis confided to Larry King years later. "Lil, one of my wives, had sweet-talked me into going out on my own to front some bands and it was driving me crazy—and I told him, 'Pops, I need you. Come be my manager. Please! Take care of all my business and take care of me. Just lemme blow my gig!' And goddamn that sweet man did it!"

Lil smiled all the way to the bank. Over the next few years, Lil devoted herself to Louis' career. Between 1925 and 1927 they recorded almost 50 songs, many of them written by Lil, including "Lonesome Blues," "Jazz Lips" and "The King of the Zulus."

When Louis recorded with the Hot Five and the Hot Seven, Lil always sat in on piano and arranged the music. She didn't perform many solos on the recordings because piano rifts were not in vogue at the time. All the time she was performing, writing and keeping Louis' career on track, she attended school. In 1928 she got a teacher's diploma from the Chicago College of Music and the following year she received a postgraduate degree from the New York College of Music.

Unfortunately, Louis' eye began to wander. They fought over his affairs, and separated on several occasions. In 1931, in the wake of Louis' New Orleans homecoming appearance, they separated for good. Lil had enough. He was making a $1000 a week and no longer needed her help. "We'll call it day," she said.

Lil returned to Chicago and focused on her own career. During the 1930s she formed two all-girl bands, one named the Harlem Harlicans. She also led a male band and became the house pianist at Decca. In later years, she took a WPA sewing class and learned to design clothes. Some of her creations, such as a cocktail gown she named "Mad Money," became famous, and Louis, himself, turned to her for the design of his dress coats. In addition, she taught French, gave piano lessons and wrote more than 150 songs, some of which -- "Struttin' With Some Barbecue" and "Original Boogie" became Louis' biggest hits. Lil wrote a song in the 1940s, "Just For a Thrill," that became a big hit for Ray Charles in the 1960s.

Sadly, Lil never stopped loving Louis. She never remarried and continued to wear the rings he had given him. She kept the cornet he played in the early days and preserved old letters and photographs. In later years, she retraced their steps, as if trying to relive the moments she shared with him, and she often visited a Michigan resort where they had vacationed as a couple.

I think time will show Lil Hardin Armstrong to be one of the grand ladies of American music—not just for her talent, which was considerable, nor for her persistent intellect, but for her admirable strength of character. She was a lady in every sense of the word, and, in some ways, more of a *man* than Louis ever was.

On August 27, 1971, six months after Louis' death, the city of Chicago held a tribute concert to honor his memory. Lil was invited to perform. Wearing a boldly patterned dress with long, elegant sleeves, she took the stage at the outdoor concert and, as if going full circle back to her Memphis roots, sat at the piano and played Handy's "St. Louis Blues." As she hit the final chord of the song—and as 2,000 fans watched in stunned disbelief—she fell over dead, the victim of a broken heart.

Lil knew how to make an exit.

E. H. Crump, c. 1930s
Photo courtesy of the Mississippi Valley Collection
University of Memphis, University Libraries

Beale Street at the turn of the century
Photo courtesy of the Mississippi Valley Collection
University of Memphis, University Libraries

Furry Lewis, c. 1960s
Photo courtesy of the Mississippi Valley Collection
University of Memphis, University Libraries

CHAPTER 2

The 1920s:
Furry, Minnie, Sleepy and Abe

In the 1920s Memphis music was dominated by four figures—Furry Lewis, Memphis Minnie, Sleepy John Estes and "Fiddling Abe" Fortas. Judging by newspaper accounts, "Fiddling Abe" was the most popular. You might say he was the white W.C. Handy of his generation. When he left Memphis in 1933 to take a post in the U.S. farm bureau, *The Press-Scimitar*, the city's evening newspaper, ran the following four-column headline in bold type:

Fiddling Abe Fortas, 22, Leaves Memphis Dancers
For High Legal Post With Uncle Sam's Farm Bureau

The reference to "Memphis dancers" was not a joke. The former U.S. Supreme Court justice—and one of the most influential men in President Lyndon Johnson's administration—was a product of the wild and woolly Beale Street music scene. The son of Orthodox Jewish immigrants who moved to Memphis from England at the turn of the century, Abe, born June 19, 1910, grew up on Pontotoc Street, a couple of blocks from Beale and about the same distance from the Lorraine Motel, where Martin Luther King was assassinated in 1968. Because his family was poor, they lived adjacent to a black neighborhood. Abe's father worked as a pawnbroker and jeweler, and was very much a player in the economics of Beale Street.

From the time Abe was a small child it was apparent to his father he needed to find his son a counterbalance to his slight, slender build. Because Abe's hands were noticeable for their delicate appearance, he encouraged his son to take violin lessons. By the age of 13, Abe was proficient enough on the violin to form a band which he named the Blue Melody Boys. The band earned $8 a night and became a popular attraction at social events in the city. It was during this period he was given the nickname "Fiddling Abe." Over the next four years, he earned enough money playing the fiddle to pay his way through a private college in Memphis, Southwestern University. He continued to perform during that time and for two years lead the school orchestra.

Abe never talked about Beale Street after he became successful, but considering the small geographic area it occupied it would have been impossible for him to avoid its gritty nightlife. Likewise, it would have been impossible for Abe not to have had at least a passing acquaintance with Memphis Minnie. They lived in the same neighborhood, competed for the same jobs, and, for the leader of the Blue Melody Boys, the allure of an attractive black woman who had a reputation for being a genius on the guitar and a slave to passion must have been difficult to ignore.

Throughout the 1920s, Memphis maintained its distinction as the murder capitol of the nation. Cocaine was sold by storekeepers in dime boxes and drug addiction soared. Police officials estimated addiction rates in the black community at between 60 to 70 percent of the population. Cocaine had been introduced into the city in 1902 with the opening of the Coca Cola Bottling Company of Memphis. The soft drink originally had been formulated by a pharmacist as a tonic and cocaine was the key ingredient. The drug was dropped from the formula in 1905, but not before local entrepreneurs forged a direct link with Columbian suppliers of the drug. But cocaine wasn't the only drug in demand on Beale. Morphine was also a popular drug and published accounts indicate it had a street value of $75 an ounce by the mid-1920s.

The city continued to be flooded with young girls, many of whom became prostitutes and cocaine addicts. Typically, the brothels contained both black and white women. White male patrons were admitted until 3 a.m., at which time black male patrons were allowed in the back door to partake of the leftovers. It was the only socially sanctioned means by which black men could have intercourse with white women. To help combat the problems caused by the influx of young girls into the city, the city organized the Woman's Protective Bureau in 1921. Under the direction of Mrs. Anna Whitmore, the bureau was charged with investigating each police case that involved a young girl.

In 1923 the bureau handled the cases of more than 1,100 young girls. That is an astonishing number when you consider that the total female population of the city was only about 75,000. A police reporter for the *Memphis Press* asked Mrs. Whitmore why so many girls were coming to Memphis: "A girl who fails to find encouragement from her parents when she is ambitious, is liable to leave home to fight it out alone .   . Other girls leave because they are unable to get the pretty clothes they desire. In the city, they think, they will be able to earn money to buy all the pretty clothes any girl could desire."

To deal with the growing cocaine problem, the city's narcotics division worked closely with the woman's bureau. In 1923, records show that 30 young female addicts where held in jail until they "got off" the drug and another 15 were sent to a hospital for treatment. "The 'cure' condemned in many cities, has been found to be successful there," reported the *Memphis Press.* "The 'cure' consists of placing the addicts in jail, and letting them stay there until they are off the drug. This has been condemned by doctors as a process of torture, which it really is. But police officials believe it is the only way to rehabilitate the addicts and place them back in society. A new world in another city is found for them so there will be no chance for their return to the land of the living dead."

Enterprising young men growing up on Beale Street quickly learned the benefits of introducing impressionable young women to free cocaine and easy money. William Faulkner often wrote about the Memphis brothels of this era in his novels, but many people mistakenly supposed his accounts to be fictitious. Of course, Memphis was not unique in that respect. Brothels were found in almost all American cities at that time. What made Memphis unique was the way drug dealers—and in those days many legitimate Memphis store owners were selling cocaine on the side—learned to pair the demand for the drug with the demand for women as a means of building economic and political empires. As a result of that expertise, Memphians developed the blueprints for the modern day drug syndicate and invented the money-laundering techniques now used by drug cartels the world over.

E. H. Crump kept a low public profile in the early 1920s. Six months after his resignation as mayor he was elected to the financially lucrative office of county trustee, a position he held for eight years. Not eager to tangle with *The Commercial Appeal*, he worked behind the scenes to strengthen his political machine, the likes of which the nation had never seen, not even in politically corrupt Chicago and New York. A profoundly cynical man, he saw a means to combine the profits of vice with the political clout of black voters in such a way as to magnify the influence of each.

Crump considered running a candidate in the mayoral election of 1919, but decided against it and, the day before the election, endorsed an independent candidate, Rowlett Paine. When Paine won by a hefty margin, as Crump knew would happen, Crump took credit for the victory. When the Ku Klux Klan flexed its muscle against Paine and others across the Mid-South whom they feared where falling under the influence of black voters, Crump saw an opening: He supported Paine for re-election against a candidate supported by the Klan. A superb editorial writer, C. P. J. Mooney unleashed the editorial might of *The Commercial Appeal* against the Klan. Mooney felt some discomfort at finding himself on the same side with Crump, but he did what he felt he had to do to stem the influence of the Klan. His leadership was recognized by the Pulitzer Prize committee in 1923 when it awarded *The Commercial Appeal* its gold medal for public service. Although it wasn't apparent at the time, Paine's re-election elevated Crump to a Southern-boy godfather status in the eyes of the Memphis underworld. He beat *The Commercial Appeal* at its own game.

In 1926, while working in his office at *The Commercial Appeal*, C. P. J. Mooney, who despised nothing on earth as much as crooked politicians, dropped dead at his desk, opening the door for his nemesis E. H. Crump to re-enter mayoral politics. The year after Mooney's death Crump jumped back into mayoral politics by offering a hand-picked candidate, Watkins Overton, to run against Paine. When the dust settled, Overton won by a margin of 19,806 to 7,080 votes.

With Mooney gone, Crump was free at last to be Boss.

*   *   *

Throughout the 1920s, Memphis music underwent significant changes. The sophisticated blues of the Teens introduced by Handy was replaced on Beale Street by its long neglected country cousin, the down-home blues. At $8 a gig, Fiddling Abe was one of the highest paid musicians in the city. There were a few good paying venues that wanted jazz bands, such as the ornate Peabody Hotel which first opened its doors in the 1920s; but most the musicians worked alone, and they performed wherever they could—in bars, at parties, barbecues, on the street corner—and their pay was measured in nickels and dimes, not dollars.

Walter "Furry" Lewis was one of the most talented bluesman to prowl Beale Street in the 1920s. Born in my hometown of Greenwood, Mississippi, sometime around the turn of the century (he was always a little fuzzy about the exact date) Furry moved to Memphis with his family as a teenager. He found work in the tent shows that came in and out of Memphis on a regular basis, and occasionally he performed with Handy's band. As Furry told it in later years, it was Handy who gave him his first quality guitar, a six-string Martin he used for decades, until he "wore it out." When Handy moved to New York, Furry went on the road with a medicine show, where he got more requests for jokes than music. He had always supplemented his income as a musician, so when he came in off the road he took at job as a street cleaner for the city of Memphis at 15 cents per hour. It was a job he would hold until 1966, when the city forced him to retire. It must have been difficult work for him. He lost one of his legs in 1916 while hopping a freight. He slipped and fell beneath the train. The wheels severed his leg and he had to learn to walk on an artificial one.

Furry is credited with inventing the bottle-neck style of guitar playing, but I am not sure how valid that claim is, though it is possible. Certainly, he was one of the best at performing in that style. He made his own bottle necks by wrapping a cotton shoestring around the base of a long bottle neck. He would set the shoestring on fire, the heat of which would enable the bottle neck to be removed in a clean break. He would slip the bottleneck over his finger and use it to fret his guitar, sliding it up and down to create the sound he wanted. He also had a unique way of using his guitar as a percussive instrument, at times using it as a rhythmic counterbalance to his fingering. In 1927 he took time off from his job as a street cleaner to go to Chicago to record five sides for the Vocalion label, which specialized in "race" music. Over the next couple of years he recorded another 18 songs, some in Memphis at a makeshift studio, for Vocalion and a second label, Victor Records.

By the time Don Nix, a major figure at Stax Records in the 1960s, met Furry in 1958 the bluesman had faded into obscurity. "I worked downtown at a TG&Y store, and I remember seeing him sweeping the street," says Nix. "He had a guitar in the little buggy he pushed. I knew who he was, but it wasn't until a year later that I actually heard him. He'd sit in Handy Park and play."

By the mid-1960s, Nix had adopted Furry. Often he let Furry stay at his house to recover from his frequent alcoholic binges. "One time I found him sleeping on these peoples' couch," Nix recalls. "He was real sick. He looked terrible and I was afraid he was going to die. I took him to my house and he stayed there the rest of the summer. One day he said, 'Don, I need some junk.' I said, 'Junk?' He said, 'Yeah, I need some souce and crackers.' So I went and bought him some rag souce (baloney). I realized that if you left Furry alone, he would bounce back if he was going to."

Sometimes Nix would spend the night at Furry's house when his girlfriend wasn't there to take care of him. She cleaned portable toilets for a carnival and was on the road during the summer months. When she was there, she took good care of him. Furry lived in a black neighborhood south of Beale. For Nix, with his middle class upbringing, staying at the two-room apartment was an exotic experience.

"It was the blues place," Nix says. "I would stay the night, sleeping in his kitchen, and not think anything about it." Nix pauses, his eyes glazing over with the memory of it. "Now I wish I could go back and stay *one more* night."

*   *   *

Throughout the 1920s Sleepy John Estes drifted in and out of Memphis from his hometown of Brownsville, Tennessee, becoming a familiar figure on Beale Street. Born in 1904, one of sixteen children, John Adams Estes grew up in a rural area where music was homemade if it was made at all. As a child he constructed a guitar out of a cigar box and a broom handle, and learned to make music on the single string he stretched along the handle. His father, a sharecropper, was impressed by what he heard and saved enough money picking cotton to buy his son a real guitar.

Sleepy John learned to play guitar by jamming with his neighbors. After mastering a few chords, he slung the guitar over his shoulder and hit the road. He performed wherever people would listen—at small gatherings, at harvest parties, at birthdays—but he never strayed far beyond the Memphis area. Usually, he received a free meal for his efforts. Every once in a while someone would give him a dollar. It was during this time he met 11-year-old Hammie Nixon, who was several years his junior. Hammie had a harmonica, so Sleepy John asked him to be his partner and go to Memphis with him. Hammie's mother wasn't too happy about that, but Sleepy John promised to bring him back the next day. They were gone six months.

For nearly 30 years, Sleepy John and Hammie performed together. Using Beale Street as a base, they worked in and around Memphis until they got wanderlust, then hopped a freight to hobo around the country until they got homesick, then they would return to Memphis. For many of the early bluesmen, playing the blues was as much a lifestyle as it was a vehicle for artistic expression. Memphis may have been home to Sleepy John and Hammie, but they never really liked the city. Sleepy John was once asked, which was the tougher town, Memphis or Chicago?

Memphis, he answered, offering his opinion that Memphis was the leader of dirty work in the world. Hammie echoed his friend's sentiments in an interview with Margaret McKee and Fred Chisenhall. "Beale Street wasn't nothing but good timers and guys walking the street and telling fortunes and conning you and cheating you," he says. When traveling, he discovered it was better not to admit his Memphis connections. "You know, when I first went to Chicago, I couldn't hardly get a room," he said. "I thought maybe it would help me to say I was from Memphis, but come to find out, everywhere I go, they'd say, 'You from Memphis? Oh, I done already rent that room out.' And finally someone told me, said, 'What you say you from Memphis for? Don't tell nobody you from Memphis, man.'"

In 1929 Sleepy John made several recordings in Memphis for Victor Records, including "Diving Duck Blues" and "Broken Hearted, Ragged and Dirty Too." The following year he cut additional sides—"Poor John Blues," "My Black Gal Blues" and "Milk Cow Blues." Over the next decade he recorded over three dozen additional songs, building a national reputation as a major country blues singer on the Decca and Chess labels. But by 1949 the party had ended. Sleepy John and Hammie returned to Memphis, where Sleepy John married and started a family, and Hammie found work as a chauffeur and cook. Two years later, Sleepy John lost his eyesight. With life in the city becoming more difficult, he moved his family to Brownsville, with Hammie in tow, and settled into the hard-times, rural lifestyle from which he had begun his life's journey.

After a decade of obscurity, Sleepy John and Hammie were "rediscovered" in the early Sixties by producer Bob Koester, who got them into the studio again and arranged for them to go to Europe on two occasions with the American Folk Blues Festival. He recorded new albums—*The Legend of Sleepy John Estes*, *Broke & Hungry* and *Brownsville Blues*—and he found a new, young, mostly white audience, but the years had taken their toll. His voice had lost its power and his failing health made performing a chore. On June 5, 1977, Sleepy John passed away. Hammie followed, as he was wont to do, in 1984, giving his traveling companion a good seven years head start.

*   *   *

Memphis Minnie, born Lizzie Douglas, grew up in Walls, Mississippi, just outside Memphis. A headstrong child, her parents called her "Kid" because she couldn't stand her feminine moniker. She had an equal disdain for farm work and, as a teen, often ran away from home for short periods to explore the bright lights and dim alleys of Beale Street. It was as a teen that she began to exploit her sexuality. An attractive woman with a petite build, she learned at an early age she had what Beale Street wanted. Of course, Beale Street had what she wanted: money and recognition.

With W. C. Handy setting musical standards for the street, Memphis Minnie (she adopted the name early in her career) did not immediately find a home for her rough-edged, country style of blues. She did what restless youngsters of that era did when they felt stifled: She joined the circus and toured the South. She learned to play the guitar at an early age and, touring the small towns that made up the circus circuit, she developed her own unique style. Circus life also taught her how to dress and capitalize on her good looks. By the time she returned to Memphis in the 1920s, Handy had moved on and the country style of blues she loved, as performed by Furry Lewis and Sleepy John Estes, was a hot-ticket item on Beale.

Memphis Minnie had a reputation as a fiery, sometimes violent, woman whose promiscuity for profit was the talk of the town. She craved sex, losing herself in its addictive surrender, and she used sex, brandishing it as a weapon to get what she wanted. Once, after a recording session for Decca, Minnie offered to have sex with Hammie Nixon and the other players in exchange for their share of the money.

Homesick James said he knew her before she got famous, when she was an outright streetwalker. Others said she liked to wear dresses when performing so that she could entice men into looking up her skirt. Not surprisingly, Minnie's music often reflected her experience as a prostitute. One song she wrote, "Hustlin' Woman Blues," tells of standing on the corner all night, not able to go home because she hadn't made enough money. Then there's "You Can't Give it Away," in which she taunts a prostitute for trying to sell something that "ain't good to eat" and "ain't good to smell." Minnie was one hell of a guitar picker, but she was no lady.

Whatever Minnie's contemporaries thought about her sexual activity, one thing was for certain: no one ever criticized her, at least not to her face. Despite her small size, her elegant jewelry and her gold-capped front teeth (a sign of status in the black community) she was feared, not so much for her physical strength as for her willingness to do whatever it took to win. Homesick James said she was tougher than any man he knew.

Men knew to keep their distance from Minnie. When angered, she would reach for whatever was handy—her guitar, a pistol, a knife—and she was not timid about using violence to get her way. Johnny Shines said Minnie had a reputation for violence that out-did anything anyone had actually ever witnessed. Attila the Hun could have learned a thing or two from Minnie. "They tell me she shot one old man's arms off, down in Mississippi," Shines told Paul and Beth Garon. "Shot his arm off, or cut it off with a hatchet, something. Some say shot, some say cut. Minnie was a hell raiser, I know that! . . . She'd work Son Joe over right on the band-stand, right in front of the whole audience. Bang, bop, boom, bop!"

Minnie dominated the Beale Street music scene throughout the 1920s, then after she recorded her first record in 1929 she dominated the national music scene, along with her husband Joe McCoy, throughout the 1940s and 1950s. She was the hottest woman blues artist of her day, recording an impressive string of over 100 records. Many of her songs such as "Bumble Bee," which she recorded in 1930, and "I'm Talking About You "became classics. As a guitarist, Minnie was without equal. Her influence extended long past her death. Guitarist Bonnie Raitt once told me Memphis Minnie was one of the reasons she became a performer, figuring that if Memphis Minnie, a woman, could play the hell out of a guitar, so could she.

After working out of Memphis for several years, Minnie and Joe moved to Chicago in the early 1930s, where Minnie established herself among the city's other blues artists. After she and Joe parted company in 1935, she married guitar player Ernest "Son" Lawlar. Throughout the 1940s, she often participated in guitar playing contests, which would find her facing off challengers such as Muddy Waters. They would take turns playing; then the audience would pick the winner. Minnie usually took home the prize, a fifth or two of whiskey, and her male challengers usually conceded defeat with dignity but not without pointing out that Minnie probably won because she was a woman and had a skirt to lift at just the right moment.

By 1958 recording sessions had become a thing of the past and bookings had dried up, so Minnie and Son moved back to Memphis, where she performed on a regular basis in black nightclubs, at fish fries, wherever she could find work. Minnie suffered a stroke, then Son died in 1961, prompting a second, more serious stroke, and she spent the remainder of her life in a wheelchair unable to speak. Sadly, she became an oddity around Memphis, a name without a voice.

In 1968, after hearing about her desperate financial situation, a British blues band held a fund-raiser in London for the ailing blues legend. Proudly they sent the check to America. A party was held at the nursing home where Minnie was living, family members were called in, a newspaper reporter and photographer showed up to document the event, and Minnie was given the money with great ceremony—a total of *$117.58*. According to a reporter, she spoke only one word: "Thanks." Surely, the party-goers were lucky Minnie was paralyzed and unable to express her outrage at such a paltry offering.

Minnie died on August 6, 1973, and was buried in an unmarked grave. In the final years of her life, she spent her days in a wheelchair, a weeping, voiceless, pitiful creature, alone and without the two things that mattered most to her, sex and music.

Sam Chatmon at home in Hollandale, 1980
Photo © Steve Gardner

CHAPTER 3

The 1930s:
Lunceford, Memphis Slim Raise the Bar

As the decade began, the Great Depression was little more than a flickering firefly on the horizon. City leaders told Memphians not to worry, that King Cotton would insulate the city from the effects of the Depression. In good times or bad, Memphis maintained its distinction as the murder capitol of the nation, a fact that attracted the attention of the national press.

By mid decade the situation had become so desperate FBI Director J. Edgar Hoover sent a special envoy to Memphis to examine the city's homicide records. Baffled by the slaughter, the FBI envoy told city officials that if they classified some homicides as self-defense, the city's murder rate would look better to the public. The police chief agreed to do that, but told reporters the real solution to the city's murder rate was for the federal government to control the sale and distribution of firearms.

The plentiful supply of alcohol and cocaine in Memphis also was the subject of national speculation. In 1931, *Redbook* magazine noted that Memphis had a speakeasy for every three hundred inhabitants, making it worse than Chicago when it came to alcohol use among the "young society set." In 1935, Colliers' Magazine, citing "7,000 professional sinners," attacked the city for its tolerance of narcotics and prostitution.

Beale Street, its dives and brothels humping the money beast like there was no tomorrow, thrived, filling the pockets of crime syndicates. But as the decade progressed and the dollars from the cotton plantations dried up, the entertainment district began a slow descent into economic oblivion. Country blues, as performed by Sam Chatmon, Bukka White and Lillie May Glover, was still the main fare in the clubs, but the more refined musical interpretations of Jimmie Lunceford and Peter Chatman, better known as Memphis Slim, exerted subtle influences on the music scene that eventually had a major impact.

Jimmie Lunceford arrived in Memphis in 1926 by way of Fulton, Missouri, where he was born, and Fisk University in Nashville, from which he received a bachelor of music degree. While teaching music at Manassa High School in Memphis, he put together a student dance band. They played in and around Memphis during the summer months, attracting a lot of attention. Encouraged by that success, Lunceford added three professional musicians in 1929, all former students at Fisk, and put together a first-rate orchestra. By 1930 the group was really cooking, but Lunceford avoided any association with Beale, preferring more staid bookings as a dance band at white society functions. The degree to which white society accepted Lunceford is reflected in the fact that radio station WREC invited his orchestra to perform live on a regular basis.

There were no black radio stations in the city at that time and racial segregation was the order of the day, except on Beale Street, where the only color that mattered was green. All over the city, restrooms and water fountains were labeled for "whites" and "coloreds." Restaurants would not serve blacks and hotels would not register them as guests. Theaters, if they admitted blacks at all, required them to sit in the balcony. The only way blacks could participate in white social events was as food servers or entertainers. I am sure black activists would today consider him an Uncle Tom—he led his orchestra with a long, white baton and dressed elegantly, a gentleman among barbarians—but I don't think he was being accommodating to white society so much as living out a fantasy of how society, white and black, should conduct itself.

Lunceford was a strict bandleader. He did not drink or use drugs. He preached to his orchestra about respectability and he would not tolerate musicians who crossed the line. If you do not respect yourself, he told them, the public will not respect your music. Considering his disdain for any deviation from his strict Protestant upbringing (his father was a choir master), it is not surprising Lunceford left Memphis at the first opportunity. After touring in the northeast, Lunceford took the group—then named the Chickasaw Syncopators, after the Indian tribe that first settled the Memphis bluffs—into New York City, where they took up residency at the legendary Cotton Club. Throughout the 1930s, Lunceford's jazz orchestra was one of the most influential in the nation.

What Lunceford learned in Memphis was very much a music phenomenon unique to the city. His gift was as an arranger, not as a composer, but in much the same way Handy blended music styles, Lunceford blended instruments with spectacular results. He played a significant role in the development of swing, and by the 1940s Glenn Miller and Benny Goodman had built upon his precise, melodic arrangements to take swing to a new level. Unfortunately, Lunceford did not make the transition during the 1940s and was content to maintain his status as a show band leader. In that capacity, Lunceford appeared in a number of movies, including "Blues in the Night."

"The music of Lunceford's mid-1930s' glory days was, for a moment in time, the very best that jazz had to offer," observes music historian Gunther Schuller. "The Lunceford band, second only to Ellington and for a few brief years even more consistent than his, reigned supreme for a while—until Basie and Goodman came along and, combined with Ellington's full maturing in the late thirties, pushed Lunceford to the sidelines artistically. But the Lunceford band at its best—and fortunately in recorded form it is still with us—was something wonderful to admire and cherish, a still timeless music, and a superior, significant part of our American musical heritage."

In the summer of 1947 Lunceford made a personal appearance at a music store in Seaside, Oregon. While signing autographs he collapsed in the store and was taken to a hospital. On July 12, at the age of 45, he died. The cause of death was listed as food poisoning. There were rumors he had been murdered, but nothing was ever proved.

While Lunceford was basking in the bright lights of New York—and Fiddling Abe was joining the faculty of Yale law school—their country cousins on Beale Street were experiencing hard times. Between 1930 and 1932, unemployment in Memphis rose from 4,000 to 17,000 as the city felt the effects of the Depression. Fewer jobs meant fewer dollars for Beale Street, but the dollars that did get there were desperate for entertainment— and cocaine.

One of the ever-present sights on Memphis streets during the early 1930s was the Memphis Jug Band, a blues group that reconfigured country music into a distinct style of blues. Using jugs to create bass lines, the musicians also made use of guitars, pianos, mandolins, harmonicas, and kazoos to create popular songs such as "I Whipped My Woman with a Single-Tree and "I Can Beat You Plenty."

Incredibly, the band recorded between 70 and 100 records between the late 1920s and 1935 for major record labels such as Victor and OKeh. The band's memberships changed over the years, but the one constant was Will Shade, who sometimes went by the name of "Sun Brimmer." The band performed in every venue imaginable, from street corners and political rallies, to juke joints across the state line in Mississippi.

Among the best of the peripatetic country bluesmen who breezed in and out of Beale Street during this time was guitarist Sam Chatmon, a member of the Mississippi Sheiks, and a relative of Memphis Slim, who spelled his name Chatman. From the turn of the century, the Chatmon family—there were at least nine full brothers and maybe as many half brothers, all the sons of a former slave—made up one of the best touring bands in the South. From their hometown of Bolton, Mississippi, they made their way through Tennessee and Illinois and occasionally into Georgia performing at white parties and picnics. They usually went by the name Mississippi Sheiks, but they sometimes called themselves the Blacksnakes or the Mud Steppers. They recorded their first records in the late 1920s, but it was during the 1930s they made their biggest impact, recording nearly 100 songs. Their most successful records were "Stop and Listen" and "Sitting on Top of the World,' which became a national hit in the early 1930s and was covered in later years by Frank Sinatra, the Grateful Dead and Cream.

In the late 1920s, Sam moved to Hollandale, Mississippi, a small Mississippi Delta farming town south of Memphis on U.S. 61, where he became a fixture on the street corner. When he performed in Memphis, either with his brothers or solo, he always traveled by bus. It would pick him up on the very street corner on which he performed and deposit him in Memphis only a block or so from Beale Street. Sam performed at festivals and clubs all over the country for nearly five decades, but he didn't like to fly and always went by bus. He once turned down a booking in Europe because he didn't like the $800 paycheck and didn't want to fly.

"My boy told me once, say, 'Oh, Dad, go ahead over there with Memphis Slim. Boy, $800 would be good for a week. You ain't going to die 'til your time come,'" Sam told Margaret McKee and Fred Chisenhall. "I told him, 'Yeah, but I'd look like a fool. I'd be way up over all that water and somebody else's time come and I had to follow him down for him to die. I'd look just like a fool following him down to die.'"

Sam never cared much for the Memphis nightlife. He preferred working in Jackson, Mississippi, or in New Orleans. Sometimes he worked as a sideman with Louis Armstrong in New Orleans. He had a high opinion of Louis' trumpet playing, but felt his singing was just "clowning." He also had a high opinion of Elvis Presley. He especially liked Presley's "Jailhouse Rock," which Sam once said knocked right at the door of the blues. Just a bit more, he said, and Presley would have walked right in.

By the end of the 1940s, Sam's musical fling had ended. He worked at odd jobs in Hollandale throughout the 1950s and 1960s. He was "rediscovered" in the 1970s and toured extensively. He appeared on the NBC television's Today Show and performed at every major festival in North America, including the Mariposa Folk Festival in Toronto and the New Orleans Jazz and Heritage Festival. He died in Hollandale on February 2, 1983.

* * *

Within a month or so after I moved to Memphis in January 1982, I went to a downtown nightclub named Blues Alley. It was there that I first heard Lillie May Glover, who liked to bill herself as Ma Rainy Two. She was in poor health and did all of her vocals seated in a chair on the bandstand. She shared billing with Little Laura Dukes, the daughter of Alex Dukes, W. C. Handy's drummer back in the old days.

While Little Laura sang, Lillie May usually napped. When it was Lillie May's turn to sing, the guitar player tapped her on the shoulder. Lillie May was a big woman and she had a big voice. Back in the 1930s, she often was compared to Ma Rainy because of the power of her voice.

Lillie May began her career in the 1920s touring with the Rabbit Foot and Georgia minstrels. By the 1930s she had settled into a regular routine on Beale Street and at the Cotton Club across the river in West Memphis, Arkansas. She never found a national audience, but for nearly 60 years she was regarded as a local celebrity. In some ways, her personal life was more interesting than her music career. A large woman, who also went by Big Mama, she developed a reputation as a street brawler and a practitioner of the ancient, black magic art of voodoo.

Beale Street had a thing for voodoo women. Almost from day one, they were there, casting their spells, and usually for a handsome profit. The practice of voodoo was illegal in Memphis, but Big Mama never let that stop her from casting a spell or two. She had a small apartment just off Beale Street. Sometimes she sent hustlers out onto the street to bring in customers, but usually word-of-mouth referrals were enough to keep her busy. She liked to tell the story of a woman who came to her for a spell that would get rid of her abusive lover. Big Mama told the woman to bring her one of his socks. She sprinkled toilet water on the sock and muttered magic over it. She told the woman that if she tossed the voodooed sock into a creek she would get rid of her lover. Later, the woman's sister showed up on Big Mama's doorstep, raising hell. She complained that her sister had fallen into the creek and nearly drowned fooling with that hoodooed sock. Big Mama, doing some quick thinking, said that it was her voodoo magic that saved her from drowning. Eventually the woman did get rid of her lover, and, of course, Big Mama took full credit for it.

Voodoo had two main purposes—or should I say *has* two purposes, since it still is practiced in Memphis: To give an enemy bad luck or to remove bad luck that has been inflicted by an enemy. Voodoo was a powerful force on Beale Street. It appealed not just to the ignorant and the poor, but to a wide spectrum of people. As late as the mid-1980s, it was still a force, an underground counterculture that had the same type of fanatical following enjoyed by some religious cults. I knew a Memphis woman who sneaked off to voodoo vendors on a regular basis. She was white, had a college degree, and came from a middle class family, but the dark and mysterious power of voodoo was too powerful for her to resist. I can see how it could become an addiction to some people.

"Why do you do that?' I asked her.

Her answer was the same one you get from cocaine addicts before they know they are addicts: "Because I like it and it makes me feel better."

Memphis crime syndicates thrived on the same business model. It didn't take them long to realize that the same people always kept coming back for more. It also did not escape his attention that practitioners of black magic also catered to a repeat clientele. People who really wanted cocaine, whose bodies craved the drug, would do anything to get it. People who desperately wanted hoodoo to remove a curse would do whatever the voodoo vendor told them to do. Even murder. Using the addictive powers of cocaine and voodoo as controls, the syndicates built a low volume, under-the-counter cocaine and bootleg whisky business into a major economic force during the 1930s.

One of those who set up a bootlegging operation in Memphis was Machine Gun Kelly, who at the time was wanted by the FBI on a kidnapping charge. For about two months, Kelly and his wife Kathryn sold whisky in and around Memphis. He must have felt safe in Memphis because my grandfather, Audie Turner, once encountered Kelly about 100 miles south of the city on U.S. 61. My grandfather was driving on the highway when he saw a stranded motorist. He pulled off the highway and helped the man change a flat tire. While wrestling with the tire, he glanced into the back of the car and saw a machine gun on the seat. After Kelly's well publicized capture in September 1933, my grandfather recognized him from newspaper photos.

So what'd you think of Kelly? I once asked.

He thought a minute, then, in typical understatement, replied: "Seemed like a nice fellah."

Bluesman Thomas Pinkston told an interviewer Kelly sold bootleg whisky to Sweet Mama's, located off Beale at 311 S. Fourth. It was Kelly's misfortune the club was owned by a woman who was having an affair with a Memphis police detective. My guess is that Kelly's arrest was not the result of a sudden devotion to civic duty by the club owner or her cop lover, but rather the result of a directive by a crime syndicate that wanted to thin out the competition.

There is no evidence Boss Crump was personally involved in drug trafficking and prostitution, but there is evidence his organization was financed by contributions from racketeers who were. In a biting article published in the January 26, 1935, edition of *Collier's Weekly*, writer Owen White linked Crump to the "commercialized vice" prevalent in the city.

"Believe it or not, that's a fact," he wrote. "Professional sinners, therefore—that is, men and women who run gambling houses, dance halls, blind pigs, policy rackets, houses of ill-fame and all that sort of thing—being cash assets for professional politicians, are not only encouraged to operate but are actually instructed to go ahead and provide everybody, both visitors and home folks, with as much wide-open wickedness as possible." White told of parties he attended at which "coke and corn" were in abundance and where "unclad" dancing girls provided the entertainment. "Memphis (and I'm not talking about black Memphis now, but white Memphis) supports a population of about 7000 professional sinners whose sole business is to provide everybody with a good time," he continues. "They do it; they make a nice job of it, while furthermore they also do something else constructive, which is to take away from legitimate business the entire financial burden of supporting the political ring that actually runs Memphis and Shelby Country, and almost runs the entire state of Tennessee."

Actually, by 1935, Crump and his organization did run the entire state. With a firm grip on the mayor's office—in 1931 Crump's candidate won by a margin of 23,684 to 869 votes and in 1935 ran unopposed—Crump looked for ways to expand the organization's influence beyond Memphis. He ran for Congress and was elected to two terms. He voted for every New Deal initiative offered by the Roosevelt administration. His loyalty was not overlooked by Roosevelt, who quietly appointed Fiddling Abe to the Agricultural Adjustment Administration in 1933.

Not particularly infatuated with Washington, D.C., but acutely aware of the economic plums there for the picking, Crump looked for someone to represent his interests. U.S. Senator Kenneth McKellar, a Shelby Country native, jumped at the chance to form an alliance with the "Boss." Together, they and their benefactors decided who would be elected in Memphis and who would win important state offices, who would get federal contracts and who would be prosecuted for crimes at the local, state and federal level. That partnership lasted nearly two decades.

Noted historian V. O. Key, Jr., whose book *Southern Politics* became a bible for the study of politics in the South, wrote about Crump in 1948 when the Boss still had political teeth. "Although Crump has no organized forces of Brown Shirts, some of his critics in the state have stayed away from Memphis in fear that a visit there would endanger their lives," he wrote. "An insult, a scuffle, a planted gun, a verdict of justifiable homicide in self-defense -- all these expectation have been worked up in the minds of such persons by events in Memphis."

Throughout his career, Crump had controlled every segment of society except one—journalists. They infuriated him. After the death of editor Mooney at *The Commercial Appeal* in 1926, Crump had a free ride until 1931. That year the evening newspaper, the *Memphis Press-Scimitar*, hired a crusading newspaperman, Edward J. Meeman, to be its managing editor. Meeman went after Crump with everything he had. He called Crump a dictator and for two decades remained a painful thorn in the Boss' side. Crump did get some relief in 1933 when *The Commercial Appeal* was purchased by James Hammond, an Arkansas banker, who pulled every journalistic tooth the newspaper possessed. Instead of news, the newspaper focused on business promotions. One day Hammond sent up a rented airplane to publicize one of the newspaper's many promotions. In the airplane were a reporter, a pilot and Crump's son, John. The airplane crashed into a Mississippi field, killing all aboard. Crump took the death of his son hard. It pushed him a step closer to madness. Hammond sold the newspaper in 1936 to its current owner, Scripps Howard, and quietly left town.

The 1930s were critical to the development of Memphis' favorite fiddle player, Abe Fortas. After his graduation from Yale, he taught at the law school for a while, where he met his wife-to-be, Carolyn Agger, a cigar smoking economist. She enrolled in law school and took classes under her husband, but the academic life was attractive to neither of them. Abe took a position with the Agricultural Adjustment Administration, better known as the farm bureau, and then quickly moved on to the Securities and Exchange Commission. Carolyn landed a job with the National Labor Relations Board, then moved over to the tax division of the Department of Justice. During that time Abe was a tireless networker. While still teaching at Yale, he met a tall, aggressive Texan, Lyndon Johnson, who worked as secretary to a Texas congressman. They became friends and often visited each other's apartments, where they took turns cooking steaks.

Throughout that time, Abe maintained his contacts in Memphis. One can imagine the glee that greeted Abe's appointment to the SEC and Carolyn's appointment to the tax division of the Justice Department by that benevolent custodian of Memphis values—Congressman Boss Crump. In a 1937 visit to Memphis, Abe went by to see his mother, who still lived in the heart of Beale Street at 525 Pontotoc. Cornered by a newspaper reporter, who asked if he still played his fiddle, Abe said he did, but only for his own amusement. He said he often played with his wife's brother, a music instructor.

"We get together and play and have a good time," Abe said. "I'm going in for serious music now and I play it rather badly."

*   *   *

Not playing for their own amusement, were Booker T. Washington White, known professionally as Bukka White, and Peter Chatman, better known as Memphis Slim. They played to put food on the table. They were both probably playing on Beale Street when Abe visited his mother in 1937.

Did the three men ever meet on the street? Did Abe take time to sample the music while he was in town, or did he spend all his time visiting his mother and meeting with his Memphis benefactors? We'll never know, but it's tempting to imagine Abe, stiffened somewhat by his straight-laced Yale education, walking the short distance from his mother's house to Beale Street, then ducking into the Green Mule or Sweet Mama's to mingle with the hot-blooded whores and coke dealers before heading back to Washington.

White had no hopes of attending Yale. An ex-con, he had moved to Memphis from Mississippi, where he had served two years in the state penitentiary. Details of the crime are sketchy. There was this crap game. A man ended up dead. White took the fall. As a guitarist, he was a master of the Delta blues—and several of his records such as "Parchman Farm" and "Aberdeen, Mississippi" are classics—but as a performer he was always just a step away from the poor house. He was a fixture on Beale Street throughout the 1930s, but he never made enough money to sustain a career. He eventually gave it up to open a secondhand furniture store.

In 1962, Bob Dylan focused new attention on White when he recorded one of his songs, "Fixin' To Die." As a result, White re-emerged from his furniture store, took his nickel-plated steel guitar out of storage and toured all over the United States and Europe, winning college audiences over with his brash voice and folksy style. He recorded a few more albums, including "Mississippi Blues" and "Big Daddy," then retired from music again, this time for good, and returned to Memphis, where he lived in a rented room south of Beale Street. He died in 1977.

*   *   *

By the age of sixteen, Memphis Slim was performing professionally in juke joints around the South. It was not an easy life. The only dependable way to get from one town to the next was by freight train. He decided to return to Memphis after a wintertime trip to Chicago that left him shivering in the bitter cold. His clothing was too thin to allow him to be a hobo in the North.

When he returned to Memphis in the early 1930s—he still would have been a teenager—he went straight to Beale Street. He hung around a club where bluesman Roosevelt Sykes, his hero, performed on a regular basis. Sykes left town one day to do some recording in Chicago and Memphis Slim saw his chance.

49

"I went in there, and I had to be drunk, because I didn't have the nerve to go in there, and started playing the piano and singing like Roosevelt Sykes, and a guy came up and asked my name, and I said it was Peter Chatman," he says. "And he said: 'You Peter Chatman's son?' and I said: 'Yes.' They were all hustlers together. He asked if I wanted to work, and I got the job, not because I was Peter Chatman's son, but because I sang like Roosevelt Sykes. And then I really had them coming in listening to me."

Memphis Slim's father was well known because he had owned a string of juke joints in Memphis and across the river in Arkansas. He was an amateur musician, but never tried to make a living at it. Despite his father's background, or perhaps because of it, Memphis Slim encountered opposition as a child whenever he showed an interest in the blues. "I was called a 'good-for-nothing-mannish boy' when I was eight and singing," he recalled years later. "Now when you start at eight, they call you 'genius.'"

As a blues musician, he was in the minority on Beale Street because he played piano at a time when most blues performers played guitar. But he played with great style. He had a tendency to do a lot of bass-note flourishes when he was in a boogie-woogie mode. By the time he got out of his teens, he was a local star. His pay was usually $1.25 a night, plus two bottles of cheap whisky. Compare that to the $8 a night Fiddling Abe earned a decade earlier. A good blues musician in those days, he once recalled, could judge his worth by the number of fights that broke out during his performance: "When you were singing and touched somebody, they started fighting, and that meant you had success."

By 1939, Memphis Slim had enough of the tough Beale Street nightlife and the low wages he earned as a performer. He moved to Chicago and recorded for Okeh Records using the name Peter Chatman. The next year he recorded for Bluebird. This time he used the nickname he had picked up on Beale Street—Memphis Slim. He joined Big Bill Broonzy's band and made a name for himself in Chicago as one of the best boogie-woogie piano players on the circuit. By 1944, he was popular enough to form his own band, Memphis Slim & His House Rockers.

Throughout the 1940s and early 1950s, he continued to build audiences with songs such as "Having Fun," "Wish Me Well" and

"Every Day I Have the Blues," but it wasn't until the late 1950s that he got caught up in the blues revival sweeping white college campuses and found a large audience. By that time he had added several outstanding musicians to his band, including guitarist Matt Murphy, who later performed with the Blues Brothers. During the late 1950s and early 1960s, he performed with Pete Seeger and Joan Baez at clubs in Greenwich Village and at the Newport Folk Festival.

It was during that time that Memphis Slim began making his first tours of Europe. He was especially popular in France, where he often was booked at the Parisian cabaret Les Trois Maillets. By 1961 his marriage was falling apart. He returned that year from a tour of Europe, took a hard look at his marriage and at his opportunities in the United States, and he promptly turned around and returned to Paris, where he married the daughter of a Paris cabaret owner and began a new life.

In 1978, Memphis Slim returned to Memphis for a homecoming performance with the Memphis Symphony at The Orpheum, an ornate theater at the western end of Beale Street. He confided to reporters he was apprehensive about returning to Memphis: "I've been to Newport. I've been to Carnegie Hall. I've been to Monterey, but coming home? I'm nervous about it."

His performance at The Orpheum marked the first time he had ever been allowed downstairs in the theater. Growing up in Memphis, he had been required to sit in the fourth balcony, the area designated for African Americans.

"I can remember when I was on Beale Street, the white people were only allowed there on Thursday nights," he told a *Press-Scimitar* reporter. "That was for the 'Midnight Rambles' at the Palace Theater, and all the police in town would be down there to protect them. Any other time that any white people went down there, they were told: 'You're on your own,' and if something happened to them, they were told: 'We told you not to go down there.' It was rough. The white police—that's all they had—didn't come down much on other nights, because it was so tough."

Memphis Slim was pleased to be honored by his hometown, but the event brought out deep seated conflicts within himself. In Paris he was a star. A real *somebody*. He had recorded over 500 songs, half of them penned by himself. He was a headliner at folk and blues festivals all over the world.

Even the U.S. Senate had acknowledged him by proclaiming him "America's Ambassador at Large for Good Will," an honor previously held by Bob Hope and Louis Armstrong. But in Memphis, indeed throughout most of the South, he was just another black blues musician. Every town in the South had one or two on the street corner.

Memphis Slim was gracious, but during the visit he struggled to come to terms with Memphis and, by necessity, his own life. "It's a pitiful thing, that when I was a young man, blues were very strong in Memphis, but later on when people realized how strong blues was going to be, they started making the black people feel ashamed of the blues, and that's why the blues is not as strong here now. Today, when I talk to people, even in Memphis, they are still ashamed of the blues. They call the blues all kinds of other names, because the black man who owned the blues is still ashamed of the blues."

Memphis Slim returned to Paris and lived another 10 years. He died there in 1988 of kidney failure at age 72. He died a long way from the home of the blues, but, in the end, home was not so much where his heart was, as where he was best able to define himself. "I didn't know I was a poet until I went to Europe," he says. "But I am a poet. Really a poet."

*　　*　　*

The decade ended with a visit on December 1, 1939, by W. C. Handy, who returned to Memphis for a heralded championship football game between two of the city's black high schools. It was billed as the Blues Bowl. The city honored Handy with a parade that began on Beale Street and ended at the stadium. Handy said a few words to the audience and then played his trumpet. For the first time in over two decades, he played the "Memphis Blues" in the city that inspired it.

"Handy was resplendent for the occasion in a black topcoat, gleaming white muffler, gray spats and walking cane," reported the *Press-Scimitar*. "The 'Daddy of the blues' certainly found that his child was being nourished and cherished in its birthplace—Beale Street."

Whatever Handy felt upon his return to Memphis, the next morning's racist headline in *The Commercial Appeal* certainly must have put it in perspective:

**HANDY TOOTS A GOLDEN HORN
-- DARKIEDOM SQUEALS IN GLEE**

Memphis Slim at the Mississippi Delta Blues Festival, 1976
Photo © Steve Gardner

B. B. King, c. 1980s
Photo © Steve Gardner

CHAPTER 4

The 1940s:
King Biscuit Time Sparks Memphis

At the start of the decade, Memphis music took a sucker punch that knocked it to its knees. The murder rate still soared. The national media still slammed the city, but now, instead of blaming poor, uneducated blacks for the high crime rate, writers blamed prominent white Memphians for their involvement in the vice trade.

In 1939, Crump announced that he was running for mayor. That shocked everyone. He already controlled every office in the city and most state offices. Why would he "step down" to run for mayor? If you look at photographs of Crump taken at that time, he resembles a cartoon character. His behavior was eccentric and bizarre, and probably would have met most legal standards for insanity. But, despite indications the city was out of control, most Memphians closed their eyes to what was going on and gave Crump a free rein. It is incredible when you think about it. He was a millionaire, yet had no job. He decided who would fill each public office, yet seldom gave public speeches. He preached morality, yet lived high off the hog on the wages of sin and corruption and seldom, if ever, attended church. He was a white supremacist, yet built his political power base on the overburdened backs of black voters.

When the votes were counted in the mayoral election, Crump won by a margin of 31,825 to *zilch* (he had no opponent). In 1940, Crump was sworn in as mayor. He promptly resigned and went to a football game. He didn't really want to be mayor. He just wanted to prove that he was still the Boss. But he wasn't finished. Abruptly, he ordered Beale Street shut down. The gin joints, the whorehouses, the casinos, the street vendors who sold cocaine, the juke joints that sold bootleg alcohol—all were shut down. Memphis musicians were tossed out on the street. Boss Crump may have been crazy, but he was no fool. While some of his supporters were still involved in vice, so were some of his enemies. His main supporters had moved on to white collar crime. That was where the real money was. The Boss may have looked like a goofball, but on the inside he was wily as ever.

Beale Street was devastated by Crump's crackdown. Black leaders had provided unquestioned support of Crump's candidates because the vice trade, as unsavory as it was, was the *only* area of the Memphis economy open to black entrepreneurs. By turning his back on the black underworld in favor of white collar machinations, Crump burned bridges between the races that would not be re-built for nearly three decades.

By then Crump had become incredibly blatant in his illegal activities. He feared no one. Extortion replaced vice collections as a source of income. In his book, *Memphis Since Crump*, David Tucker tells the story of a Michigan businessman who came to Memphis to open a jewelry store on Main Street.

"The city building inspector informed him that the front of his building violated the city code and would have to be rebuilt," says Tucker. "The alarmed jeweler called his contractor, who assured him that the problem was political rather than structural. 'Do you have any insurance from Mr. Crump?' the builder asked. 'I suggest you take at least part of your insurance from E. H. Crump and Company.' The jeweler purchased a policy from Crump, and the city inspector promptly approved the new store."

Memphians did then what they do today in the face of organized crime: They looked the other way. That myopic view mystified and enraged people in other parts of the country. In 1946, the *Washington Post* used Memphis as an example of how unsuspecting Americans could be enticed into fascism. "Memphis, Tennessee, should be a warning to the whole country," proclaimed the newspaper. "The city is a perfect example of the ease with which Americans with a philosophy of efficiency and materialism can succumb to fascism and like it. The majority of the citizens of Memphis lick the boots of their notorious tyrant, Mr. E. H. Crump, not because they have to. They lick his boots because it pays. Like all fascist rulers, Crump has the support and admiration of big business."

The vice crackdown of 1940 did not result in the closing of all the nightclubs on Beale Street, but since it eliminated the source of much of the ready cash spent in the clubs, it crippled the ability of musicians to make a decent living. Many blues musicians stayed on the street, but most moved on to greener pastures. West Memphis, Arkansas, took up the slack by accommodating some of the prostitutes and drug dealers, and nightclubs with gaming tables popped up along the river in the shadow of the Memphis skyline. Memphis musicians looked for opportunities wherever they could find them.

Out of Crump's crackdown, or perhaps because of it, Memphis music, by that time a life force embedded deep in the belly of the city, looked toward new technology for ways to survive. It would find nourishment and then re-birth first in radio, then in the recording industry.

As the decade began, Lillie May Glover was still performing on Beale Street, as was Sam Chatmon and Sleepy John Estess on a sporadic basis, but one of the most enterprising bluesman of the early 1940s was Rice Miller, known professionally as Sonny Boy Williamson 2. Born in Mississippi around 1910 (the actual date is disputed), Sonny Boy spent much of the 1930s as a itinerant musician, performing with Robert Johnson and others. Much of his early life is a historical blur because in later years he told different stories to different people. He appropriated his professional name from John Lee "Sonny Boy" Williamson, a Chicago blues musician who was murdered outside a Chicago nightclub in 1948. Miller was using the name long before the other "Sonny Boy" died, and despite a number of outstanding records by the Chicago "Sonny Boy" on the Victor label in the mid-to-late 1940s, there can be no doubt Miller was the more important musician of the two. He was a wizard on the harmonica and his vocals were earthy and passionate. He was probably the first bluesman to ever use the harp as a lead instrument.

In 1941 Helena, Arkansas, a Delta river town located about 60 miles south of Memphis, got its first radio station. It was christened KFFA, call letters meant to show deference to an organization that was popular in that area, the Future Farmers of America. Since the economy was almost exclusively agricultural, the radio station designed its programming to appeal to a rural audience. That usually meant country music and crop reports. The nearest large city was Memphis. Technically, Helena residents, being loyal Arkansans, acknowledged Little Rock as their capital; but since, like most Delta towns in Arkansas and Mississippi, black residents composed a significant percentage of the population, they considered Memphis their spiritual capital.

To travel to Memphis, it was necessary to either ride the train (usually too expensive) or take the ferry across the river to Delta Landing. The ferry, incidentally, was operated by Harold Jenkins, country singer Conway Twitty's father. From Delta Landing, they would drive about 15 miles to U.S. 61 and then have a straight shot into Memphis.

Sonny Boy often worked the juke joints around Helena. KFFA went on the air at a time when he was looking for ways to supplement the loss of income caused by Crump's crackdown. When he heard about the radio station, Sonny Boy, as enterprising in life as in art, got an idea. He talked to the white station owner about airing a blues show. The owner liked the music, but told him he would have to have a sponsor. He sent him over to talk to Max Moore, owner of the Interstate Grocery.

When he heard Sonny Boy's idea, Max was very interested. He had his own line of flour and corn meal and saw a blues show as a way to market his products in the black community. He agreed to sponsor the show. Since King Biscuit was the name of his flour, they decided to call the show King Biscuit Time. To promote the corn meal, he re-named it Sonny Boy Corn Meal. He took a picture of Sonny Boy sitting barefoot on a tow sack and splashed the picture on the package.

King Biscuit Time aired daily at noon. Sonny Boy became a household name, not just among blacks, but among whites. The format of the show was simple: 15 minutes of live blues, interspersed with commercials for King Biscuit Flour and Sonny Boy Corn Meal. The show was broadcast from the KFFA studio on the fifth floor of the Helena National Bank building. It was on the air from 1941 to 1981, doing for the blues what the Grand Ole Opry did for country music. For many years, the show replaced Beale Street as a venue for Memphis musicians.

During that time, the show had two white announcers, Hugh Smith and Sunshine Sonny Payne, both of whom were on the KFFA payroll. I never met Smith, but I met Sunshine in 1988 when I produced a weekly radio syndication based on the old King Biscuit format. Sunshine, then in his sixties, was one of my announcers.

The first time I met Sunshine was in a Memphis studio just prior to taping. He seemed reserved to the point of timidity, but when the tape started rolling, the big booming voice that had been a trademark for King Biscuit Time for four decades filled the room with the resonant good humor that made him a household name in the Delta. Small in stature but stocky in build, he was always immaculately dressed, a walking advertisement for the well-mannered Southern gentleman. I liked him right away.

Sunshine told me about his first meeting with Sonny Boy. Two things stuck out in his memory. Sonny Boy showed up at the radio station wearing a derby hat and Sunshine had never seen a derby hat. The other thing was Sonny Boy's appearance.

"I don't mean to be insulting, but he had a nose just like a buzzard's beak," Sunshine says. "A lot of the blues performers called him the Buzzard Beak."

Sonny Boy put together a house band of outstanding musicians. Alternating on guitar over the years were Robert Junior Lockwood, Houston Stackhouse and Joe Willie Wilkens. Usually on drums was James "Peck" Curtis. Joe "Pine Top" Perkins came down from Memphis to play piano. They would all show up at the studio a few minutes before the show was scheduled to air. The musicians sat down to play, but Sonny Boy stood and faced the microphone at eye level. Everyday Sunshine would ask him what he was going to sing so that he could announce it and everyday Sonny Boy would say he didn't know yet. But when the show began, he sang and the band played on cue, usually something they made up on the spot.

"When he came in, he always had a big smile on his face," says Sunshine. "He would greet all the musicians and naturally the guy who would be hosting the show, in most cases myself. After that, everything was strictly business. He got serious. He didn't want anybody to foul up. He wanted you right then and there on the spot to do your thing and do it right. That was the easiest way to make him mad. He got real serious about his music."

Pinetop Perkins, who was on the show on a regular basis from 1943 to 1948, agreed with Sunshine on that point. "Me and Sonny Boy could get along all right," he says. "He was kinda' crabby, but he never did bother me too much."

Sonny Boy was paid $15 a week, which, when compared to normal wages of that era—50 cents to one dollar a day—was good pay, especially for a 15-minute workday. As a result of the program, Sonny Boy's fame spread throughout the decade. In the late 1940s, he sold his idea of a blues format to a radio station in West Memphis.

For a while, he did both shows, living in Memphis and commuting to Helena and West Memphis. Then in 1951 he teamed up with Elmore James and recorded his first record, "Dust My Broom." At around that same time he recorded about 20 songs for a label based in Jackson, Mississippi. By 1955 he was ready for the big time. He went to Chicago and signed with Chess Records. The resulting releases, "Bring It On Home," "Don't Start Me To Talkin,'" a Top 10 hit on R&B charts in 1955, and "Help Me," established Sonny Boy as one of the leading bluesmen of the post war period. An excellent songwriter, his songs were marked by biting wit and a fatalistic view of society. He went to Europe in 1963 and played a significant role in the development of the British blues-rock invasion that hit America with a vengeance in the 1960s. While in Europe he performed with the Yardbirds and the Animals, who later offered American audiences their own version of Sonny Boy's "Bring It On Home."

Sonny Boy went back to Helena during the late 1950s and early 1960s (maybe once every two years) but when he did he always stopped by KFFA to perform on King Biscuit Time. When he returned in 1964, Sunshine ran into him on the street before he went by the studio. Sonny Boy told him he had come home to die.

"No one ever knows when they are going to die," Sunshine told him. "That's God's thing."

Sonny Boy shook his head knowingly. He rented a room upstairs over the Dreamland Cafe. A few months later, in 1965, Sunshine was at the radio station when he got word Sonny Boy had died in his sleep.

"I didn't believe it," he says. "I felt somebody was kidding me. They used to try to wake him up and they couldn't get him awake. That was the first thought that entered my mind, that somebody was snow-jobbing me. When I actually saw his body, I knew he was gone and it hurt."

Years later Sunshine still couldn't talk about it without the grief slipping into his voice. The two races may not have eaten or slept together during those segregationist years, but they cared about each other and often forged lifelong friendships. Sunshine was devastated by Sonny Boy's death. "I felt kind of dead myself," he says, eyes watering up after all those years. "I cried."

*　　*　　*

Sonny Boy Williamson ignited a spark in Memphis with his radio program. It was a slow burning fuse that didn't detonate until 1948, but throughout the early to mid-1940s it inched forward with a slow, steady burn. One of Sonny Boy's regular listeners in Indianola, Mississippi, was a youngster named Riley Ben King. When King Biscuit Time went on the air in 1941, King was 16 years of age. He attended school in cold weather and worked in the cotton fields in warm weather. For King and thousands of other working black youngsters like him, King Biscuit Time was the main source of entertainment. "We would be in the fields and we would go home for lunch," King says. "We hurried so we would be there when 12:15 came so we could catch the King Biscuit program. I heard them so long, it seemed like I really knew them."

Riley Ben King went on to become the legendary B. B. King, but that was later, much later, and in the interim King Biscuit Time not only entertained him, it gave him a vision of a better life. He could hear black men participating, not just in the mainstream of Southern life, but in the forefront of new technology. Just as important he could hear black men and white men bantering on the airwaves, communicating man to man. It instilled a sense of pride in him.

In 1946, B. B. King went to Memphis to visit his cousin, bluesman Bukka White. He stayed several months, making the rounds of the clubs with Bukka, watching him perform. Back home in Indianola, King sang in a quartet, but Memphis was the big time and he didn't have the nerve to ask Bukka, or anyone else, if he could perform. Instead, he found work as a laborer and spent his earnings partying on Beale Street like everyone else.

"Where I came from, they only had one nightclub," King says. "They had several on Beale. People seemed more into what was happening. Where I came from, you wore your work clothes to work and you came home in them. On Beale you couldn't tell people were working. Everybody would be dressed up and looking neat in the evenings. They had places to go for socializing that we didn't have at home."

Beale Street also offered a more liberal view of race relations than he was used to in Mississippi. "It was different, somewhat. Most of the white people I saw were people who had stores on Beale Street. They seemed to be accommodating. Everyone knew each other. You didn't see the race thing until the police came around. I remember this squad car we called Number One. They weren't too friendly when they came around. But most of the people, the people who worked in the stores, they treated you kindly."

As visits with relatives are prone to do, this one ran out of steam after several months and King returned to Indianola to work on the plantation. In 1947, he visited Bukka again; then in 1948 he moved to Memphis to stay. He took the guitar Bukka had given him as a child and he started performing, using the name Riley King. His first job was at the 16th Street Grill across the river in West Memphis. He was paid $12.

Years later, King laughs when he thinks about it. "I had been working on the plantation for $22.50 a week—and I got paid $12 for one night! I had never heard of that much money in the world."

King took the money and ran, all the way back to Beale Street, where he started performing on a regular basis. By 1948, West Memphis was wide open. Whorehouses, gambling halls, dope dins, all the exotic pleasures that had fled Memphis, found a home in West Memphis. Performing in one of the whorehouses on a regular basis was a 38-year-old Arkansas farmer, Chester Burnett. During the day he was a typical field worker. He looked the part, too. A large, muscular black man with an enormous face and a rock-solid jaw, he didn't always take time to change from his farmer's overalls when he went into town. Apparently, no one cared. With a booming, rough-edge voice that bellowed like a demon in the throes of a godly presence, he captivated his audiences and vocally wrestled them into submission.

It didn't take long for West Memphis radio station KWEM to hear about Burnett. By then he was using a stage name, Howlin' Wolf. The station offered him a job as a deejay and as a featured performer. For 15 minutes a day, Howlin' Wolf talked, sang; then after the farm reports and advertisements for fertilizer and assorted farm products were run, he sang and talked some more. Sonny Boy Williamson had proved in Helena that radio and the blues were a solid mix, so when he approached KWEM about doing the same thing there, the station jumped at the idea. For a time Sonny Boy and Howlin' Wolf were filling the airwaves with their down-home humor and captivating performances. B. B. King told me that it was Sonny Boy who gave him his first radio exposure. King, a fan of Sonny Boy's show, showed up at the radio station one day and asked Sonny Boy if he would put him on the air.

"He made me audition for him," King recalls. "But he must have liked what he heard because he put me on the show that very day."

As an art form, the blues had been airborne in Arkansas and some parts of Mississippi for seven years, but Memphis had been slow to utilize black programming. All that changed in a big way in 1947 when the owners of radio station WDIA, two white men named Bert Ferguson and John Pepper, decided to convert to an all-black format. The station was losing money and they figured they had nothing to lose by giving it a try. In 1948 there were no black radio stations in America, so they had to make it up as they went along. Not only did Ferguson and Pepper want the station to air black music, they wanted to staff it with all-black personnel. No American radio station had ever done that. It was a revolutionary concept that would radically change American broadcasting.

For their first deejay, they hired Nat D. Williams, a popular columnist for the black-owned newspaper, *The Tri-State Defender.* When Williams went on the air with a program called "Tan Town Jamboree," the station was flooded with letters of protest from white listeners who demanded that Williams be taken off the air. But the station owners wouldn't budge. Not only did they keep him on the air, they expanded black programming.

America watched the experiment with afar.

Listening with great interest was Riley King.

Early in 1949, King summoned all the courage he could muster and walked into the WDIA studios at 2074 Union. For what seemed like an eternity, he stood at the picture window of the control booth, watching Nat. D. Williams. During a break, Williams poked his head out the door. What you want, son? King said he wanted to make records. He wanted to be a big shot and get on the radio. Williams liked what he saw. He called over the stations owners, Ferguson and Pepper, and when King left the station that day he was the host of his own daily program. The 10-minute show was scheduled to air each day at 3:30 p.m.

"Mr. Ferguson started this product called Peptikon and it was my job to advertise it," King says. "It was a competitor to another tonic called Hadical." King wrote the jingle himself. Fifty-four years after the fact, the jingle was still fresh in his mind when he sang it for me in 1995:

Peptikon sure is good. Peptikon sure is good.

You can get it anywhere in your neighborhood.

Within a month, King, using the name Beale Street Blues Boy, had become one of the most popular deejays at the station and his program was expanded to 15 minutes. He abbreviated his name to Blues Boy, and then shortened it even more to "B. B." The program attracted so much attention, Lucky Strike cigarettes decided to co-sponsor it, becoming the station's first national advertiser. To play piano on the Lucky Strike jingles, and to vocalize when necessary, Pinetop Perkins was recruited by King. Pinetop would later move on to become Muddy Waters' pianist and a recording artist in his own right, but in those days he divided his time equally between Memphis and Helena, doing whatever it took to survive.

64

When I first met Pinetop Perkins it was in the late 1980s during one of his infrequent visits to Memphis. I picked him up at his hotel and drove him to the office of my syndicated radio program, Pulsebeat—Voice of the Heartland, where we planned to record an interview for future use on our blues program. He appeared weary, but he was in an affable mood, eyes twinkling.

We had only gone a block or two before he nervously coughed and cut his eyes toward me and said, "Are you one of those journalists who don't like to pay for interviews?"

"Afraid so," I answered.

"I thought so. Well, would you consider making a donation of a fifth of whiskey to the cause?"

"Certainly," I said, wondering how much he was being paid for his Beale Street gig with Little Mike and the Tornadoes. Probably not very much. After all these years of performing with legends such as Muddy Waters, Pinetop was still what he'd always been, one of the best sidemen in the business.

Once we arrived at the studio, which was located in the basement of a Midtown Memphis high-rise, he fell into conversation with my announcer, Kim Spangler, whose cheerful voice and excited demeanor quickly put him at ease. One of the things on my mind was what he saw as the biggest difference between the blues he played in the 1930s, 1940s and 1950s and the blues that was being played in the 1980s.

"Now people are squeezing the strings more than they did back in the olden times," he explained. "Back then it was all about picking a guitar, not squeezing the strings. I used to pick myself years ago. Before I got a muscle cut out of my arm in Arkansas I used to double between piano and guitar."

Pinetop disclosed that he had borrowed the "Pinetop" moniker from Clarence "Pinetop" Smith, a boogie-woogie pianist from Alabama who often worked with Ma Rainey. He was killed in a barroom shoot-out in 1929, but not before establishing his rhythmic piano flourishes as a critical ingredient in 1920s ragtime.

"I was just a kid," Pinetop said, explaining his decision to adopt the name of an already established performer. "I grew up near Belzoni, Mississippi, on Honey Island plantation . . ."

He didn't have to finish the sentence. I grew up in the Mississippi Delta twenty minutes from Belzoni (pronounced with an 'a' at the end) and I understood that he mentioned his birthplace as a way of explaining that he came of age in unsophisticated surroundings. Why would he make a name for himself using another man's name? Because knowing the do's and don'ts of building a music career was beyond the reach of anyone in Belzoni, especially a kid.

Ironically, there was some continuity involved with his morphing from Joe Willie into Pinetop in that he first got paid for playing music in 1929, the year the original Pinetop died. If Pinetop Smith didn't need the name anymore why couldn't he borrow it? "I played blues on the guitar first," he said. "Back in those days, you worked [in the fields] for 50 cents a day. You worked hard all day for 50 cents. If I got two dollars a night [playing the blues], that was four days work in the fields."

Certainly, that was enough to turn anyone's head. Asked what kind of work he did in the fields, he answered, "I worked the mules, planting. I never could chop cotton. Couldn't pick it either. But they always found something for me to do."

I was naturally curious about what a man of Pinetop's experience would consider the greatest blues song. "B.B. had the best blues," he said. Next was Albert King. I liked to play with Little Milton, but he and I couldn't see eye to eye. Now when it comes to the best blues song, I'd say one put out by St. Louis Jimmy—'I have had my fun, if I don't get well no more.'"

Actually, that was the first line, not the title. When James Burke "St. Louis Jimmy" Oden wrote the song, he called it "Goin' Down Slow." The song, which conveyed the reflections of a dying man, had been recorded by Aretha Franklin, the Animals, and Duane Allman by the time the conversation with Pinetop took place. The song reflected his own feelings at that time that his best years were behind him. "I've had my fun in life."

Kim reacted in surprise. "Not having fun anymore?"

"No, I try to play so that other people can have their fun."

After the interview, I drove Pinetop back to his hotel, detouring to a liquor store.

"What's your pleasure?"

"Seagram's Seven."

I dropped him off at his hotel, the brown-bagged bottle dangling at his side. He was stooped somewhat and walked with an unsteady gait. No way did I think he would live another 23 years. He passed away in 2011, but not before receiving richly deserved accolades from his home state of Mississippi.

*   *   *

The impact WDIA had on the development of American music—and American culture—was far-reaching, both economically and spiritually. To put it in perspective, consider that blacks in 1948 were still restricted by law as to where they could eat, sleep or socialize. Racism was not an unreasonable attitude, it was the law of the land. The hit records in 1948 were Dinah Shore's "Button and Bows," Spike Lee's "All I Want For Christmas Is My Two Front Teeth and Kay Kyser's "Woody Woodpecker." The top grossing movies of 1948 were "The Road to Rio," with Bob Hope and Bing Crosby, and "Red River," with John Wayne and Montgomery Clift. With few exceptions, black culture was all but invisible to white America.

B. B. King treaded ground no one had ever walked. It was like being the first man to set foot on the moon. King still marvels at the experience.

"Bert Ferguson had rules that were different from any other place I had ever gone," he says. "At the station, you gave honor to whom honor was due. You didn't have to say, 'yes sir' or 'yes mam," simply because a person was white. Most of us learned at an early age that you respected people. But if a person was named Tom, then you called him Tom. Of course, you never addressed a lady by Laura or Lucille unless they were at a level with you. If it was a married lady, it was Mrs., but you didn't have to do it because she was white. Mr. Ferguson will be Mr. Ferguson to me for the rest of my life because I respected him. The atmosphere was like it would be today if you went to the American Embassy in Russia. You feel like you are at home. That's the way I felt at WDIA. It wasn't intimidating. It was like a college of learning for me."

For King, WDIA was a safe refuge in a land seething with danger. Crump may have closed the door on black musical aspirations with his Beale Street crackdown, but WDIA, located just two blocks off Beale Street, had inexplicably risen out of the ashes of that despair to give new hope to a new generation typified by B. B. King.

Bolstered by his success on radio, King recorded four or five songs in WDIA's Studio A for Bullet Records, a company based in Nashville. Unfortunately, the company went out of business shortly after the songs were recorded. But King pushed on. In 1949, he recorded a song on mobile equipment set up at the YMCA. The song, "3 O'clock Blues," was released in 1950.

Memphis had become a hotbed of recording activity for black musicians. But since there were no studios, sessions were held wherever they could find an empty room. Most of the sessions were for record companies based in Chicago. By the late 1940s, Chess Records had recruited a talent scout from Mississippi named Ike Turner. He would later find international fame as leader of the Ike and Tina Turner Revue, but in those days his first big "find" was Howlin' Wolf, whom he recorded on portable equipment for Chess in 1948.

Across town from WDIA, a white employee of radio station WREC watched with great interest. Sam Phillips had moved to Memphis in 1945 to work at the station, and, after four years, the ambitious Alabamian was on the lookout for new opportunities. What he heard on black radio in 1948 and 1949 excited him. White radio had overproduced pop music and folksy announcers. Black radio had Howlin' Wolf, Sonny Boy and B. B. King. The airwaves exploded with the sexual bravado of liberated black manhood— and the women of Memphis were noticing.

Something was in the air.

Johnny Cash in the studio, 1950s
Photofest

CHAPTER 5

The 1950s:
Revolution in the Air

Sam Chatmon didn't look like anyone else I knew. He had a bushy, white beard at a time when most men were clean-shaven. He wore funky hats. Not the straw work hats or cloth baseball caps worn by most of the field hands, but arty, be-bop hats that solicited double-takes. But it wasn't the clothes, or even the beard, that most set Sam apart. It was his icy blue eyes. Unlike most of the black men you'd meet on the streets of the Delta town of Hollandale, Sam looked you straight in the eye. It wasn't a stare. He just looked straight at you. There wasn't anything creepy about it. It was like crossing a railroad track and looking up to see the light of a freight train bearing down on you. You paid attention.

After my father died in 1952, my mother, my sister and I moved to Hollandale, to live with my maternal grandparents. My grandfather had a department store on Main Street and I worked there on Saturdays from the time I was eight. That was when I met Sam Chatmon. He would come into the store and sometimes I would wait on him. I remember selling him white cotton socks packaged three pair for a dollar. I would also see him on the street corner near Booth's Drug Store. He leaned back against the building out of the sun and played the blues late in the afternoons and into the evenings. I must have walked past him a thousand times. He was a gentle man and I never heard him raise his voice above a murmur. Sometimes I would stop and listen. He was the first person I ever saw play guitar. That was the only time Sam would not look you straight in the eye, when he was playing guitar and singing. His eyes had a faraway look to them then.

Many a summer day I stood on the sidewalk in the hot sun, watching him play his guitar, his foot keeping time on the concrete. Once after he stopped playing he motioned down to a tin cup just to the right of his chair.

"Know what that is?" he asked.

I shook my head.

"It's a tip jar."

"That doesn't look like a jar to me."

He shook his head back and forth, stopping just short of rolling his eyes. Then he launched into another song, finding solace in the groove.

Sam Chatmon was an important part of my growing up in the 1950s. It was because of him that I traded a 6mm Italian carbine for a Sears Silvertone acoustic guitar that I learned to play while sitting on the back steps of my home.

When Sam Chatmon wasn't sitting on the street corner, gathering a crowd, few of whom ever made the tin cup ping, or working as a night watchman at the cotton gin, he was waiting for the bus that would take him to Memphis to help lay the groundwork for a cultural revolution. There were dozens more like him, white and black, all drawn to Memphis from across the South, as if by a beacon.

There were two sides to Memphis in those days. On the outside, it was a Norman Rockwell painting. In 1950, it was chosen the "Nation's Cleanest City." The murder rate plummeted. So did drug addiction. Prostitution, gambling and cocaine were holed up across the river in Arkansas. Boss Crump outlawed the sounding of car horns and the city was given a national award for being the nation's quietest city. To make sure his cleanup was being enforced, Crump perpetually drove about the city in his chauffeur driven limousine. If he saw a piece of paper, he got out and picked it up. If he saw a pothole, he sent a stinging reprimand to the city engineer. By the end of the decade, the national press was in love with Memphis. *Look* magazine gave the city an award for urban renewal.

Beneath the surface, Memphis was primed for revolution. Dozens of Sam Chatmons infiltrated the city, performing in the few clubs left on Beale Street or on the street corners, but mostly looking for opportunities to make records or be heard on the radio. The contrast between white and black Memphis had never been greater. The economic boom brought about by World War II had lulled white Memphis into a cultural complacency. In 1950, the hit records were Patti Page's "The Tennessee Waltz" and Red Foley's "Chattanooga Shoe Shine Boy." Two of the biggest grossing movies were "Cinderella" and "Cheaper By the Dozen." There was no talk in white Memphis of making records or getting on the radio. It was as if half the city had an erection and the other half was asleep on the porch.

Black Memphis throbbed with jive talk. Hey, man, let's *do it.* Everybody had a scam to get on the radio or make records. Beale Street had once been the place for action. Now talk was king. That and high fashion. Clothing stores, such as Lansky's, sold bright, gaudy apparel, pimp duds that symbolized the simmering passions on the street. By 1950, B. B. King was a major celebrity in the black community, but he was by no means the only celebrity. Howlin' Wolf had his fans. So did Ike Turner (and not far away in Nutbush, his future wife, Annie Mae Bullock). Before long they were joined by Little Milton, Junior Parker, James Cotton and Bobby "Blue" Bland. Using modern technology—radio and the recording industry—black Memphis, not thinking it, mind you, but feeling it, quietly redefined Beale Street, priming the Revolution with generations of sweat piped in from the plantations.

U.S. 61 was the pipeline that supplied the Revolution with foot soldiers. Because U.S. 61 runs through Hollandale, my hometown was a beneficiary—and sometimes a training ground—for the Memphis experiment. In the summers, I often waited until dark, then walked two blocks downtown and climbed the chinaberry tree next to the icehouse. I peered across the railroad tracks into Blue Front, the black entertainment strip that during the day appeared deserted and run down, but came alive at night with teeming crowds that packed the nightclubs, all-night cafes and brothels, and I listened to the forbidden music that made the night air come alive with exotic rhythms and sweet harmonies. I watched pickup trucks and cars filled to capacity dodge pedestrians in the dimly lit street and I saw brightly dressed prostitutes dance in and out of the headlights as the music of Jimmy Reed, Little Milton and dozens of other faceless musicians wafted overhead to melodic heights and then fell stone-like across the tracks on the white side of town. There were no juke joints for whites in Hollandale in those days. That privilege was reserved solely for the town's black residents, who made up about 80 percent of the population.

* * *

Radio was the key to the magic taking place in Memphis. It instilled pride. It energized emotions. "All of the radio stations prior to WDIA were informative, but they didn't seem to touch us where we lived," says B. B. King. "When I left home in Indianola, every time I heard something about a black person it was when they did something wrong. It was never praising them. Rarely would you hear of anything positive being done by a black person. WDIA was like a light."

With two notable exceptions, white Memphis just didn't see it.

In 1950, a 15-year-old immigrant from Mississippi, where his father worked in a store owned by a family member of mine, Elvis Aron Presley, lived with his parents in a two-bedroom apartment in a housing project not far away from Beale Street. His first summer in Memphis he worked as an usher at a movie theater, but the next summer he got a more lucrative job as a $27-a-week worker at Precision Tool Co. Elvis wasn't like the other boys. He sang at high school programs and at church gatherings. Beale Street intrigued him, and he started hanging out on the street, listening and watching, soaking up the atmosphere, but still keeping his distance. Before he knew what had happened, he was making the talk, doing the walk.

In 1950, Sam Phillips took the plunge. After two years of listening to black radio, and feeling the excitement, it was so raw it was sexual in its overtones, he leased space in a building at 706 Union and opened Memphis' first recording studio. He called it Memphis Recording Service. At that time, Union was the main east-west thoroughfare that connected mid-town with downtown. Traffic on Union was usually heavy. Directly across the street from Memphis Recording Service, with a small triangular median in between, was the east end of Beale Street. Several blocks to the west was the entertainment district. Phillips wasn't on Beale, but, from his front door, he could *see* Beale Street, and that counted for something. Phillips rounded up all the black talent he could find and started recording. The idea was to record songs that could be sold to Chess in Chicago or Modern/RPM on the west coast, the two main labels that signed black artists.

At the start of the decade, B. B. King became the undisputed leader of the pack when his song, "Three O'Clock Blues," made the national R&B charts. It was the first time a Memphis radio personality had placed a hit record on the national charts, but it would not be the last; it would happen again in the 1960s with Rufus Thomas and once again in the 1970s with Rick Dees. Despite the notoriety the record brought him, King kept his day job at WDIA, but continued performing at local clubs and recording at every opportunity for the Los Angeles-based Bihari brothers.

"We went to homes, the YMCA, wherever the Bihari brothers could find me," says King. "They would set up portable equipment and put blankets against the wall to make it sound better. Then I learned about Sam Phillips' studio and the company I worked for made a deal with Phillips' studio that anything I wanted to record, and they had the time to do, they would let me in."

Joining King, first as his chauffeur, then as a musician, was Bobby "Blue" Bland. Born in Rosemark, Tennessee, his family moved to Memphis when he was a child and he grew up singing in churches around the city. Even though B. B. King was just five years his senior, Bland idolized him and jumped at the chance to become his driver as he toured around the Mid-South. Eventually King, recognizing his talent, invited him to join his band. Years later, Bland looked back on those days with affection. The only bad part was the pay. "We worked for Sunbeam Mitchell at Beale and Hernando and we got about $5 a night, with food," says Bland with a laugh. "But it was a good time."

Bland did some sessions in 1951 with Ike Turner, and one of the songs, "Cried All Night," was released on Modern. His career came to a sudden halt in 1952 when he was drafted. After his discharge in 1954, he was signed by the Texas-based label, Duke Records. From 1954 to 1972, he recorded a number of Top 40 hits for Duke, including "Cry Cry Cry," "Stormy Monday Blues," and "Turn on Your Love Light," an upbeat tune that became enormously successful with white college audiences in the 1960s. Like many of his sessions, "Turn On Your Love Light" was recorded in Nashville. It was raining that day, he told me. "We didn't really think it would do anything," he says. "But it turned out to be one of the biggest things we ever did."

74

Bland still lives in Memphis, and with the exception of a seven-year stint in Texas, he has always made the city his home. Sadly, Memphis has never claimed him, perhaps because he recorded in Nashville for a Texas label. I once asked him about Memphis' neglect of its blues heritage. His reply could be applied equally to the city's appreciation of his career. "Memphis is sorta' swishy, swatchy," he sniffed. "But they will never get rid of the label, 'Home of the Blues.' W. C. Handy saw to that."

*   *   *

B. B. King did some recording at Memphis Recording service, but not much. Phillips was trying to sell his own discoveries to Modern/RPM and the Bihari brothers apparently thought it wise not to get too cozy with the wild man from Memphis. In the beginning, Phillips would record anything that moved. Weddings, speeches, birthday greetings, nothing was beneath the dignity of Memphis Recording Service. If it made a sound, Phillips could give you a good reason for preserving it on tape—and for a fair price. But Phillips was a dreamer. He wanted to make records like the ones being played on the radio. Pop music was out of the question. There were no musicians in Memphis sophisticated enough to do pop. Country was the hottest thing going, but Nashville had that tied down, and, besides, there didn't seem to be any country artists in Memphis. That left R&B. With R&B talent scouts from Los Angeles and Chicago visiting Memphis on a regular basis, Phillips knew the odds for success were better if he concentrated on black music. In those days the market for R&B among whites was almost non-existent. Few whites purchased R&B records. They might listen on the radio, especially if no one was looking, but they wouldn't be caught dead buying the record.

In February 1951, Ike Turner brought his band, the Kings of Rhythm, into Phillips' studio. Phillips booked the session on the recommendation of B. B. King, who had heard the group in Mississippi. With Turner's band was Jackie Brenston, a new saxophonist who had written a song called "Rocket 88."

When they recorded the song, Brenston, not the regular vocalist, did the vocals. Chess bought the master. To the surprise of everyone, the record went to No. 1 on the national R&B charts.

Not only was "Rocket 88" the first No. 1 record Chess ever had, it was the only No. 1 record Ike Turner ever had, with or without Tina.

Many people consider "Rocket 88" the first rock 'n' roll record ever recorded. That is debatable, since there were a number of similar songs recorded around that time that could quality for that honor, but what is not debatable is where the first rock 'n' roll record was recorded. Phillips' Memphis Recording Service owns that distinction.

Lightning had struck for Phillips. His studio, still in the toddler stage, had produced a No. 1 hit record. Encouraged, he stepped up his efforts to recruit black talent. It was a courageous thing to do. Segregation was still the law of the land. Socializing between the races was not just frowned upon, it was *against the law.* If he had taken Ike Turner and Jackie Brenston into the cafe next door to celebrate the success of the record, they all would have been arrested. Years later, when asked why he had focused on recording black music, he attributed it to the fact that while growing up on a farm in Florence, Alabama, one of the black laborers, Uncle Silas Payne, often sat him on his knee and sang to him. When the R&B records he recorded with black artists became hits with white teens, Phillips was not surprised.

"These records appealed to white youngsters, just as Uncle Silas' songs and stories used to appeal to me," says Phillips. "To city-born white children who had never had an Uncle Silas, it was something new, and it became their nonsense—like fairy tales."

To hell with the law, Phillips was on a mission. His memories of Uncle Silas—and his obsession with success—propelled him with a reckless abandon for the social consequences. A stream of talented black musicians poured into his studio: Walter Horton, Doctor Ross, Joe Hill Louis, Willie Johnson -- and, of course, Howlin' Wolf.

Phillips had heard Howlin' Wolf on the radio, so he had this visual image of him in his head, but when he first came into his studio in the summer of 1951, Phillips could scarcely believe his eyes. The Wolf stood at six-feet-six and had the largest feet Phillips had ever seen. Howlin' Wolf was his stage name; his friends called him Big Foot Chester.

76

If Phillips, who is in the five-feet-six range, felt intimidated, it gave way to awe when the Wolf cranked up his band. Phillips later said that watching the Wolf sit in his studio, his enormous feet spread apart, the veins on his neck bulging, his eyes burning with fire as he sang and played his harmonica, was one of the greatest shows on earth.

When he performed, the Wolf was as raw as the Arkansas earth he tilled as a farmer. His voice had a primeval quality to it. It was not a big, deep voice as you might expect; it was long and dark, like a tunnel, filled with the anguish, or angst, as it would be called in the 1980s, of a thousand painful lifetimes. Despite his size, the Wolf had a vulnerability, expressed in his voice, that was appealing, and that was a major contributor to his later success. White people loved the Wolf for the same reason they loved King Kong. They wanted him to be *their* giant.

The Wolf recorded two songs during that first session, "Moanin' at Midnight" and "How Many More Years." More sessions followed. Phillips placed some of the songs with Modern/RPM, then, after a dispute with that label, sold the Wolf's next masters to Chess. Modern/RPM responded with a lawsuit against Phillips and Chess. Then, while Phillips was recording the Wolf for Chess, Modern/RPM hired Ike Turner as a talent scout and asked him to record the Wolf for them.

Turner set up a portable studio and re-recorded the first two songs the Wolf had done with Phillips. By September, Howling Wolf had records from both Chess and Modern/RPM on the national R&B charts. Years later, he admitted he had "messed up" by doing dual sessions, betraying the man who first took a chance on him, but he attributed the competition to a dispute between Turner and Phillips. Howling Wolf's last session with Phillips was in July 1952. Leonard Chess ended the rivalry by taking him away from both Phillips and Modern/RPM. He offered him $4,000 in cash and a new car if he would move to Chicago.

Phillips couldn't compete with that, and Modern/RPM didn't know about it, so the Wolf turned his farm over to his brother-in-law and loaded up his new car and struck out for Chicago, where he lived until his death in 1976. He signed an exclusive contract with Chess and had a number of R&B hits over the years, including "No Place To Go," "The Red Rooster" and "Smokestack Lightin.'" By the late 1950s, his primitive style of music had fallen into disfavor with black audiences and he was looked down upon by black jazz musicians, who considered his rough edges an embarrassment.

The Rolling Stones re-discovered Howling Wolf in 1964 and introduced him to the British public. From that point on, he performed almost exclusively for white audiences. In 1970 he teamed with Eric Clapton, Steve Winwood, Bill Wyman and Charlie Watts in a London studio to record an outstanding album, *The London Howlin' Wolf Sessions*, released by Chess in 1971.

It was an important session for the blues rockers—Beatle Ringo Starr even sat in on one song--but if they thought that Howling Wolf, by then in poor health, was in awe of them, they were mistaken. Outtakes from the session reveal a somewhat paternal Howling Wolf, reminiscent of Phillips' Uncle Silas, willing to explain chord changes but resistant to Clapton's invitations to join in where he didn't want to join in.

*   *   *

Frustrated by his dealings with the record labels in Chicago and Los Angeles, dealings which he considered marred by questionable business tactics on their part, Sam Phillips decided to start his own record label in 1952. He called it Sun Record Company. The label's first release was "Drivin' Slow," by saxophonist Johnny London. People told Phillips he was crazy to start his own label. They told him he couldn't compete with the majors. But he didn't believe them, not even when "Drivin' Slow" proved a bust.

For a year after that failure, he put Sun Records on the back burner, while he struggled to keep the studio going. Meanwhile, he still had his day job at the radio station. He also had a night job at the Peabody Hotel, where he monitored the equipment for big band broadcasts from the roof top.

By 1953, he was ready to gear up Sun Records again. WDIA had just added a new deejay, Rufus Thomas. A high energy announcer, with a glib delivery, the 36-year-old Thomas had toured with the Rabbitfoot minstrel shows since leaving high school in 1936. Going from town to town (they called it the chitlin circuit) he learned the basics of being an entertainer. "It was truly an experience," Thomas explained to me. "They had high stepping dancers, comics, singers, they had it all. That was during the days of separation, where the whites were on one side and the blacks were on the other. Man, we had some of the greatest shows ever."

Thomas looked like a winner to Phillips. He was a high-profile announcer on WDIA and had nearly 20 years experience as a minstrel entertainer. Phillips invited Thomas into the studio to record a song called "Bear Cat." Phillips released the record and held his breath. It was a hit. Encouraged, Phillips released two more songs—"Just Walking in the Rain" by the Prisonaires and "Feelin' Good" by Little Junior Parker. Both were hits. By 1954, for reasons that never have been explained, though it would not be unreasonable to attribute it to the difficulties he was having keeping the loyalty of black artists, Phillips lost interest in Thomas and the other black artists on his roster.

I asked Thomas about that in 1989 and was surprised to hear an undercurrent of bitterness in his voice when he talked about it, even after all those years. "Sam dropped all of the black artists," says Thomas. "That is the only thing I dislike about the whole picture—Sam not carrying along the good black artists with the good white artists."

*   *   *

As it happened, 1952 was a big year for Memphis. Not only did it mark the birth of Sun Records, it was the year Kemmons Wilson opened America's first Holiday Inn. But it was two years earlier, in 1950, that the fireworks really began. That was the year Tennessee's new senator, Estes Kefauver, and arch-enemy of Boss Crump, took over as head of the Senate Crime Investigating Committee. Over a two-year period, Kefauver used the committee hearings, many of which were televised, to expose a vast network of organized crime in every major crime city but one—Memphis.

Looking back, it is obvious Kefauver used the hearings to taunt his enemies in Memphis. He had no intention of exposing them (not all of his supporters in Memphis had clean hands), but he obviously wanted his enemies to know he could expose them.

79

Whatever his motivation—it could have been merely defensive, to protect himself and his Memphis supporters, or it could have been offensive, a genuine desire to combat organized crime—the results mesmerized the entire nation. The Accardo-Guzik-Fischetti syndicate in Chicago and the Costell-Adonis-Lansky syndicate in New York were exposed by Kefauver, as were syndicates in St. Louis, Kansas City, New Orleans, Tampa, Las Vegas, Cleveland and Detroit. The media was so enthralled by the process, no one noticed Kefauver had omitted Memphis from his inquiry. That is incredible when you consider all the national press Memphis had received, castigating the city for its tolerance of organized crime and official corruption. For some mysterious reason, the fact that the "murder capital" of America for the past four decades had escaped the committee's scrutiny was overlooked by the press.

When the committee issued its findings, it said organized criminals had infiltrated legitimate businesses, ranging from liquor to sports to news services. The results of Kefauver's excursion into the underworld were predictable. All of the gangsters identified by name said they were innocent and had never heard of organized crime. After receiving death threats, Kefauver stepped down from the committee in 1952, citing a desire to work for "international peace."

*   *   *

In early 1953, Scotty Moore, a guitar picker fresh out of the Navy, went by Memphis Recording Service to talk to Sam Phillips about the Starlight Wranglers, a country group he was fronting. At that time, Sam was using the studio for two types of recordings-- vanity recordings for weddings and birthdays, and speculative recordings for sale, hopefully, to record companies. Since Sam was still concentrating almost exclusively on black artists, the Starlight Wranglers did not fit into either category.

Sam wasn't eager to put out a record on a country band, but he had an open door policy and he didn't discourage Scotty from hanging out at the studio. At every opportunity, Scotty talked up the exploits of the Starlight Wranglers. Finally, Sam relented and let the group into the studio. The session produced a record, "My Kind of Carrying On," that, according to Scotty, sold "12 copies, maybe."

Undeterred, Scotty continued to hang out at the studio, talking to Sam, watching people come and go. It was during that time that Elvis Presley stopped by the studio to do a vanity recording, a birthday greeting for his mother. Since his family had moved to the projects, his musical interests had grown, but, for the most part, he preferred gospel music. He often attended gospel concerts at a downtown theater, Ellis Auditorium. On one occasion he summoned the courage to go backstage to meet the performers.

For years, Memphis had been a hotbed of activity for gospel music. Just as the major labels sent recording teams to the city to record blues musicians, so did the labels that specialized in gospel music send teams to record Christian music. Thus, the city that invented the "devil's music," the blues, also was a major center for Christian music.

The Memphis-based Blackwood Brothers, one of the most successful gospel recording groups in history, often performed at Ellis Auditorium. That was where Presley met J. D. Sumner, the bass singer for the Blackwood Brothers. They remained close friends for the remainder of Presley's life.

By the time Presley walked in off the street to do that recording for his mother, the Memphis airwaves were dominated by blues and gospel music. There was an excitement in the air that was palpable. Like the scent of honeysuckle, it was so strong you felt you could reach out and touch it. I felt it sitting in a chinaberry tree in Hollandale. Presley felt it every time he turned on his radio, every time he stepped out onto Beale Street. What he felt when he recorded that birthday greeting at the age of eighteen, one can only imagine.

Marion Keisker, Phillips' secretary, was there when Presley made the recording. She was impressed enough by Elvis that when she took the four dollars for the recording she asked for his name and address in case her boss ever needed a singer.

About a year later, during one of Scotty's daily pilgrimages to the studio, Scotty, Sam and Marion went next door for a cup of coffee. Scotty figured that if he knew what Sam was looking for, he would give it to him. Tired of hinting around, he finally tried the direct approach.

"What exactly are you looking for?" Scotty asked point-blank.

"I'm not real sure. Something different. It can't be the same old, same old, like everybody else is doing."

It was at that point that Marion joined in the conversation.

"Mr. Sam, you remember that boy who came in to record that song for his mother?"

"Yeah, I remember him. He was a dark haired boy."

"Well, you said you thought he had a pretty good voice. Why don't you get him to come in and try it?"

"Yeah, I'll probably do that."

"That was all I needed to hear," recalls Scotty. "I worried him to death."

From that day on, Scotty's daily visits to the studio always began with the same question: "Have you called that boy yet?" Finally, Sam relented and told Marion to give Scotty Presley's name and phone number.

"When I saw his name," Scotty later recalled, "I said, 'what kind of a name is this?'"

"I don't know," said Sam. "It's his name. Give him a call. Ask him over to your house and see what you think about him.'"

Scotty talked to Elvis and made arrangements to meet at Scotty's house the next day, a Sunday. Scotty also invited his bass player, Bill Black.

Scotty's wife, Bobbie, was looking out the window when Elvis arrived. He was wearing white buck shoes, a white lacy shirt and pink pants with a black stripe down the legs. She told Scotty that if *he* was coming inside, she was going out the back door.

When Elvis came in, Scotty was impressed at how clean and neat he was. "He sang everything from Eddy Arnold to Billy Eckstine," says Scotty. "It was uncanny to me how he knew so many songs. Bill came over and listened for a little while and got up and left. I told Elvis I would talk to Sam and we probably would be in touch."

After Elvis left, Bill, who lived down the street, returned to compare notes with Scotty. "I asked him what he thought," says Scotty. "He said he thought he had a pretty good voice. I said I thought he had good timing."

The following night, Scotty stopped by the studio after work to report to Sam, who still seemed unsure about the venture. Sam suggested that Scotty and Bill bring Elvis in so he could see how Elvis sounded on tape. About a week later, on July 5, 1954, they got together in the studio. Scotty, at age 23, played guitar. Black was on bass. Elvis, at age 19, did the vocals and also played acoustic guitar. Sam was in the control room.

They did several songs, none of them very impressive, but they knew they were just experimenting. It was not meant to be a real session. They would record a song, then Sam would back the tape up and they would record the next song over the previous one. During one break, Elvis jumped up and started playing his guitar.

"I mean he was beating the fire out of that guitar," says Scotty. "Then he started singing, 'That's All Right Mama.'"

Sam stuck his head out the control room door.

"'What are you doing?" asked Sam.

"'We're, just goofing around," Scotty said.

"'Well, it didn't sound too bad through the doors. Try it again."

"We did it three or four times for Sam and he put it on tape," said Scotty. "He played it back for us and said, 'Yeah, that's good. It's different. What is it?' I said, 'Well, you said you were looking for something different.'"

"That's All Right Mama" had been written and recorded in 1940 by blues singer Arthur "Big Boy" Crudup. Elvis almost certainly heard the song on WDIA. But when Elvis sang it, it didn't sound like a blues song. It was . . . . well, different. Sam knew he had a record. He told them he needed a song for the B side. Bill jumped up and started slapping his bass, singing "Blue Moon of Kentucky," in a high falsetto voice. Elvis joined in. Sam stuck his head out the door and hollered above the music: "That's the one."

Finally, Sam had the "something different" he had been looking for. Within two weeks, they had the record pressed and ready for radio. Marion took Elvis by the *Press-Scimitar* to meet the entertainment writer, Edwin Howard. An item appeared the next day in the newspaper. Years later, Howard wrote that Elvis had been very shy during the interview and let Marion do most of the talking. When Elvis spoke, he recalled, it usually was to say "yes sir" or "no sir." His hair was brushed back in a ducktail and his face was covered with pimples. He wore a "funny looking" bowtie. He wasn't what you'd call a lady killer.

Sam took "That's All Right Mama" to Dewey Phillips (no relation), a deejay at WHBQ who was doing for white radio what WDIA had done for black radio. Sam and Dewey were good enough friends that Sam could take tapes by for Dewey to play on the air during his "Red Hot and Blue" show. If listeners called in, Sam knew he had a hit; he would rush back to the studio and cut an acetate recording on equipment he had in the studio. When Dewey played "That's All Right Mama," the station's white listeners went wild. Elvis was the talk of the town. Sleepy Eyed John, a deejay for a country station, picked up on the flip side, "Blue Moon of Kentucky." At night, Sleepy Eyed John moonlighted as an announcer at a nightclub called the Eagle's Nest.

Jack Clement, a guitarist and singer in a band that was playing the Eagle Nest at that time, awoke one morning to hear Sleepy Eyed John introducing "Blue Moon" on his radio show. "Sleepy Eyed was saying, here's the record everyone is screaming about," recalls Clement, who pauses to sing a few bars of "Blue Moon" for me. "I said,' Oh, man, that's it. I want to hear that again. It was an instant hit from day one."

A week and a half after the record was released, Elvis performed at the Overton Park Shell, an outdoor amphitheater. The afternoon show, headlined by country crooner Slim Whitman, was a dud. When Elvis returned for the evening performance, he was nervous. He sang an up-tempo song. The audience went wild. The women screamed and shouted.

"That's when he got into all that shaking," recalls Scotty, who played guitar that night. "When Elvis played the guitar standing up, he would go up on the balls of his feet and keep time to the music. He was doing it, I'm sure when we cut the record. When we did the show, all those people started screaming and hollering and we didn't know what was going on. When we went off stage, someone made the comment that it was because Elvis was shaking his leg. From then on, he just starting adding a little more to it and made it into a fine art. But it was a natural thing for him."

Sam knew he had a hit with Elvis. What he didn't know was how to package him. The songs they recorded were bluesy, but they weren't blues and, even if they were, he couldn't package him as a blues singer since white men didn't sing the blues.

84

Earlier that year, Louis Armstrong had come to Memphis for a performance on Beale Street. A newspaper story described Armstrong as "the great negro trumpet player" and announced that he would be giving "a show for whites at 8 p.m. and a dance for negroes at 10:30."

No, Sam knew that it wouldn't do to bill Elvis as a rhythm and blues performer, not at a time when race mixing could land you in jail (or worse). The songs had a country feel to them, but Elvis wasn't like any other country singer making records.

Sam compromised. Since "rock 'n' roll" had not been coined, Sam, or his secretary, made up a phrase he thought represented a mix of the two styles. He billed Elvis as the "Hillbilly Cat." By the end of the summer he succeeded in booking the "Hillbilly Cat" on the Louisiana Hayride, a top-rated country radio show broadcast from Shreveport, Louisiana.

On October 16, 1954, as Elvis walked onto the stage of the Louisiana Hayride, Boss Crump, at age 80, lay dying in his bed at 1962 Peabody Avenue in Memphis. He had fallen ill earlier in the summer. As Elvis performed that night, initiating a new era in American music, life flowed from Crump's ravaged body. He died that night without appointing a successor to his empire. What he thought of the music emanating from his radio all summer is not known.

* * *

Buoyed by the success of Elvis' record in Memphis and his reception at the Louisiana Hayride, Sam Phillips booked Elvis anyplace and every place he could. John Evans, who would later play keyboards on the first No. 1 record recorded in Memphis, "The Letter," recalls seeing Elvis perform at the grand opening of a laundry down the street from his house. "My brother held me up to where I could see," says Evans. "People came from all over the neighborhood and swarmed down on the place."

Sam loaded up his car with records and promoted them at radio stations across the South. Then he sent Elvis, Scotty and Bill out on the road. Soon "That's All Right Mama" and "Blue Moon of Kentucky" were solid hits across the South. For the first time, Sun Records looked like a viable business. Sam stopped scheduling sessions with black musicians and focused all his efforts on Elvis. When they returned to Memphis, the trio performed at local venues and worked in the studio with Sam. Through the summer of 1955 and into the fall of 1956, a string of regional hits flowed out of the studio, including "Mystery Train," "Baby, Let's Play House" and "Good Rockin' Tonight."

It was during this time that Jack Clement met Elvis. With the success Ray Price was having on the country charts, Sleepy Eyed John organized an 8-piece western band at the Eagle's Nest. Jack was the lead singer and the MC. Elvis, Scotty and Bill were booked as the floor show, which meant Jack introduced them each night.

"The first time, Elvis said, 'Give me a big build up, Jack,'" he recalls. "I said, 'OK, I will.' When they came on, just the three of them, with Elvis on acoustic, Scotty on electric guitar and Bill slapping the bass, it was magic. My girlfriend, Doris, was there. I later married her. Elvis was always flirting with her, but he didn't get her. I got the girl that time."

Although Sam, Elvis, Scotty and Bill didn't coin the term "rock 'n' roll"—that honor went to Cleveland deejay Allan Freed—they invented and then defined the music that took the name. Two months after Elvis, Scotty and Bill recorded "That's All Right, Mama," Michigan-born Bill Haley made the Top 20 with a rhythm and blues song, "Shake, Rattle and Roll" that danced around the fringe of rock 'n' roll. The following year, he had his only No. 1 hit, "Rock Around the Clock," a song that cemented his role in the development of rock 'n' roll, thanks to a movie of the same name that featured both Haley and Freed.

It didn't take long for the major labels to feel the tremors radiating from Memphis. Sam received many offers for Elvis over the next year, but turned them down. Then, in the summer and early fall of 1956, something happened to make Sam change his mind. Abruptly, in November 1955, he sold Elvis' contract to RCA Records for $40,000 ($35,000 to Sam and a $5,000 advance to Elvis). Everyone in the music industry was stunned. It was a bad deal. Why would Sam sell an artist for peanuts? It is one of the great mysteries of rock 'n' roll history.

In a 1959 interview, Sam said he did not regret the decision. "Selling that contract gave us the capital we desperately needed at the time for expansion," he said. "To understand why I have never regretted the decision, you have to remember something. At that time, most of the experts thought Elvis was a flash-in-the-pan. Even RCA wasn't sure they had made a good deal."

What no one knew at the time was that Sam had borrowed $25,000 from Holiday Inn founder Kemmons Wilson to start up an all-female radio station that would be given the call letters WHER. Once the loan was paid off, according to the agreement, the two men would become equal partners. Selling Elvis's contract allowed Sam to pay off Kemmons and then begin the partnership. In time it would lead to a record label named Holiday Inn Records.

Not only had Memphis, within a period of seven years, given birth to rock 'n' roll, the first all black radio station, and the first national motel chain, it now was the home of the first all-female radio station. A sign was hung over the control room: "Doll Den." Two attractive and effervescent sales executives were given the keys to a Rolls Royce and told to sell, sell, sell.

Memphis sizzled with excitement. It's not surprising dreamers flocked to the city in droves. It was the only place in America where a shy country boy could become a king, where black men and white women could not only get on the radio, but have a hand in management. For those who had been shut out of the system, Memphis offered new hope. The Revolution was underway.

One of the first to respond was Carl Perkins, who drove in from Jackson, Tennessee, to introduce himself to Sam Phillips. Within twelve months he would be followed by Johnny Cash from Arkansas, Jerry Lee Lewis from Louisiana and Roy Orbison from Texas. Carl wasn't sure what to expect when he walked into the studio. After an audition, Sam signed him to a recording contract.

"I'd sent tapes to every record company I could," says Carl. "I'd get them back and they'd say, 'We don't know what it is and we don't know what to do with it.' Most of the tapes were never even opened."

If the majors didn't know what to do with Carl, Sam certainly did. The first song they recorded was one Carl had written while living in the projects in Jackson. He titled it "Blue Suede Shoes." It was released early in 1956 and immediately became a hit on all three charts—pop, country and R&B.

Meanwhile, RCA had taken Elvis to Nashville for a session. In January 1956, they released the first single, "Heartbreak Hotel." As "Blue Suede Shoes" and "Heartbreak Hotel" battled it out on the charts, Carl appeared the clear winner. Arrangements were made for him to receive a gold record for the song on the Perry Como show in New York. In late March, Carl and his band left a concert in Norfolk, Virginia, to drive to New York.

Outside of Wilmington, Delaware, they were involved in an accident that sent Carl to the hospital. A little over three weeks after the accident, "Heartbreak Hotel" went to No. 1 on the Billboard charts. "Blue Suede Shoes" stalled at No. 4. Fate, as if to rub Carl's nose in his misfortune, gave the No. 2 slot to Perry Como for "Hot Diggity/Jukebox Baby."

Elvis sent a wire to Carl suggesting that Carl might have been No. 1 if he had not had the accident. Carl recovered from his injuries quickly enough to receive a new car from Sam Phillips on April 10. Carl told a reporter he was going to drive the dark-blue Cadillac "mighty careful." Carl's photo with the car appeared the next day in the *Press-Scimitar*. That was the last major attention he received from the press for nearly 30 years.

Back in the studio with Sam, Carl followed "Blue Suede Shoes" with "Your True Love" and "Pink Pedal Pushers," but his career fizzled quickly until the 1960s, when the Beatles recorded three of his songs—"Match Box," "Honey Don't" and "Everybody's Trying to Be My Baby."

Sam took Carl's plunge in stride and moved on to the next man in line, Johnny Cash. Sam had signed Cash to a contract early in 1955 and the first release, "Hey Porter," backed with "Cry, Cry, Cry," was a hit, as was the follow-up, "Folsom Prison Blues."

But Sam apparently thought Johnny was too country to fit the new rock 'n' roll mold and with the success of Elvis (and then Carl), Sam gently nudged Johnny to the back burner. Despite his day job as an appliance salesman, Cash stayed busy writing new songs. When Sam called him back in the studio after Carl's automobile accident he was ready. In 1956, he scored with three self-penned Top-10 hits: "I Walk the Line," "There You Go" and "So Doggone Lonesome."

Elvis now recorded solely in Nashville, but he still lived in Memphis and he stopped by Memphis Recording Studio on a regular basis. Like everyone else, he quickly became a Johnny Cash fan. By then Colonel Tom Parker had become Elvis' manager. Since Parker also managed Johnny Cash's future wife, June Carter, a member of the popular Carter Family, he often booked them together at fairs.

"I used to do a little comedy act in the beginning and do my little set and then Elvis and Scotty and Bill went on," June once explained to me. "I was introduced to Johnny Cash by Elvis. He used to go into every little cafe and play Johnny Cash records. He used to tune his guitar by listening to 'Cry, Cry Cry' . . . I met Johnny Cash because Elvis was such a fan of his."

Johnny Cash became Sun Record's biggest selling artist, with sales surpassing those of Elvis while he was with Sun. It was during that period that Roy Orbison entered the picture. Johnny heard him perform in Texas and suggested he send a demo to Sam. Roy sent in a tape of "Ooby Dooby,"an up-tempo song written by some of his schoolmates. Sam liked the song and called him, but when Roy told him Johnny Cash had recommended him, Sam snapped that Cash didn't run his studio and hung up. When he cooled off, he offered Roy a contract and re-recorded "Ooby Dooby." The song, with a solid rockabilly riff and nonsense lyrics, did well, but wasn't a major hit.

By the summer of 1956, Sam decided he needed some help in the studio. Jack Clement had a job in a hardware store, but he performed at night and on weekends. That summer he set up a studio in a garage on Fernwood Street with a truck driver, Sam Wallace. As they were learning to use the equipment, Jack did a recording session with Billy Lee Riley in a radio station. He took the tape in to Memphis Recording to be mastered and when he told Sam he was setting up a garage studio, Sam offered him a job.

If you ask Jack if he was hired as an engineer, he will laugh. He prefers the word "operator," since he considers engineers technical experts and not music experts. "Actually, I was one of a new breed," says Jack. "Prior to that, everyone who had run a board had been an engineer. I was a musician. So suddenly a musician is playing with those knobs instead of an engineer. I did a lot of things wrong. But some of them worked. That was the neat thing about doing things wrong--sometimes it works."

On June 15, 1956, Jack Clement reported for his first day of work at Memphis Recording. He remembers the date because it was on June 15, 1948, he had enlisted in the Marine Corps. June 15 was one of those reoccurring dates that demanded his attention.

The first artist Sam assigned to Jack Clement was Roy Orbison. Sun already had released "Ooby Dooby" and was in need of a strong follow-up. "Musically, Roy was ahead of his time," says Jack. "He wanted to do things in the studio that were a little bit over our heads production-wise. Memphis wasn't quite ready for that. We didn't have organized vocal groups and strings. He was thinking orchestrally. He was wanting to cut what he ultimately did cut. I told him, and he never let me forget it, that he would never make it as a ballad singer."

Jack and Roy became good friends, and Roy moved into his house while they were working together in the studio. Roy was shy, says Jack, but not as withdrawn as he appeared later in life. "We went out at night and hung out," says Jack. "Roy was a lot of fun. He was very comfortable with the people around us. Now if you brought in other people, he might be a little shy, but he was very comfortable with our little group. He was a genuinely nice person. Always was."

Jack's official job title was engineer, but with Sam staying less and less at the studio, Jack organized the sessions, booked the players and operated the equipment. He recorded a number of songs with Roy—the better cuts were "Rock House," "Sweet and Easy to Love" and "Mean Woman Blues"—but they never got another song that did as well as "Ooby Dooby." Sam wanted Jack to push Roy more toward rock 'n' roll and Roy wanted to be a ballad singer. Frustrated, Roy left Sun Records in 1957 and moved to Nashville, where he wrote and recorded the hits for which he is best known—"Oh, Pretty Woman," "Cryin'" and "Blue Bayou."

That fall, Jack was in the studio when the receptionist came into the control room and told him there was a man in the outer office who said he played piano like Chet Atkins played guitar. Jack invited him into the studio. "I'm Jerry Lee Lewis," the man says, running his words together, making his name sound like one word.

"Sure enough, he played 'Wildwood Flower' on the piano and it sounded like Chet Atkins licks," says Jack. "I said, 'Can you sing?' He said, 'Yeah,' and started singing these wonderful George Jones songs. I taped four or five songs. I asked him if he knew any rock 'n' roll. He said, no. I liked the tapes so much I played them for anybody who came in the door. For some reason, I didn't get around to playing the tapes for Sam for several weeks. I was busy, he was busy, whatever."

When Sam heard the tapes, he told Jack to schedule a session with Jerry Lee, but before he could call him, Jerry Lee showed at the studio sporting a newly grown goatee. Jack thought he looked pretty scruffy looking and gave him hell. Jack told him that if he would stick around town a few days, they would cut some songs. That suited Jerry Lee just fine.

Sam was in Nashville attending a disk jockey's convention when they did the session. They recorded a song he had written, "End of the Row," then they tried four or five other songs. Nothing really clicked. Jack asked if he knew, "Crazy Arms." Jerry Lee said he knew a little of it. Jack turned the tape on. The bass player was in the bathroom. The guitar player had put down his instrument. It was just Jerry Lee on piano and the drummer. Jack let the tape run because he figured they would redo it when the bass player returned. "There wasn't anything but drums and piano on the record, except at the very end when the guy who was playing bass walked in and picked up the electric guitar and made a bad chord because he thought we weren't recording. That's all there was to 'Crazy Arms.' It was on tape, so we went on to something else."

After Jerry Lee left, Jack listened to the tape again. He fell in love with "Crazy Arms." He played it for everyone who came into the studio over the weekend.

"The next Monday, when Sam came in, we went back into the control room," says Jack. "I put the tape of 'Crazy Arms' on. It started and before it ever got to Jerry Lee's voice, Sam reached over and stopped the tape.

"He said, 'I can sell that. Just from the piano intro.'

"Then he wound it back and played it through. That night he made an acetate and took it to Dewey Phillips and Dewey started playing it and everyone wanted to buy it. Now that was when the music business was fun. We make a tape on Thursday and it's on the radio the next Monday and on sale in the stores the next Thursday."

Based on public reaction to "Crazy Arms" and "End of the Road," Sam offered Jerry Lee a contract and promised to use him as a session player whenever possible. Meanwhile, Jerry Lee went out on the road, shocking audiences by kicking his piano bench across the stage and jumping up on top of the piano. That fall ,Johnny Cash, probably at the suggestion of Jack Clement, took Jerry Lee out on the road with him.

"He gave me my first tour," says Jerry Lee. "We left town in a '57 Buick and I was getting $100 a day and I thought I was getting rich. We went all over Canada on gravel roads and wore the car completely out. When I got home, I had $60 in my pocket."

In December, Sam scheduled a session with Carl Perkins. He told Jack to bring Jerry Lee in off the road and book him on piano for the session. While Carl and Jerry Lee were rehearsing, Johnny Cash showed up. Carl had invited him to the session and was expecting him. Then, to everyone's surprise, Elvis strolled into the studio. He often stopped by when he was in town.

"Elvis played the piano for about an hour and then Jerry, he was brand new, he asked if he could play the piano," says Johnny. "Well, when Jerry sat down at the piano, Elvis didn't play it anymore." Johnny laughs. "*Nobody* followed the 'Killer.'"

As the four of them gathered around the piano, Sam called a newspaper reporter—the photo would later be dubbed the "Million Dollar Quartet—and Jack turned on the tape machine.

"I set up a couple of microphones here and there in the room and started taping," says Jack. "I wasn't trying to make a record. I kept that going for an hour and a half or so. Some people say Johnny Cash is not on the tape. He says he is. I'm not sure."

Unfortunately, nothing substantial resulted from the session. The songs recorded by the Million Dollar Quartet weren't released until 1981 and the only good thing to come out of Carl's individual session was "Matchbox," which was not a hit for Carl, but was a hit for the Beatles.

Nineteen fifty-six ended with Elvis firmly entrenched as the king of rock 'n' roll. It was a good year for Memphis music. Elvis had four No. 1 hits: "Don't Be Cruel/Hound Dog," "Heartbreak Hotel," "Love Me Tender" and "I Want You, I Need You." Carl scored with "Blue Suede Shoes" and Johnny had a string of country and regional hits. Elvis became a movie star with the release of *Love Me Tender*. By the end of the movie's run in 1957, it had grossed $4.5 million, making it the tenth most profitable movie of the year. At the top of the list was *The Ten Commandments* with Charlton Heston, which grossed $18.5 million.

By 1957, Memphis was soaring. In a year that saw Pat Boone, Frank Sinatra and Perry Como all score with No. 1 hits, Memphis countered with Jerry Lee Lewis' "Whole Lot Of Shakin' Going On," which peaked at No. 2, and another string of No. 1 hits from Elvis: "All Shook Up," "Jailhouse Rock," "(Let Me Be Your) Teddy Bear," "Too Much" and "Love Me." Elvis starred in his third movie that year, *Jailhouse Rock*, but it was the beginning of the end for Elvis the artist. Between 1956 and 1972 he starred in 33 movies.

His music took a back seat to his film career, but Elvis, by then earning $1 million a picture, was too busy savoring his success to notice what was happening to his music or to his friends. To impress his mother, he bought a two-story, limestone mansion in Memphis for $100,000. He kept the name that came with the house—Graceland.

Unnoticed in the commotion over the motion picture deals, was the way Elvis' band was being pushed to the sidelines. By then Scotty and Bill had been joined by D. J. Fontana on drums. When Elvis filmed *Love Me Tender*, the music director, Ken Darby, refused to use Scotty, Bill and D.J. in the movie. He wanted to use his own trio. Elvis' manager Tom Parker agreed to exclude them from the soundtrack. To make it up to the Memphis boys, Elvis flew them to Hollywood to record "Too Much" and his second RCA album, *Elvis*.

It was a nice gesture, but it was too little, too late. When they began, they had a 50-25-25 split agreement. Elvis got half and the other half was split by Scotty and Bill. When D.J. joined the group, he was given a salary of $100-$125 a week. Then Elvis' manager got involved.

"We discussed it and decided that Bill and I would go on salary, too," says Scotty. "They decided to make a corporation out of Elvis. We got $100 a week when we weren't working and $150 a week when we were. Later it went up to $200."

That arrangement worked for a while, but when Elvis started making $1 million per movie and they were excluded from the soundtrack, it created waves. "We had to buy our own meals and clothes," says Scotty. "When it got to where he was really raking in the bucks, and we were at the same level, well ... our union wasn't strong enough, so the only thing to do was to quit."

Scotty, Bill and D.J. walked out in 1957. Elvis did a few shows without them, and then Parker asked them to do the state fair in Dallas for two weeks and a tour of the northwest that took them to Seattle, Spokane and Los Angles. They agreed to do it for $250 a show, but when the tour ended they went their separate ways. Scotty didn't see Elvis again until he performed in Elvis' CBS-TV special in 1968.

After the departure of Scotty, Bill and D.J., Elvis' music sank into a soundtrack mindset, but with the enormous success of the movies no one, least of all Elvis, noticed that his music had lost the raw, reckless, Memphis-homeboy synergy that had made him a recording star. Elvis would have many hit records over the years, but not until he returned to his Memphis roots in 1969 would he again make a good record.

If 1957 was an ominous year for Memphis music, 1958 would prove to be disastrous. Jerry Lee would have a No. 2 hit with "Great Balls of Fire," but would then self-destruct by marrying his 13-year-old cousin. Elvis would have two No. 1 hits with "Don't" and "Hard Headed Woman" and a No. 2 hit with "Wear My Ring Around Your Neck," but he would be devastated by a double whammy: In March he was drafted into the Army and in August his mother died of a heart attack. Elvis was devastated by his mother's death. Some say he never recovered from the loss.

Not happy with the way his career was progressing at Sun Records, Johnny Cash signed with Columbia Records and moved to Nashville in 1958. Jack Clement was working with Johnny at that time and still considers the breakup a mistake for both Johnny and Sam.

"I think Johnny left because he got his feelings hurt," says Jack. "One day Johnny dropped by and wanted to talk to Sam or have lunch or something and Sam was too busy. He was doing something with Jerry Lee. I think John felt slighted. I think that's what started it."

Johnny says Jack played the role of "Henry Kissinger" between himself and Sam. After Johnny signed with Columbia, Sam sent Johnny a curt letter instructing him to come into the studio to complete the recordings agreed to in their contract. When he showed up at the studio, Sam wasn't there. Sam left instructions with Jack to get everything he could out of Johnny.

"I did every song that Jack asked me to do," says Johnny. "I really don't think I would have done it for anyone else in the world. I could have played off sick or pulled this or that excuse. Jack said after we got to working, 'I don't like this any better than you do.' I said, 'Well, I'm really kind of enjoying it.' I recorded everything he asked me to do."

The session produced enough material for Sun Records to release Johnny Cash singles long after he was gone.

Jerry Lee was stunned by public reaction to his marriage. Before the marriage took place, he told Elvis what he was going to do. Elvis thought he was joking. When he convinced him that he was serious, Elvis reportedly said: "God bless you, Jerry Lee. You just saved my career."

Sam advised him not to do it, but Jerry Lee was hardheaded. Why would people get made about that, he reasoned, when they approved of all the other outrageous behavior he engaged in? Jerry Lee was fond of telling about the time he and Elvis went to a party at Jack Clement's house and got buck naked and rode motorcycles around Memphis at 2:30 a.m. Jack doesn't remember the incident now, but admits it may have happened without his knowledge.

* * *

By 1959, Johnny Cash and Roy Orbison were gone, Elvis was in the Army, Jerry Lee was being ridiculed by the press and his concerts were canceled by nervous promoters, and Carl Perkins had returned to the juke joints from which he had sprung.

Despite the hard times, Sun Records scored a No. 4 hit with Bill Justis' instrumental, "Raunchy." When a reporter asked Sam Phillips in 1959 if rock 'n' roll was dead, he answered an emphatic "no," adding that it was simply "modifying the beat." But as the decade ended, Sam prepared to move into a new building on Madison Avenue, leaving the old Memphis Recording Service vacant.

That fall, three black students integrated the all-white Memphis State University. That sent shock waves through the community, but it would be several years yet before the public schools would be desegregated. As the decade ended, it was still against the law for black Memphis residents to eat in white restaurants, go to white movie theaters or check into white hotels.

As editor of the *Press-Scimitar*, Edward J. Meeman maintained that newspaper's dominance over its sister publication, but there was a new star in the ascendancy at *The Commercial Appeal*. In 1957, Michael Grehl began work at *The Commercial Appeal* as an obit writer. By the end of the decade he was well on his way to becoming its managing editor. Under his direction, the morning newspaper would assume the leadership role formerly held by the *Press-Scimitar*. Grehl may have missed the birth of Sun Records, but he would be there to direct news coverage of the second flowering of Memphis music in the 1960s and he would be instrumental in its attempted re-birth in the 1980s.

Elvis Presley
Photofest

Estelle Axton, c. 1995
Photo courtesy James L. Dickerson

The Mar-Keys: Top, clockwise: Don Nix, Terry Johnson, Duck Dunn, Wayne Jackson, Packy Axton, and Steve Cropper
Photo courtesy of Don Nix

Petula Clark found a home in Memphis
Photo courtesy of the Mississippi Valley Collection
University of Memphis, University Libraries

CHAPTER 6

The 1960s:
Sweet Soul, Southern Rock & Slick Pop

At the age of 40, Estelle Axton had settled in for the duration of middle age. After teaching grades one through eight in a one-room school in Middleton, Tennessee, she moved to Memphis, where she got a job as a bookkeeper at Union Planters Bank. With a husband, two children, and home in suburbia, she had everything, statistically speaking, an American woman of the 1950s could want. The social, economic and music revolution taking place in Memphis did not interest her in the least. She was more concerned with raising a family and earning a living.

Estelle's younger brother, Jim Stewart, was more introspective. By age 28, he had served a two-year stint in the Army, earned a degree in business from Memphis State, accepted a job in the bonds department of First National Bank in Memphis and married Evelyn White, who worked for the same bank. But beneath the banker's exterior—he wore schoolteacherish glasses and conservative business suits with a white shirt and black tie—simmered a passion for music. Jim Stewart led a double life.

While attending classes at Memphis State, he played fiddle in a series of swing bands and occasionally performed on WDIA, which, in its early years, sandwiched brief country segments between its staple R&B formats. On weekends, he sometimes played at the Eagle's Nest, where he once met Elvis. "I remember (him) . . . telling me he was going to have to quit, because they couldn't afford gas to go on the road," says Jim. Of course, Jim would never have told his co-workers about playing at the Eagle's Nest or hanging out at a black-format radio station, nor would he have told them when he bought a tape recorder and dreamed of making records. Jim wrote a country song, "Blue Roses," and asked Fred Bylar, a radio announcer, to sing it. He thought Bylar, with his radio connections, would be able to get them a record deal. He couldn't, and Jim watched with disgust as his first recording disappeared into the Black Hole of American music. Jim

101

blamed the failure on their equipment, or lack of it, and the fact they had to use a garage for a studio.

"So, Jim came to me," says Estelle. "He played the song for me, even though I was more into popular music than country music. He said, 'Would you like to get in the music business?' I had never thought about it. I said, 'Well, I don't have any money.'

"He said, 'I know you don't have any money, but you have a house and you have several years paid into it. Maybe you could mortgage it. All we need is $2,500.'

"I talked to my husband. He said, no way. He wasn't into music and just wasn't interested in it. I had to talk to him for a long time and convince him that if we invested in something, it might come out, even though none of us knew anything about the recording business."

Estelle's husband was understandably hesitant. They had bought the house in 1940 for $3,800. Their monthly payments were low--$23.63 a month—so a $2,500 mortgage would take a big bite out of the equity they had in the house.

"Back then, that was a lot of money," recalls Estelle.

Then she chuckles. "We sold it later on and got $50,000."

In the end, Estelle was victorious. With the $2,500 she received from the mortgage of her home, she and Jim bought a one-track Ampex recorder and set it up in a vacant grocery store in Brunswick, a small community just outside Memphis. They named their new company Satellite Productions (Russia's Sputnik had made satellite a household word). For about a year, they experimented with the equipment, recording the store owner's 16-year-old daughter. When it became obvious Brunswick didn't have a deep talent pool, they looked for a place in Memphis. "We knew we would have to get into Memphis to be close to the talent," she says.

Enter Lincoln Wayne "Chips" Moman, a 22-year-old guitar picker who had hitchhiked to Memphis at the age of 14 from his home in Georgia. As a child, he had lain awake at night listening to black gospel music with the radio hidden beneath the covers, the sound turned low so his father, Abraham Lincoln Moman, would not hear and suspect he had secret dreams. His father was a former professional baseball player, a Southern jock, and, although he later was proud of his son's success—"Music was born in him, I reckon," he once told me. "I don't see how he does it myself. It's amazing to me."—he did not feel music was something his son could make a living at.

By contrast, Chips' mother, who played piano, encouraged his interest in music, first by buying him a ukulele when he was three in exchange for a visit to the dentist, then later by getting him his first guitar, a Gene Autry model, from Sears Roebuck.

For several years, Chips was in and out of Memphis, as he traveled around the country as an itinerant laborer. He chopped onions in Texas. He painted houses and service stations all over the South. "For a kid my age, I was really successful," recalls Chips. "I was making $400 to $500 a week. I painted fridges, post offices, flag poles, anything. When I got a chance to play in bands, I just did it. Some people just got to play it, can't help it."

By the late 1950s, he had made a name for herself as a session player in California. "People would hire me as a guitar player, but they were really hiring me to put the sessions together," says Chips. But he was unhappy living away from home and returned to Memphis, where he painted by day and played music by night. Chips met Jim shortly after he bought the tape recorder and played guitar on Jim's abortive "Blue Roses." By 1960, fate would throw Chips together with Jim and Estelle for the beginning of the Second Revolution in Memphis Music.

When Chips heard Jim and Estelle were looking for a place to put a studio in Memphis, he found them a bargain, an empty movie theater on East McLemore. "The guy who owned it, rented it to us for $100 a month," says Estelle. "Can you imagine a whole theater for $100? We ripped out all of the seats and put a partition down the middle to compact the sound."

They put the tape recorder up on the stage where the screen used to be and they opened a record store in an abandoned barber shop next door.

"When I was working at Union Planters, I took orders from the people I worked with," says Estelle. "They would tell me what they wanted and I would go to Popular Tunes (a record store) and buy records for sixty-five cents and sell them to them for one dollar. I took that profit and bought enough records to set up a record shop."

Chips, Jim and Estelle were an unlikely threesome. With his arms marked with self-inflicted tattoos and a cocky attitude shaped by years of survival out on the road as a teenage vagabond, Chips was a social rebel with a penchant for playing cards and hustling pool (he wasn't given the name Chips for nothing). Jim was the quintessential Walter Mitty, a mild-mannered banker who kept whatever rebellious thoughts he had to himself. Estelle was a slender, outspoken 40-year-old redhead with two kids, a nervous husband and a $2,500 mortgage. I never saw the three of them together at the same time, but knowing all three of them, I can imagine what it was like. Estelle would have spoken her mind, Chips would have disagreed on principle, citing his experience in a man's world, and Jim, disagreeing with both of them, would have shaken his head and said nothing. There were rough days ahead.

As Jim and Estelle ripped out theater seats, Memphis music underwent major changes. In 1960, Sam Phillips closed the doors at Memphis Recording Service and moved into his new studio at 639 Madison, changing the name of his company to Sam Phillips Recording Service. In the spring of 1959, Sam and Jack Clement had a falling out that in retrospect resembled a signal flare from a sinking ship.

"We'd been recording all day," recalls Jack, who by then had become Sam's right-hand man. "There was this guy named Cliff who was one of Elvis' entourage. He hit another member of Elvis entourage over the head with a tennis racket and Elvis threw him out of the house. For some reason, Cliff was staying with me. At that time, I lived over in Frasier, which was across the river. It got into the evening and Bill Justis had been having a few cocktails and Sam came in and he had a few cocktails. Cliff also had a few cocktails. I wanted to go home because it was snowing and I wanted to get across the bridge before it froze up. So somehow I worked in the control room and Sam was there telling jokes and they were having a big party. I said, 'Cliff, we need to go.' Sam interpreted that as meaning 'You don't want to stay here and talk to this idiot.' In the meantime, him and Justis had been arguing. I just wanted to go home."

Jack and Cliff left. When he returned to the studio the next day there was an envelope addressed to him. "Sam had fired me," says

Jack. "I saw another envelope there for Justis. He fired him, too. The next day I think he was sorry about it and we probably could have reconciled, but I was ready to go. Sam still don't know to this day why he fired me. We still argue about it."

Jack moved to Beaumont, Texas, where he set up a studio for a while; then he moved to Nashville, where he produced a number of hit albums for Johnny Cash. Sam had a minor hit in 1960 with Charlie Rich's "Lonely Weekends," but not since Jerry Lee Lewis recorded "Breathless" and "Great Balls of Fire" in 1958 had he had a major hit. In 1963, after Rich's contract with Sun Records expired, he signed a contract with RCA-Victor. Sam sent a telegram to RCA notifying them that he still had a verbal agreement with Rich. RCA suspended the contract and Rich sued Sam for breach of contract. The lawsuit was settled, Rich moved to RCA and his first release, "Big Boss Man," was a hit. But it was the beginning of the end for Sun Records.

Jumping ship before the decade ended were three of Sam's session players: Ray Harris, Bill Cantrell and Quinton Claunch. They teamed with a group of Memphis investors, including Joe Cuoghi, the owner of Poplar Tunes, one of the largest wholesale and retail record distributors in the South, to start up a new label, Hi Records. They built a studio in a black neighborhood on South Lauderdale and named it Royal Recording Studio. Impressed with the success of Bill Justis' hit instrumental "Raunchy," Cuoghi decided to build the label's reputation on instrumentals with a repetitive R&B groove. Hi's first hit came in 1960 with Bill Black Combo's "Smokie Parts 1 & 2." Co-founder of the Bill Black Combo was Reggie Young, a native of Oscelo, Arkansas, who went on to become one of the best session guitarists in the country. Over the next 10 years, the combo racked up 18 more hits. Playing on some of those sessions was saxophonist Ace Cannon, who scored with a hit solo effort in 1961, "Tuff."

At that time, the best band in town belonged to Willie Mitchell, a light-skinned black trumpet player whose pencil-thin mustache and dapper good looks made him a big hit with the ladies. In 1995, I was driving into Memphis when I tuned my radio to a rock station. The deejay, commenting on a ceremony the night before at which Willie Mitchell had won an award, took a call from a young girl, who judging by her voice, was in her early twenties and notably white.

"Wasn't Willie Mitchell the best looking thing you've ever seen?" gushed the caller. The deejay paused. "But he's in his sixties or something, isn't he?"

"He might be," said the caller. "But he was still the best looking man there."

Hi Records recruited Willie, first as a trumpet player, then as an arranger and producer. To turn out the instrumentals Hi wanted, he put together a first rate house band that included Al Jackson on drums and Lewis Steinberg on bass. Royal was the first studio to allow black and white musicians to work together in an atmosphere of equality. It was still illegal for blacks to go to white theaters or use white restrooms, but, at Royal, the two races worked together as equals.

In March, Elvis was discharged from the Army. He returned to Memphis, but he wasn't given much time to relax at Graceland. Within two weeks he was recording new material at a Nashville studio. Without even knowing the name of the first release, record stores had placed advance orders for 1.2 million singles. No one was surprised when the first release from that session, "Stuck On You," went to No. 1. After recording six songs in two days, Elvis reported to Hollywood to star in his next movie, *GI Blues*. It grossed $4 million that year, but it was a terrible movie, even Elvis was embarrassed. He asked the Colonel to find him better roles.

Elvis returned to Nashville in April for another two-day recording session. The Colonel was pushing him hard. "Stuck On You" had dropped from the charts by July and Roy Orbison had scored with a hit, "Only the Lonely." One of the songs from Elvis' April session, "It's Now Or Never," went to No. 1 in August and stayed there for five weeks. It was his biggest selling single of all time, with sales exceeding 20 million. By fall, he was filming another movie, *Flaming Star*, which offered him his first dramatic, non-singing role. Under the guidance of Colonel Parker, Elvis became the biggest star in America in 1960, but he paid a stiff price for that stardom. His music entered a period of decline that would not be reversed until the end of the decade. Instead of building movies around his music, his handlers adapted his music to the movies.

Despite the financial success of his comeback year, Elvis was miserable. That Christmas he sent for Priscilla Beaulieu, a 14-year-old ninth grader he had met in Germany. The following year, Elvis asked her father if she could live in Graceland under the supervision of his father. In 1962, she moved into Graceland and enrolled at Immaculate Conception High School.

When Jerry Lee Lewis found out, he must have been livid. He had done the "right thing" and married his teenage cousin, yet it cost him his career. Elvis was living in sin with a teenager and no one said a word. Where was the justice?

By 1964, Jerry Lee's sales on Sun had dwindled to a trickle, so when his contract came up for renewal he left Sun and signed with Smash. His first album on Smash did well on country charts, but didn't make a dent in the pop charts. Under the circumstances, he had no choice but to become a country artist. As a rock 'n' roller he was history.

* * *

As Jim and Chips worked to get the new studio at Satellite Productions organized, Estelle stocked the record shop. Without the profits generated by the record shop that first year, it is doubtful the studio would have survived. Both Estelle and Jim kept their day jobs. When they got off work at four, Jim went to the studio and Estelle went to the record shop, which she kept open until nine.

The first few sessions Jim undertook were unproductive. Then one day Rufus Thomas stopped by to pitch an idea to him. They had met at WDIA when Jim played his fiddle on the country segment. Rufus had written a song, "Cause I Love You," he thought would make a good duet. He suggested he sing it with his 16-year-old daughter, Carla, who was then performing with a popular high school group, the Teen Town Singers. Jim liked the idea.

"In May of 1960 we brought out 'Cause I Love You' on Satellite," says Jim. "I didn't know what rhythm and blues was then, but I was in what you'd call a soulful environment. It sold about 15,000 locally, and to us that was like having a million-seller."

107

When Jerry Wexler, head of Atlantic Records in New York, was tipped off by a pressing plant operator as to how many units of "Cause I Love You" were being sold, he called Jim and Estelle and offered to distribute the record. It wasn't a hit, but it did sell 35,000 units nationwide, giving Jim and Estelle their first national exposure as record executives. They were offered $1,000 for the master, plus a small royalty on sales. Estelle breathed easier about her mortgage. They signed what they thought was a leasing and distribution deal with Atlantic. Years later they discovered it was something else, but for the moment, at least, they were in high cotton.

Rufus and Carla recorded more songs, but they didn't sound like hits. One day they were sitting around the studio, tossing around ideas. "It was then that Carla said, 'I've got a song.'" recalls Estelle. "She said it was called 'Gee Whiz.' As soon as Jim and I heard that song we knew it was a hit. It's funny. When you hear a song, you know if it's got something in it that will sell."

Jim and Estelle used part of the $1,000 they received from Atlantic to record "Gee Whiz." They hired strings and asked Chips to produce the session. When Wexler heard the recording, he signed Carla to a five-year contract and released "Gee Whiz" on Atlantic. In March 1961 it went to No. 13 on the pop charts, establishing Carla as a star and Satellite Productions as a major player in the music business.

"It took me a while to see the significance of what I was getting into," says Carla. "What I thought was fun, was a business. Being young, black and in the Sixties, it was a thrill to just record."

To understand her feelings, consider that six months after "Gee Whiz" became a hit, Memphis desegregated its public school system, but it would be another year before blacks, including Carla, would be allowed into movie theaters or permitted to use the public library. To the rest of the world, Carla was a teen queen; but to most of Memphis she was still a *nigger* who would have been arrested if she had gone to a movie theater.

*   *   *

At Satellite Productions racial integration was in full bloom, as it was at Hi Records. As usual, music led the way in Memphis.

Once Jim and Estelle got the studio cranked up, Chips was given free rein. He had used black players occasionally in his bands, so he thought nothing about using them in the studio. Booker T. Jones was one of the first young black musicians Chips worked with in the studio. Booker, though still a teenager, was playing bass then with Bowlegs Miller and Willie Mitchell at the Flamingo Club. He switched to organ after hearing Jack McDuff's combo one night at the club. McDuff used an organ and played the bass keys himself. Booker was so impressed he took piano lessons.

"No one was playing organ much then," says Booker. "I was able to get attention and get a job by playing the organ. But it fascinated me because I had heard Ray Charles and I liked the way he played it."

After Chips saw Booker playing with pros like Willie and Bowlegs, inviting him to the studio seemed like a natural thing to do. Most of Memphis was totally unaware of what was happening musically in the city. There had always been two co-existing cultures in the city, one white, the other black. Now there were three. White, male teens, witnessing the success Elvis, Jerry Lee and the others had with members of the opposite sex, saw music as a way to score with girls. In the beginning, rock 'n' roll was more about sex than art. For that reason, teenage boys all over the city schemed to get into the studio with Chips. Among them was Packy Axton, Estelle's son. Some of his high school friends, Steve Cropper and Donald "Duck" Dunn, put together a guitar band they called the Royal Spades.

"My son was determined to be a musician," says Estelle. "He wanted to get in the band that Steve was in."

Since the Royal Spades didn't need another guitar player, Packy learned to play sax. "He drove us crazy learning to play that thing," says Estelle. "He knew a little about music, but not much. He learned it himself. He never took lessons."

When Packy asked Steve if he could join the band, Steve told him they didn't need a saxophone. Then Packy told him his mother owned Satellite Productions: "You know, the studio where Chips Moman works." Instantly, Packy became a Royal Spade.

Jim wasn't that crazy about his nephew hanging round the studio (it would have offended his long-suffering sense of professionalism), but Estelle pushed it and Chips was desperate for musicians. Chips worked up a three-chord, instrumental riff with keyboard man Smoochy Smith during an intermission one night at a nightclub. He used the Royal Spades to flesh out the song in the studio. He did take after take, using whoever was in the studio, adding a trumpet, additional saxophones, but as far as he was concerned the song never jelled. Jim never liked it, either. Chips took the tape to Nashville during the Carla Thomas sessions and got no reaction from the people he played it for there. When the tape came back, it had an erasure.

"I thought it was a hit," says Estelle. "I keep bugging Jim. Then I started in on Chips. I said, 'Look, this is a hit record.' They said, 'forget it.' Finally, I got them to agree to it. They said for Packy to get the tape mastered and take it down to the pressing plant. That's when we discovered 16 or 18 bars had been wiped out."

Estelle called Jim at the bank. "He said, 'Well, we did that song 50 times, get Packy to find another front end, same tempo, and let him splice it on the front and that's what Packy did. Whenever I hear that song, I can still hear the splice. There's about a half a note difference."

Satellite released the song, "Last Night," in July 1961. By then the Royal Spades had become the Mar-Keys. They renamed themselves the Marquees, after the movie marquee outside the studio, but when no one could pronounce it, they changed it to Mar-Keys. To Jim's and Chips' enormous surprise, "Last Night" went to No. 2 on the pop charts in August, becoming the hottest selling record in Memphis music history. Estelle felt vindicated. Maybe there was a place for women in the rock 'n' roll business after all.

Jim and Chips organized a touring band to promote the record. Thus the Mar-Keys became Steve Cropper on guitar, Duck Dunn on bass, Packy on sax, Smoochy Smith on keyboards, Terry Johnson on drums, Wayne Jackson on trumpet and Don Nix on baritone sax. That group of musicians would become the core of what later would be known as Stax Records. One unexpected result of the notoriety of the record was the threat of a lawsuit from another company named Satellite. To avoid a legal hassle, Jim and Estelle adopted the new name, Stax, by combing the first two letters of their last names. Some copies of "Last Night" were sold on Satellite and others on Stax.

The Mar-Keys could hardly believe their good fortune.

"It was a high school band that lucked into a hit record—just seven people trying to have a good time," recalls Don Nix. "It was the big time to us. At that time, guys our age doing that was really crazy."

Not surprisingly, Memphis ignored their success. It was an attitude musicians would expect from Memphians for the remainder of the century. "You get to where you don't expect them to (be supportive)," says Nix. "I remember at the time not caring. I didn't want to be famous in Memphis. I wanted to be famous in New York City. That was where all the girls were."

*   *   *

With two hits under their belts, Jim, Estelle and Chips slapped Stax Records into overdrive. Estelle used the record store as a workshop. Whenever Packy and his friends came by the studio, Estelle pulled them into the store and told them about the records that were selling and why she thought they were hits. She did the same thing with young black musicians. In effect, she became both a housemother and an educator.

"I was a mama to all of them," says Estelle. "If they were having some personal problems, they would come to me. I was there when they needed somebody to talk to because Jim wasn't that type of person. They couldn't talk to him. Having the record shop was the most important thing for those writers and musicians in the studio. They could come to the record shop and see what customers were buying and why."

Chips, with his cocky attitude and his reputation as a rebel of the Marlon Brando variety, was a magnet for the teenage boys who flocked to the studio. Unlike Jim and Estelle, neither of whom spent much time associating with musicians away from the studio, Chips performed in the local clubs and was looked up to by younger musicians. He became the unofficial talent scout for the label. One of the first people he brought into the studio was William Bell, a 22-year-old black singer who had made a name for

111

himself in the local club scene. He played a song for Chips and Jim that he had written himself. They recorded the song as a demo, but when they played it back they liked it so much they released it as a single. The song, "You Don't Miss Your Water," was a smash hit in the South and made the national pop charts. Bell was drafted by the U.S. Army shortly after the record was released and was out of the Stax loop for a couple of years, but the mold for future Stax hits had been set. Jim, Estelle and Chips had found a soulful "sound" that would not only define the record label, but change the direction of American music.

In the summer of 1962 only one Memphian had a hit record, and that was Elvis, with his imminently forgettable single, "She's Not You." Despite the success of "Gee Whiz," "Last Night" and "You Don't Miss Your Water," Jim wanted something for the country charts. He set up a session with a country singer and asked Steve Cropper to play guitar, Booker T. Jones to play keyboards, Al Jackson to play drums and Lewis Steinberg to play bass. While waiting for the country singer, who never showed, the musicians jammed to kill time.

Jim had heard Booker and Steve play a slow blues song, "Behave Yourself," in the clubs. They decided to record it. "Jim didn't want to release it without a B side, so he said why don't you guys record something for the B Side and we'll have a record," says Booker. "Steve and I knew each other, and we had been fooling around together with some chords and stuff. We had this idea for 'Green Onions.' We had been fooling around with it on the piano a couple of weeks before . . . Something just caused me to play it on the organ this time. It sounded a lot better on the organ than it did on the piano. That was a thrill for us to see that come together by accident."

"Green Onions" peaked at No. 7 on the pop charts. Whereas "Gee Whiz" had been a joint effort among Jim, Estelle and Chips, Jim had not been involved with "Last Night," and neither Estelle nor Chips had been involved with "Green Onions."

Tempers flared. Egos were bruised.

"Jim and Chips had a disagreement," says Estelle. "Chips was trying to take over the place. That's when the breakup came between Jim and Chips. I think their agreement was that if Chips

112

would come back in a couple of weeks and agree to go along with Jim, then he would accept him back."

Memories grew fuzzy over the years, but it appears the breakup occurred after it dawned on Chips that he was helping build a company in which he had no equity. "Chips wanted half the company," recalls Estelle. "I was left out and I was the one who put all the money up for it."

Whether Chips asked for 50 percent or 25 percent is immaterial since, considering the dynamics involved, it was a conflict that had no solution. Estelle had mortgaged her home to put up the money. There was no way she was going to take less than 50 percent. Jim wasn't about to become subordinate to his sister, not when the whole thing was his idea, his dream. Chips had the rough appearance of a Southern roustabout, but beneath that exterior was the sensitive underbelly of an artist. How could he give his heart and soul to a company that considered him nothing more than an expendable employee?

Jim and Chips had words. Harsh, bitter words, according to witnesses, and Chips stormed out of the studio and found a lawyer who would file a lawsuit against Stax Records.

Amid that chaos, Booker T. & the MGs were born. Steinberg was replaced on bass by Duck Dunn, giving the group a racial mix of two whites and two blacks. "Steve and I had a little bit more rock 'n' roll in us and Booker and Al were the R&B—and the mixture worked," says Duck. "We were just playing with the people we loved to play with. We never though about it as a racial thing."

"For us, music had no color," says Cropper. "What went on politically, we were not involved with . . . there were a couple of instances on the road later, when we ended up leaving in the middle of something, but that only happened a couple of times . . . If we went to a place and played in a town where things were segregated, we just stayed on the outskirts of town. We didn't worry about it."

In the studio, Cropper filled the leadership void created by Chips' departure. Using Cropper as a band leader and a producer, Jim merged Booker T. & the MGs and the Mar-Keys to form the nucleus of his studio band. I once asked Jim how he got the idea to use that unique blend of harmonic instrumentation for which Stax was famous. Jim laughed. He said the Stax horn sound developed because he couldn't find any Memphis singers who could get along well enough in the studio to sing background. The horns were a substitute for human voices. I asked Estelle the same question. She, too, laughed and said, "I think that when 'Last Night' came out so well, that's when they started paying attention to horns."

Into this cauldron of creativity tiptoed Otis Redding.

There are differences of opinion on whether he showed up at Stax Records by accident or design. Some accounts have him driving Johnny Perkins and the Pinetoppers to Memphis from Macon, Georgia, for a scheduled session. Others say his appearance was planned. However it happened, Jim had some time after he completed the session with Perkins and he suggested Otis give it a try. Booker T. Jones had to leave, so Steve Cropper moved over to organ. Perkins played guitar, Lewis Steinberg was on bass and Al Jackson was on drums. They recorded a couple of songs, one a Little Richard sound alike and the other an original tune written by Redding called "These Arms of Mine." Everyone was impressed with Otis' voice, but no one was particularly impressed with the results of the session.

When he returned to the studio the next day, Booker listened to the playback. "I had never heard of him but you could tell there was something special about him," says Booker. "'These Arms of Mine' seemed new and different and it was obvious that this man had quite a future."

Jim released the record locally on his new subsidiary, Volt, but there was little reaction. To help things along, he gave a Nashville deejay a percentage of the publishing on that one song. The record died in Memphis, but the Nashville deejay played it so often, it became a minor regional hit.

Jim didn't invite Otis back into the studio until June 1963, nine months after the first session. They recorded two songs, "That's What My Heart Needs" and "Mary's Little Lamb," both disasters. Otis was slow to develop, but everyone knew there was something there. "That voice was different," says Estelle. "The way he expressed his songs—he didn't do them like anybody else."

Otis returned in September and recorded one of his own compositions, "Pain in My Heart." The song scored on the R&B charts. Finally, Otis was on his way. By then, Booker T. & the MGs were one of the hottest groups in America. Encouraged by that success, Willie Mitchell, across town at Hi Records, stepped up his efforts to put together an instrumental group. Not to be outdone, Rufus Thomas brought Jim a new song he had written titled "Walking the Dog."

"It was a nursery rhyme," says Rufus. "We used to do it in the neighborhood—Mary Mack dressed in black—this may sound strange but I played all the games in the neighborhood, the girls' games as well as the boys'. So it was a nursery rhyme from when I was a child."

"Walking the Dog" was an enormous success, particularly with college students, who associated it with the newest dance craze, the Dog. Some people consider "Walking the Dog" one of the first rap songs ever recorded. The song was so successful an emerging British rock group, the Rolling Stones, recorded their own version on their debut American album the following year.

*   *   *

With "Walking the Dog," Stax had its fourth biggest hit to-date. It peaked at No. 12 on the pop charts in December 1963, but in November, as it was holding at No. 17, President John F. Kennedy took a bullet in the brain in Dallas, Texas. As Vice President Lyndon Johnson ascended to the presidency, one of the first people he called was Memphis' own Fiddling Abe Fortas, who quickly became the second most powerful man in Washington.

Fortas and Johnson were opposed to setting up a commission to investigate Kennedy's assassination, but public pressure was such that Johnson had no choice. Perhaps with a view of controlling the results, Johnson put Fortas in charge of setting up the Warren Commission. In addition, he became the President's chief advisor on civil rights and his unofficial minister of culture. It was Fortas who helped draft legislation for the Kennedy Center for the Performing Arts.

Fortas projected a complex, dual image. On one hand, he was a high-profile lover of music and culture. He stepped up his musical

115

performances and entertained often at his Georgetown home. On the other hand, he was a cynical, behind-the-scenes operator, whose services were offered to the highest bidder.

In June 1964, Martin Luther King was jailed in St. Augustine, Florida, for trying to enter a "whites only" restaurant. In July, President Johnson signed the historic Civil Rights Act of 1964. "The purpose of this law is simple," said Johnson. "It does not restrict the freedom of any American so long as he respects the rights of others . . . It does say that those who are equal before God shall now also be equal in the polling booths, in the classrooms, in the factories and in hotels and restaurants and movie theaters and other places that provide service to the public."

In 1964, the first full year of the Johnson presidency, Fortas urged his friend to go to Memphis to give a speech on the Tennessee Valley Authority. Fortas told him it would be good politics, but the record does not indicate exactly who he wanted the President to meet in Memphis and why he thought it would be a good idea. By 1965, Fortas had become invaluable to the President. As a result, Johnson decided to put him where he would be of the most help. He appointed him to the U.S. Supreme Court. Shortly after the appointment, he autographed a photograph for his friend: "For Abe," Johnson wrote on the photograph, "the Isaac Stern of the Supreme Court. My first *string* man."

Neil Diamond recording in Memphis
Photo courtesy of the Mississippi Valley Collection
University of Memphis, University Libraries

The Gentrys at Overton Park Shell in Memphis
Photo courtesy of Mike Gardner

117

Rufus and Carla Thomas, c. 1979
Photo courtesy of the Mississippi Valley Collection
University of Memphis, University Libraries

CHAPTER 7

The 1960s:
Hits From Stax, American and Hi

In the summer of 1964 two carloads of student musicians from the University of Mississippi, better known as Ole Miss, struck out for Memphis for a late-night rendezvous on Beale Street, the importance of which would not be understood for nearly two decades. The students left behind a campus that only two years earlier had been racially integrated at gunpoint by federal marshals. The campus was still seething with racial tension, as, indeed, was the entire region. When President John F. Kennedy had been assassinated in Dallas the previous November, the Ole Miss campus had erupted into rebel flag-waving celebration at the news.

In the two Memphis-bound cars were six male members of a band named The Strokers and one female student, who had hitched a ride at the last minute. I was the keyboard player. I rode in the car with Bunker Ex Hill, the bassist, and a blonde coed Bunker had met on the way to pick me up. The coed carried a box of fried chicken in her lap. The other four band members rode in the second car. Since it was a school night and a violation of school policy for coeds to not sign into their dorms by 11 p.m., the coed left with the knowledge she would be risking expulsion. For that reason, she declined to give us her name. The less we knew, the safer she felt. The less we knew, the safer *we* felt. She was dressed in a pink skirt and sweater and her makeup had a pinkish tint to it, so we called her Pink Lady. That suited her just fine.

In 1964 Ole Miss had a reputation as a party school. That reputation was well deserved. It was one of the largest venues in the country for popular music. On any given weekend there were probably as many nationally known recording acts performing at one of the dozen or so fraternity houses than there were in New York or Los Angeles. Music was everywhere. Rock, rhythm and blues, pop, even jazz were common. I remember a weekend in which I listened to Julie London, backed by the Bobby Troup

119

band, sing her scorcher, "Cry Me a River," Rufus Thomas sing his 1963 hit, "Walking the Dog," and Hot Nuts steam up a frat house with ribald lyrics meant to bring blushes to the coeds' cheeks. As often as not, the bands that performed on campus were composed of black musicians from Memphis. The racial politics of the era were strident, but students were always willing to park their prejudices at the door for the sake of a decent party.

Despite the students' devotion to music, there were only two or three local bands that performed on the campus on a regular basis. The Strokers played once or twice a week at sorority "swaps," and on weekend nights at the fraternities. Ole Miss students were accustomed to the best bands in the country. To be accepted by them was a compliment of the highest order. I don't know how good The Strokers were. I do know the band's name was a source of controversy. Once I was riding in a car with several people I had just met. A young girl, a freshman, asked me if I had heard of a band called The Strokers. I said I had. She said she had never heard the band, but it had nearly kept her out of college. It seems her mother had heard of the band and told her daughter she could not enroll in Ole Miss as long as The Strokers were prowling the campus. After weeks of tearful pleading she was allowed to enroll on condition she not get within 100 yards of the band. She made a solemn vow to keep her distance. I could have ruined her day by confessing my identity, but didn't.

For whatever reason, The Strokers were booked at the Flamingo Club in Memphis. It was on Hernando Street, just off Beale Street, in gritty downtown Memphis. On the way to Memphis, we listened to our favorite radio station -- WDIA, a black Memphis station that featured black announcers and black music. Rufus Thomas was probably the most famous announcer identified with the station. The Pink Lady sat between Bunker and me in the car. She said very little. All her efforts were focused on the box of fried chicken.

"Yum, yum," she said as she licked each bone clean as a whistle. "I could do this all day long." Her long, pink tongue flicked with serpent-like accuracy. We left a trail of chicken bones along the Interstate, a whiff of perfume emanating from each bone.

It was almost dark when we pulled up outside the Flamingo Club. By 1964 the Beale Street district had become a seedy, dilapidated caricature of its former self. The Flamingo Club was an all-black club. We knew that, but, despite the racial tensions of the day, thought nothing about performing there. Black musicians had performed at Ole Miss for years. What we didn't know then—what I didn't discover until more than two decades later, when I was living in Memphis and working for *The Commercial Appeal*—was that all-white bands simply did not perform in black clubs in Memphis. The Strokers earned a footnote in history by becoming one of the first—if not the first—all-white bands to perform in a black nightclub in Memphis.

At dusk, the tall urban shadows bobbed and flickered in the fading light, transforming the most innocent of pedestrians into potential muggers. It was then I discovered that most of the band members, including myself, were packing pistols. I protested that much firepower. The pistols were collected and put into a canvas bag for safe-keeping. The bag was given to me to keep on the bench behind the organ. The idea, as one band member explained it, was that in the event of trouble I could squeeze off rounds with one hand and with the other hand toss the extra pistols to the band members.

That night the Flamingo Club was packed with several hundred black patrons. We decided to play some new music we had worked up. That spring a new British band called The Beatles had released their first American album. We thought their music showed promise. To the bafflement of everyone in the club, we opened with several Beatles songs.

The audience was stunned.

"What kind of music is that?" a man in the audience shouted. "That music don't do nothing for me."

Suddenly, a young black girl leaped onto the stage. She ran up to the microphone. "How 'bout a little honky tonk?" she said. The crowd went wild.

As the band belted out a raunchy Bo Diddly number in the key of E, the young girl began to take off her clothes. She was a professional stripper, or a shake dancer, as they were called in those days. Pink Lady sat perched on the organ bench to my left. On my right was the bag of pistols. Pink Lady squirmed during the strip tease. The song ended and the stripper gathered up her clothes. She looked at the band and smiled.

"That's real good," she said.

"I'm hungry," Pink Lady said. "I wish I had more chicken."

We kicked off with another R&B song and stayed in that groove for the remainder of the night. There was a second British band that had released its first American album that year. They called themselves the Rolling Stones. Their first album sounded like a tribute to Memphis music. Since we had worked up songs from that album, including Rufus Thomas' hit "Walking the Dog," we added them to our playlist that night. After our first set, we heard a commotion in the audience.

A line of perhaps a dozen women snake danced among the tables. Or were they women? Lord, no. They were men, part of a transvestite review! For one dollar the patrons could have their photographs taken with the transvestite of their choice. Each time they snaked past the bandstand, the transvestites gazed up at the band and shouted out, "kiss, kiss, kiss."

As we began the second set, the club manager took the stage. Without saying a word to us, he announced that Tommy Tucker, whose song "Hi-Heel Sneakers" had been a tremendous hit on college campuses, was there in the club and was going to perform with the band.

We were stunned.

As the audience went wild, Tommy Tucker, wearing a dapper suit, jumped up onto the stage. He turned to the band. "You know my song?" he asked. Luckily, we did.

Tucker sang with us for the remainder of the evening. The audience loved him and forgave us our earlier transgressions. At the end of the night, Tommy Tucker asked us if we would back him at an upcoming engagement at Club Paradise, the biggest blues supper club in the city. We jumped at the chance. We loaded up the cars and went to Club Paradise, where Tucker met us. When the deal was proposed to the club manager, he looked at Tucker with amusement. The manager shook his head.

"Not with no white band, you ain't," he said.

Tucker apologized to us and we parted company. On the long drive back to Memphis, I started nodding off. I was around 5 a.m. "Why don't you put your head on my shoulder and get some

122

sleep," Pink Lady said. Her shoulder was hot and sweaty, and I slept like a baby.

I had an 8 o'clock class across the street from the cafeteria, so Bunker dropped me off there. Pink Lady said she would join me. We made an strange looking pair in the cafeteria. I was still dressed in my band uniform: a pink shirt, a burgundy blazer and white pants. And, of course, Pink Lady looked imminently wise than she had been when we left. As we approached the checkout counter, Pink Lady touched my arm.

"Let me treat you," she said.

She pulled out a thick wad of bills and paid the cashier.

Later that week, we performed at a frat party, where I saw a boy who would go on to become a conservative political leader in the state of Mississippi, sidle up to an attractive coed with long blonde hair who was standing with her back to him, her arms outstretched, palms down on the table edge. He walked right up behind her, unzipped his pants, and plopped his penis down on top of her hand.

"Know what that is?" he said breathlessly.

Without looking at her hand, she turned and looked him squarely in the eye and—answered sweetly, "If it was bigger, I'd think it was a penis."

He withdrew in fast order and faded into the shadows.

*   *   *

In 1965, Beale Street resembled a ghost town. The night life was gone and only a few stores remained. Windows were boarded up. Trash littered the sidewalks. Bill Browder, who later changed his name to T. G. Sheppard and found success as a country music artist, started work as a sales clerk at Lanksy's, a clothing store on the west end of Beale. For years, the store specialized in gaudy, pimpish clothing, but with the sudden burst of recording activity in Memphis it became a favorite shopping place for musicians.

Elvis shopped there frequently. So did the Stax and Hi artists, and visiting musicians. "It was basically a black area, but a lot of white entertainers came down to Beale to buy clothes," says Sheppard. "Elvis would come down to buy from Lanskys because they carried all those loud clothes entertainers like to buy."

After Chips Moman left Stax, the label faltered throughout 1964 and placed no hits on the pop Top 20. The only Memphis artists who made the charts that year were Elvis, with the embarrassing "Kissin' Cousins," and Roy Orbison with his monster hit "Oh Pretty Woman." Of course, 1964 was the year the Beatles invaded America and totally dominated the charts. By April the Beatles held the top five slots on the pop charts with "Can't Buy Me Love, "Twist and Shout," "She Loves You," I Want to Hold Your Hand" and "Please Please Me."

If 1964 was one of the worst years in Memphis music history, then 1965 was one of the best. Over the next five years, Stax would do its best work; Hi Records would come into its own; Sam Phillips' studio would have one last hit; and Chips Moman would accomplish recording feats that seem incredible in retrospect. By then Chips had settled his lawsuit with Jim and Estelle and used the money to set up his own studio on the north end of town in a rundown, mostly black, neighborhood. He named it American Recording Studios. He assembled a first rate studio band, made up of Reggie Young on guitar, Bobby Wood on piano, Gene Chrisman on drums, Mike Leech on Bass and Bobby Emmons on organ.

Despite the flurry of activity at Stax, American and Hi in 1965, the biggest hit of the year was a song recorded at Sam Phillips' studio. A Dallas, Texas, native, Domingo Samudio, had been performing with his band, The Pharaohs, in Texas and Louisiana since the early 1960s. While working the club circuit, they made their way to Memphis and Phillips' studio, where old rockabilly hand, Stan Kesler, recorded a session with them for MGM Records. Within twelve weeks after "Wooly Bully" by Sam the Sham & The Pharaohs was released, it went to No. 1 on some pop charts and No. 2 on others.

American's first hit was an up-tempo rock song, "Keep On Dancing," which was recorded by a group of white Memphis teenagers who called themselves the Gentrys. The song peaked at No. 4 on the pop charts. Chips never liked the song—he once told me he hated the song so much he mixed it with the sound turned off, setting the mix by the meter alone—but it opened the door for other, even bigger hits. For the first time since Elvis' early recordings, Memphis was viewed by the outside world as a potential source of pop hits for the white market.

American's next big hit came from Sandy Posey, the studio receptionist who scored with a No. 14 hit, "Born A Woman." But since it takes more than two hits to sustain a studio, producers and musicians, and Chips worked night and day to make ends meet. He engineered sessions for whatever he could get; he continued playing in bands; and he fought a deep depression that almost immobilized him at times.

"I wouldn't turn anything down," says Chips. "There was a 10 year period in which I might have averaged three hours of sleep a night. I recorded one time for nine days without going home. I would fall unconscious behind the board and people would pick me up and shake me and say, 'Can you do one more mix?'—when they should have taken me straight to a hospital."

Chips was swimming upstream and had to claw and scratch for everything he got. Thirty years later, I asked Estelle Axton how long it took for the hard feelings between them to fade away. "I don't think they ever did," she said. "I think Chips was going to prove that he could do it—and he did. There's no doubt he was talented."

Frustrated with a record label's refusal to pay him money owed him, Chips went to New York to collect the money himself. He was warmly greeted by the record executive, but when Chips asked for his money, all he got were excuses. Chips grabbed the record executive by the lapels and dragged him over to a window of the skyscraper.

"You've finally pushed me to the point when I'm ready to die for this," Chips said. He pushed the record executive against the window. "Is this something you're ready to die for?"

Chips left with his check.

Extreme as Chips' behavior was on occasion, it was behavior Jim Stewart should have emulated in his dealings with Atlantic. Though he didn't know it at the time, he was being drawn into a financial morass from which he would never be able to extricate himself. No longer content to merely distribute the records that emerged from the studios at Stax, Jerry Wexler assumed a more activist role by signing artists to Atlantic and then persuading Jim to work with them in Memphis. Among the first were Sam Moore and Dave Prater, who recorded under the name Sam and Dave, and Wilson Pickett, whose first session at Stax produced his signature song, "In the Midnight Hour."

By 1965, the Stax family had grown. Jim brought Al Bell aboard as national sales director. Although Booker T. Jones and Al Jackson played prominent creative roles at the label, there had been no blacks involved at the executive level. Bell was a tall, aggressive black man, who had been a successful deejay at a Memphis radio station. He was Jim's opposite and that offered a much needed balance. Cropper still was working both as producer and guitarist, using players from the MGs and the Mar-Keys, but new faces started showing up in the studios. Homer Banks, who worked as a clerk in Estelle's record shop, and Isaac Hayes and David Porter, made their way into the studio by way of Estelle's "workshops."

"I was really close to the writers," says Estelle. "Maybe my earlier experience as a school teacher may have had something to do with that. I'll never forget how David Porter became a writer. He was working at a grocery store across the street from the studio. The minuet he got off, he'd come over to the record shop and talk to me. He was so young they wouldn't let him in the studio. He wrote a song and wanted my opinion. That song had eight sheets of words. I said, 'No way, David. You have to concentrate it, shorten it.' I would play him records that were hits. Today, he gives me credit for teaching him how to write songs. It makes me feel so happy I helped someone. He and Isaac Hayes are the best writers around."

By the time David Porter was old enough to get into the studio, he found one of his school chums, Isaac Hayes, already there playing piano on sessions. They teamed up to write songs, with David doing the words and Isaac the music. After the first few sessions with Sam and Dave didn't yield any hits, David and Isaac submitted some of their ideas. One of their first songs, "Hold On, I'm Comin,'" gave Sam and Dave their first hit and set a direction for Stax that established it as the leader of Southern-based soul. They followed that up with "Soul Man."

Meanwhile, Otis Redding was slowly building up a fan base with a string of records, that while not hits, always seemed on the verge of being hits. Everyone knew Otis was going to be big. They just didn't know when he was going to be big.

"Otis was not our biggest-selling Stax artist," says Jim. "But he was one of the most talked about and recognized. He started developing a market and was always good for a certain amount of sales. And each one he did would surpass the others. He was a superstar in Europe when he was best-known over here among blacks and college kids. But it was obvious he was going to eventually be a pop star."

Otis' non-threatening, unisex voice was perfect for the times. He was sexual, but without orientation. White college students, particularly those at Ole Miss, wanted their soul music sweet as iced tea. It supported their view that blacks, at their core, were a benign race, who possessed a glorious view of the world. Sweet soul music was never a reflection of the black experience so much as it was a creation of white college students who idealized the black experience. It is a little understood reality that most of the sweet soul music created in the early years was done to satisfy a white college audience. Black music, when written by and for a black audience, had a hard edge. Otis wanted no part of that. His kinship was to the white Southern boys who wanted their soul sweet. It is the reason he worked so well with Steve Cropper.

David Porter saw two sides of Otis. "You know Otis didn't talk the way he sang," says Porter. "He might sing like a kid with a speech problem sometime but offstage he was soft-spoken and quite articulate. Another thing. When Otis strutted the stage he walked pigeon-toed, but off-stage, he didn't walk that way. When he was onstage that personality just came out of him and it would just knock you out. Otis worked on his style and even after he was rich and a polished performer, he could maintain the raw edge, the emotionalism of his music. That's because he was a pro."

Collaboration was the key to success at Stax. Jim worked on the principle that if you have the best musicians, the best songwriters and the best singers in the country, something good just had to happen. Interestingly, while the same core group of musicians played on all of the recordings made in the studio, seldom did Jim

127

ever pair his artists with each other. The major exception was Otis Redding and Carla Thomas.

"We were in Memphis at the same time," says Carla. "Most of the time, when we got together it was for a social gathering and never in the studio. When we got together this time Jim Stewart said, 'Hey, everyone is doing duets. Why don't you and Otis?' First, it was kinda' something that was thrown out for fun. I said, 'Hey, I'm used to singing soft ballads like 'Gee Whiz.' I don't know if I can keep up with Otis Redding."

The song Jim had in mind was "Tramp," a pre-rap extension of the trademark Stax groove. The song featured dialogue between Carla and Otis in which Carla berated him for his country ways, but Carla wasn't sure she could talk to Otis that way. Otis was a star. "They said, 'Oh, talk to somebody like you're mad and be yourself," she says. "It worked." The song reminded Carla of Rufus' hit, "Walking the Dog."

"My father's stuff really started that rap stuff," says Carla. "I remember he did a record called, 'Jump Back, Baby Jump.' He sang that to us when we were little kinds when he was down on Beale Street."

What impressed Carla about Stax in those days was the way everyone pitched in to offer ideas or constructive criticism. "We were young and we did a lot of playing around in the studio," says Carla. "We weren't all that sophisticated. We didn't have 16 tracks like they did in New York. We sat there and threw out ideas. The horns might say, 'Hey, how about a little something there,' and Duck (Dunn) might say the same thing. It was all put together by us. All those merging of ideas."

That sense of camaraderie extended past Stax's immediate family. While I was a student at Ole Miss, I often spent time in the rehearsal rooms in the building where music classes were taught. I had formed a band called The Dynamics that featured a trumpet and sax (and I played sax), but I wanted to play keyboards and went by the rehearsal rooms every day after class to practice on the piano there. Late one night I was pounding away on the piano, trying to get "Green Onions" right, when there came a knock on the door. A guy a few years older than myself stuck his head in the door and asked what I was doing. I told him and he offered to show me a better way to play "Green Onions." He said he was from Memphis and played in a band. I asked what band. He said he had played keyboards with the Mar-Keys on their smash hit "Last Night," a song I played at least once a day in my dorm. For years after that, it was a point of pride for me that Jerry Lee "Smoochy" Smith had taught me to play "Green Onions."

*   *   *

Not to be outdone by the magic that was happening at Stax and American, across town at Hi Records Willie Mitchell had been put in charge of production. He developed a competing instrumental style, exemplified by the 1964 hit, "20-75," and set out to discover black artists who could reflect his own sophisticated view of Memphis soul.

Don Bryant had been the singer with Willie's band for years, so it was natural for him to record with him first. "Don't Turn Your Back On Me," their first soul release, was a big hit in the South in 1965 but didn't make the national charts. Willie kept recording. For several years, Hi and Stax shared the same rhythm section with Al Jackson on drums and Lewis Steinberg on bass, but Willie's concept of instrumentation was different from the Stax sound. A Stax, the horns offered rough edges and melodic repetition. At Hi, the horn sound was smoother, more sophisticated.

Willie needed singers who could complement the sound he had in mind. One night Willie was at the Rosewood Club listening to his friend Bowlegs Miller perform, when Bowlegs invited a 19-year-old woman in the audience to sit in with the band. At five-foot-three and 99 pounds, Ann Peebles didn't take up much space on the stage, but when she sang, her voice filled the room. As soon as he heard her sing, Willie knew he had found what he was looking for. After the set, Bowlegs introduced them and they sat down to talk.

"Where do you live?" asked Willie.

"St. Louis," she said.

"Not anymore," answered Willie.

Ann Peebles didn't move to Memphis right away, but she commuted on a regular basis to work with Willie in the studio. In 1969, they released the first single, "Walk Away." It did well on

129

the R&B charts, but didn't make the pop charts. Willie paired her with Don Bryant and other writers who were working with him in hopes of getting a break-out song. The pairing was more complete that Willie expected: Don Bryant and Ann Peebles fell in love and got married.

As Willie waited patiently for Ann to develop into the artist he knew she could become, he kept working with new artists. Another of the female singers he started working with in 1965 was Anna Mae Bullock, who had been brought to him by Ike Turner. By then she and Ike had married and she changed her name to Tina Turner.

Willie worked with Tina from 1965 until 1977, recording 17 albums with her, and although she enjoyed a lot of success with Ike, she didn't become a superstar until the mid-1980s. In 1988 I asked Willie if he had been surprised by Tina's strong comeback.

"I don't think Tina ever needed to make a comeback," says Willie. "She was always there. She always had the talent, the looks, everything."

Of course, Willie had sound economical reasons for being excited about Tina's good fortune. "Ever since she recorded, 'Let's Stay Together,' which was written by myself and Al Green, people have been calling, wanting to know if I had any more songs like that."

Working with Ann Peebles and Tina Turner in the mid-to-late 1960s, Willie felt like he was on the right track with female singers. What he needed more than anything else was a strong male vocalist who could complement his instrumental sound. Fortune smiles on him in Midland, Texas, in the summer of 1968. He had scored that year with another instrumental hit, "Soul Serenade," and he was touring to promote the record.

"It was real hot that day, like 112 degrees," laughs Willie. "We pulled the bus up to the club in Midland. This guy runs up to me. He says his name is Al Green. He said, 'I'm stranded here. Can I work with you tonight so I can get back home?'

"So, we went in to rehearse. I heard him sing. I said, 'Hey, man, you've got a neat style.' He was about 20. I said, 'Why don't you go back to Memphis with me. Let's work on some stuff. You could be a star. He said, 'How long would it take to do it. I said about eighteen months. He said, 'I don't have that long to wait'.

"When the show was over, we got stranded in the lot because a car wouldn't let us out of the driveway. Finally, Al comes and jumps in the bus and we took him back to Memphis. It was eighteen months exactly when 'Tired of Being Alone' was a million seller." In Al Green, Willie, at long last, had found the voice he'd been searching for.

*   *   *

On August 19, 1966, the Beatles performed at the Memphis Coliseum. The Ku Klux Klan had pickets outside the coliseum because of comments John Lennon had made about the Beatles being more popular than Jesus Christ. The police were asked to keep an eye out for firearms. By the time they took the stage, John, Paul, George and Ringo were basket cases. Halfway through the performance someone threw a firecracker onto the stage and George Harrison nearly fainted.

The Beatles' manager, Brian Epstein, arranged a visit to Stax while they were in Memphis. T.G. Sheppard was working there by then as a record promoter. He remembers seeing them walk down the hall. "I kind of freaked out," he says. "They were talking about recording at Stax and the word got out. A mob of people showed up. They were big fans of Otis Redding and people like that. I guess they just wanted to see where all those records were cut."

As usual at Stax there was a lot of confusion about the reason for the visit. Jim and Estelle had learned the music business by using the bootstrap approach. They learned the hard way that people didn't always do things for the reasons they said they were doing them. It made them cynical.

"I don't think they ever meant to come (to record)," says Estelle. "They just wanted to get something stirred up for their concert."

The debacle left Estelle so distraught she refused to buy Beatles albums for the record shop. "As I look back, it's funny. But then I was in tears."

The following year, the entire Stax stable went to Europe as part of the Stax/Volt Revue. While the tour was in London, legend has it the Beatles stopped work on their Sgt.Pepper album to take in a performance. Carla Thomas says she has always heard that, but never saw them at the performance.

131

"What pleased me is that I was the only artist out of the bunch of folks on the tour who performed at a club called the Bag of Nails," says Carla. "Booker played for me, but I was the only vocalist. In that little club was Paul McCartney and the fact that he was there says something about the Memphis sound."

By January 1967 the Memphis sound was on the verge of a major overhaul. The Mar-Keys had broken up as a touring band in 1965 and the singer who fronted the band on the road, Ronnie "Angel" Stoots, formed a group he named Ronnie and the Devilles. But after a couple of years of getting nowhere in the club scene, Ronnie ditched the Devilles to start up another group. The three remaining members of the Devilles—Danny Smythe on drums; Gary Talley on guitar; and Bill Cunningham on bass—started looking around for a singer and a keyboard player. Smythe brought John Evans into the group to play keyboards; then they focused on finding a singer.

"Danny said, 'We need somebody who can sing like a nigger,'" says Evans. "In those days that word was not such a derogatory term. Danny admires black music and more than any person I know. They asked me if I knew anybody. At that time, it would not have been a viable alternative to have a black member in the band. I called a friend and he said, well, there's this guy who was in a talent show. I said, well, is he any good? He said, yeah, but I don't really know why."

Evans found out that his name was Alex Chilton and he gave him a call. He was surprised to find out that he was only 16 (they were all 19), but he invited him to an audition. Three years difference at that age is a lot, and that concerned some of the guys in the band, but they figured they could overlook the age thing if he could really sing. If they had prepared themselves for the age difference, they had not prepared themselves for what they saw when he arrived for the audition. All the members of the band were dressed in the preppy fashions of the day—Gant shirts, Gold Cup socks and Bass Wegens loafers.

"There was a dress code without having a dress code in those days," says Evans. "Alex came in wearing a faded black T-shirt, jeans with holes in the knees and that was not acceptable in those days—and a blue jean jacket, and no one wore those except farmers, blue collar workers, you know, trailer park people, for heaven's sake. On top of that, he comes in cold weather and he had on a men's dress scarf, like you would wear with an overcoat."

But when Alex sang, he transformed himself into a gritty soul singer, so they forgave his eccentric dress and asked him to be their singer. Later they discovered his mother owned an art gallery and his father was a jazz musician. They lived in the gallery, and, in the minds of 19-year-old musicians, that explained Alex's eccentricities. They started doing gigs as the Devilles.

As the Devilles were re-grouping, Chips Moman and Dan Penn, an Alabamian who had jumped to American from Fame studio in Muscle Shoals, Alabama, were booked as players for a session at Fame with a Memphis-born singer named Aretha Franklin, There was a buzz out about her, and Chips and Dan both were anxious to see if she measured up. She had been signed to Atlantic by Jerry Wexler, who had decided to record her in Muscle Shoals after Jim Stewart had turned down another one of Wexler's "deals" to record her at Stax. Wexler knew it would piss Jim off if he invited Chips and Dan to the session. For Dan, a hard-core country boy who was seldom without sun glasses and a cigarette dangling from his lips, it was a chance to return to a neck of the woods in which he felt comfortable. They recorded one complete song, "I Never Loved a Man," and laid down the track for a song written by Chips and Dan, "Do Right Woman."

With the success of "I Never Loved a Man"—it peaked at No. 9—Wexler sent for Moman's rhythm section at American. They went to New York and completed an album within one week. Other songs on the album were "Natural Woman" and "Chain of Fools." One of the songs recorded that week, "Respect," had been released earlier by Otis Redding.

Aretha liked the song and wanted to record it herself. Of course, the Memphis boys were happy to oblige. What better way to stick it to their competitors across town than by re-doing their work? In June, Aretha Franklin's version of "Respect" zoomed to No. 1 on the pop charts, only two weeks after its release. Otis Redding was stunned. None of his records had cracked the Top 20.

Spirits soared at American. Aretha hadn't recorded at American, but she had used American players and Memphis songs—and she herself was a Memphian—so there was a feeling, at the very least, that they were headed in the right direction. Sometime between the New York session and the success of "Respect," Dan Penn was approached by a deejay about the Devilles. Dan talked to Chips about the group and he told him to give them a shot. Dan arranged for them to come into the studio for a 10 a.m. session and notified them the day before. He sent word for them to pick up a tape of original songs he had put together for them to learn. That night John Evans and another band member stopped by the studio to pick up the tape.

"Dan wasn't there, but he had left the tape there with our names on it," says Evans. "So we went back and listened to the tape. There were three tunes on it. 'The Letter' was the only one we could stand to listen to. It was short, very simple."

When they returned to the studio the next morning, they got the second jolt of their young careers (Alex's avant garde appearance had been the first of many shocks). "Dan was wearing Bermuda shorts that came down to the middle of his knee caps," recalls Evans. "If that weren't nerdy enough, he was wearing a white T-shirt with the sleeve rolled up around a pack of Lucky Strikes. He was the darnest thing to see. He was wearing high topped tennis shoes with athletic socks rolled up."

Dan informed them that Chips wouldn't be coming in that day. He would be their producer. They looked around the studio. Dirty ashtrays and food were piled up everywhere. It looked dark and foreboding.

"We didn't know what to think," says Evans. "Dan was primarily a writer, but he worked as an engineer. Dan, thinks, 'Uh, huh, here's my chance to do something.' I think it was the first tune he had ever produced."

Evans showed the other guys in the band the chord progression for "The Letter"—Dan suggested to Alex that he pronounce aeroplane in three syballes—and 33 takes later they had a record that re-defined the Memphis sound.

"The Letter" was released on Mala, a New York-based label that specialized in music for black markets. By then the Devilles had changed their name to the Box Tops. To the surprise of everyone involved, especially the group's 16-year-old lead singer,

"The Letter" peaked at No. 1 in September 1967, thus becoming the first No. 1 pop hit ever recorded in Memphis by Memphis artists.

Chips Moman was elated with the success of "The Letter," even if Dan Penn, who had never produced anything in his life, had produced it; but it seemed to confirm his worst fears about what could happen if he didn't stay in the studio 24 hours a day. He would never let *that* happen again. For the next five years he would eat, sleep, work and play at the studio, working at a fanatical pace and never, ever, again take his eye off the console board. Creatively, it would pay off. He would produce a string of over 120 hit records at American, one of the most impressive feats in American music history. Physically, it nearly destroyed him.

Chips began his second flowering (the first had been at Stax) with Wilson Pickett, whom Jerry Wexler had brought up from Muscle Shoals, and Bobby Womack, a songwriter and guitarist who had played on some of Pickett's previous sessions. Chips cut hits with Pickett, then turned around and cut hits with Womack.

"I gave Wilson Pickett all my songs," says Womack. "Every time he asked for another one, I gave it to him. I was so happy. He got his whole album down and then they said, "Bobby, you're next.' He walked out of the studio and they said, 'Well, what do you want to cut first?' I didn't have a damn song left. I tried my best to write something. Chips came in and said, 'Hi, Bobby, how's it going?' I didn't tell him I had given Pickett every song I had. I started playing 'Fly Me to the Moon,' and Chips said, speed it up. That's a smash. Let's cut it.' It was about 2 o'clock in the morning. He never knew that 'Midnight Mover' and the others were on the Pickett album. They'd have really shit in their pants if they had known that."

In those days, everything Chips touched became a hit. He cut another Top 10 hit with the Gentrys ("Cry Like a Baby"), then followed that up with Dusty Springfield's "Son-Of-A-Preacher Man," B.J. Thomas' "Hooked on a Feeling" and Neil Diamond's "Sweet Caroline." Then he got word that the King himself, Elvis Presley, wanted to work with him. Despite his recent failings, there was no one in music any bigger than Elvis.

*　　*　　*

135

In the summer of 1967 Otis Redding and his band, the Bar-Kays, played the Fillmore in San Francisco. There were there several weeks, so Otis rented a houseboat instead of staying in a hotel. The bay, with its ever present dock and soothing sounds, had a mystical attraction to a Southern boy raised in inland Georgia. It gave him an idea for a song. That fall Otis took a couple of months off to recuperate from minor throat surgery. Since they were booked on December 8 at Vanderbilt University in Nashville, he decided to spend several days in Memphis before the concert date, with the hope of doing some recording. He told Steve Cropper he had a song.

"Otis was always writing," recalls Steve. "Every time he came to Memphis to record, he always had 14 or 15 ideas. A little piece of this, a little intro there. He played me what he had, and it was only the first verse. I sat there with him and within about half an hour we had written the other two verses and the bridge."

The song, "(Sitting On) The Dock of the Bay," was unfinished when Otis left to perform in Nashville. Otis had played acoustic guitar on the track, but Cropper had not dubbed in his electric guitar. Nor had he added the sea gulls and ocean waves that appeared on the final version. "The day we cut that song, Otis and I looked at each other and said, 'This is a hit,'" says Cropper. "Not everybody in the studio agreed with us, but we knew in our own minds that this would be his biggest record. In this business, you know when you have a winner."

Jim Stewart wasn't so sure since it deviated from the tried-and-true Stax formula. But if he was less than enthusiastic, he can be forgiven since he had other, more pressing, matters to deal with. Unknown to the musicians, Stax was in the midst of a major crisis. Jim's relationship with Wexler had been deteriorating all year. Wexler was playing up to Chips, offering him money to help keep his studio afloat, while distributing the records produced at Stax.

In October 1967, Atlantic announced it was being acquired by Warner Bros., but Wexler assured Jim he would be staying on and nothing would change in the Stax/Atlantic relationship. But that was not the case. *Everything* was about to change.

The Atlantic/Warner Bros. merger meant that Stax and Atlantic would have to renegotiate their contract. It was then that Jim found out that his relationship with Atlantic was not what he had thought.

Unknown to Jim, the original agreement had transferred ownership of the Stax master tapes to Atlantic. It was spelled out in the fine print, but Jim had not understood it. That meant that all that Stax owned was a name and the future work recorded by the label's artists. Atlantic owned everything they had recorded to date. It was the business equivalent of a date rape. Jim was screwed, just as every Memphis player from Handy forward had been screwed by the writing in the fine print.

That news probably didn't surprise Estelle, who had never particularly cared for Wexler. After "Last Night" was released, she complained to Jim that Wexler was not promoting it. He told her to call him and talk to him about it.

"I did, and I told him that it had been a hit in Memphis and a record that could be a hit in Memphis could be a hit anywhere," says Estelle. "Well, he didn't like my attitude at all. He called Jim back. He said, 'Don't let your sister get on the phone anymore to me. I don't want to talk to her.'" Estelle laughs. "Well, I proved him wrong. I knew it was a hit."

After the Nashville performance, Otis flew to Cleveland, Ohio, in his new, twin-engine Beechcraft to appear at Leo's Casino. The next morning, December 10, he called his wife before heading out for a performance in Madison, Wisconsin. She later recalled he sounded depressed.

Two weeks earlier, the Atlantic deal with Warner Bros. was concluded. Did Otis know he had become a pawn in Stax's negotiations with Atlantic? Did he know he was the only real bargaining chip Jim had to get a better deal with Atlantic?

Had Otis been approached by a third party and pressured to leave Stax? Had he received a secret offer from Atlantic that enticed him to leave Stax? Had he said, yes? At age 26, Otis had one of the brightest futures in pop music.

On board the Beechcraft with Otis were Bar-Kays Ben Cauley, Jimmy King, Phalon Jones, Ronnie Caldwell and Carl Cunningham, and pilot Richard Frasier, a 26-year-old flight instructor with 1290 total hours. It was a cold, wintery day when they left Cleveland. At 3:25 that afternoon, moments before they were scheduled to land, Ben Cauley awoke to feel the plane spinning out of control in the rain.

The Beechcraft crashed into the frigid waters of Lake Monona three miles from the Madison runway. After impact, Cauley grabbed a seat cushion and stayed afloat until help arrived. He looked for Otis and the others. They were nowhere to be found. He was the only survivor.

The timing of the crash certainly seemed suspicious. The report issued by the National Transportation Safety Board said the cause of the crash was "undetermined." The report said the left wing and the left propeller were never found. That meant the plane probably broke up in mid-air and separated from the fuselage. Had the plane been sabotaged? If the plane was spinning, as Cauley reported, that would indicate the possibility of an explosion on the left wing or the possibility the engine cowlings had been loosened prior to take-off, causing the engine to drop from the wing. Unfortunately, federal officials could not make a determination of the cause of the accident without the wing fragments.

Three months after the crash, "(Sittin' On) The Dock of the Bay" was the No. 1 pop record in America. It was the first—and only—No. 1 record Stax would ever have, and it could not have come at a better time. Sadly, Otis never heard the finished record. That fact would haunt Cropper for the rest of his life.

Despite the success of the record, the future of Stax was in doubt. By May, Jim had three options: he could sell out to Atlantic and watch Stax be shut down and absorbed by the larger company; he could try to make it as an independent (against overwhelming odds); or he could find a buyer who would allow Stax to stay in business as a separate label. Jim and Estelle decided to sever their relationship with Atlantic and sell to Gulf & Western. Estelle flew to New York to personally give the "bad news" to Wexler (oh, what a glorious moment that must have been for her) and Jim and All Bell flew to Los Angeles to sign the deal with Gulf & Western.

But there was more to the deal than that. Estelle, the heart and soul of Stax, stepped out of the picture entirely as the result of a buy-out. "I saw they were going to beat me out of part of mine, so I dealt with them and got my part before they gave up on Stax," says Estelle, who surrendered her interest in the label for 4,000 shares of Gulf & Western stock and an annual salary of $25,000 for five years. The agreement also called for her to stay out of the music business for five years. With Estelle out of the picture—and no women around to call them to task—Jim and Al Bell decided to take Stax in a new direction. They wanted to play hard ball.

* * *

From the time of Otis' plane crash and Estelle's buyout, events were overtaking not just Memphis, but the entire nation. On Feb. 1, 1968, Priscilla Presley gave birth to Lisa Marie, giving Elvis his first and only child. But news of the Vietnam War and presidential politics overshadowed Elvis' good fortune.

On March 31, President Lyndon Johnson went on television to announce a unilateral halt of bombing about the 20 parallel in Vietnam. Then he stunned the nation with an announcement he would "neither seek nor accept" his party's nomination for President. Ostensibly the most hated man in American politics he stepped aside.

Abe Fortas' fortunes continued to rise. His vote was the deciding vote in the 5-4 Miranda decision that extended the Fifth Amendment's privilege against self-incrimination to include police interrogation. That year Earl Warren announced he was retiring as Chief Justice. Johnson nominated Fortas to replace him.

The war in Vietnam had made 1968 one of the most convulsive years in American history. The President had been made a virtual prisoner in the White House by antiwar protests. His political allies were beginning to desert him because of his war policy.

Johnson's problems were heightened when it was disclosed that Abe Fortas, while a Supreme Court justice, had accepted a "consultant's" fee from a Florida businessman. After the story was reported in the press, Fortas gave the money back, but it was too late. The businessman already was under investigation by the Securities and Exchange Commission.

Eventually, the businessman was convicted on stock manipulation charges and sentenced to one year in federal prison. Fortas' acceptance of the money was scandalous and the Senate, charged with approving his appointment as Chief Justice, balked and stated its intention to hold the nomination in abeyance until

139

after newly elected President Richard Nixon took office.

Sen. Robert Griffin of Michigan, who led the fight to block the nomination, received death threats. Tennessee Sen. Howard Baker spoke out in opposition to Fortas' nomination, as did Hamilton S. Burnett, the chief justice of the Tennessee Supreme Court. Saying Fortas' lack of ethics made him "sick," Burnett called for the justice's impeachment. Fortas had "violated every principle of honesty," he said. Fortas resigned a year later, bringing to an end the public service career of Fiddlin' Abe, Memphis's most politically connected musician.

On April 4 civil rights leader Martin Luther King, Jr. was shot to death by an assassin at the Loraine Motel, only two blocks from Abe Fortas' home. In the wake of King's assassination, outraged blacks rioted in 80 cities, including Memphis.

Nationwide, 29 people died and 2,000 were injured. It was the most widespread racial unrest in American history. Mobs of angry blacks roamed city streets, looting and setting fires. Memphis officials set a 7 p.m. curfew and called in National Guard troops. If there was ever a turning point in Memphis music, a point beyond which there was no return, it was the King assassination.

Don Nix and Duck Dunn were standing in front of the studio when the rioting began. "There was a lot of activity," recalls Nix. "People were moving around in the streets." But they weren't overly concerned. Stax was located in a black neighborhood, but they knew every shopkeeper on the street. It was inconceivable to them that anyone would hurt them.

"We went back inside and Isaac (Hayes) said, 'Man, ya'll better go home. Let me carry you and Duck home."

They said no.

Then they began to see smoke on the horizon.

Jim and Estelle decided to close the doors at Stax. They stayed closed for a week. "Jim took all the masters home," says Estelle. "We didn't know what might happen. The building might go up in flames. Out of respect we closed until the riots were over and things settled down. We were protecting ourselves."

Estelle smiles, sharing a secret. "I don't think they ever knew we took all the master tapes out of there."

After the riots ended, Jim put a chain link fence around the back entrance to the studio. The gates had locks. "I thought that was when the music started dying," says Nix. "After that, you couldn't go back out on the street. That was my neighborhood. We spent more time there than we did at home."

*   *   *

The summer of 1968 must have been especially bleak for Elvis. He had a brand new baby girl, and he was still demand as a movie actor, but his music career was stone cold dead. He had not had a Top 10 hit since June 1965, when "Crying in the Chapel" peaked at No. 3, two slots below "Wooly Bully." If he turned on the radio, he heard songs by the Byrds, the Beatles, the Rolling Stones and, perhaps worst of all, a whole gang of Memphis people turning out records at Stax, Hi and American.

Elvis was a relic—and he knew it. If he watched television or read newspapers, all he heard or saw was talk of race riots and anti-war demonstrations. He became a virtual prisoner in Graceland.

"There was a period of time for a few months when it was really tough," says T.G. Sheppard, who spent a great deal of time at Graceland at that time. "There was a big fear of people breaking into Graceland to kidnap him or Lisa Marie. I remember being in the den, then all of a sudden everyone was scrambling because someone had called the house and said someone had climbed over the wall and had something in their hand and they were pointing it toward the house. Everybody was outside and Elvis was freakin'. He grabbed his gun. There was a fear in him that I had never seen before. He started talking about wanting gun turrets on top of the house and it rubbed off on everyone else. Everybody was scared."

In June he recorded a TV special for NBC that was broadcast on December 3. It was a big hit and writers who had not written about Elvis in years began talking about his "comeback." Elvis needed a new album to build on the momentum of the TV show. Colonel Parker began making plans for him to return to Nashville, but at the last minute it was decided that it should be recorded in Memphis. They turned to the man who, at that moment, was the hottest producer in America—Chips Moman.

In January 1969 Elvis showed up at American with his entourage. He had not recorded in Memphis since 1955. No one was sure exactly what to expect. Chips' studio musicians, known as the 827 Thomas Street band, would be putting down the tracks. Elvis hadn't worked with *real* musicians since the early years he was on the road with Scotty and Bill. "He obviously hadn't had any direction in a great while," says Moman. "If he had, I don't think he would have cut all those junk records he cut. When I told him he was off pitch, his entourage would come up and say, 'Oh, don't tell him that.'

"Well, why not? I saw quickly I did not want to go on the speaker and say, 'Hey, man, da-dah-da' every time he did something wrong, I walked out into the studio and into the booth where he was singing and I had a quiet conversation with him. He took direction great. But I'm not sure Elvis would've taken direction over the monitors where fifty people could hear me say he was flat. That would blow things out of proportion. But if you do it quietly, one on one, it was no problem at all." Adds Chips with a laugh: "He wasn't the world's greatest singer, but he had a sound. I worked with people who were more talented, but nobody bigger."

A pattern quickly developed in the studio. "When he went at it, he was either on or off. If he was off, it was better to do it another day," says Chips. "A lot of people didn't understand how I could get him to do so many takes. I would have him sing a song twenty or thirty times, over and over. Back up and fix little lines that he would miss. He went through it without a problem."

The best work done at the session, which lasted about two weeks in January, and another week in February, was done when Chips and Elvis were alone in the studio. "We did the best work before everybody would come in," says Chips. "Some of the things we did was to cut the tracks before he got there and put his voice on it when he arrived. One of the things I missed with Elvis was his old band. I always liked Scotty and Bill and DJ Fontana. I thought they were really unique. In my opinion, up until the 827 Thomas Street band cut him, no one took an interest in his music after Scotty and Bill were gone. I was just a job for him. You can hear it on the records. Everything was rushed. I always thought it was sad that Scotty and Bill didn't stay their whole careers with him. They were unique together. It's hard to carry that on vocally."

Chips recorded enough material during those sessions to fill out two albums. Most critics consider the session to have been the most productive since Elvis early Sun sessions. Among the songs recorded were "In the Ghetto," which gave Elvis his first Top 10 song since "Crying in the Chapel," "Kentucky Rain," "Gentle on My Mind," "Any Day Now" and "Suspicious Minds," which peaked at No. 1 in November. It would be Elvis' last No. 1 record.

Elvis' career was given new life. In December 1969 Chips and Al Bell of Stax were honored in Atlanta by 1,000 radio and recording executives at the annual Bill Gavan Radio Program Conference. Bell was named "recording executive of the year" and applauded for his promotional efforts. Chips was named "producer of the year" and cited for his work with Elvis. "It's a wonderful honor for me," said Chips. "But my staff at the studio should receive most of the credit. They make the music. I just turn the knobs and make a few suggestions."

Memphis was on top of the heap.

Charlie Rich in Memphis
Photo courtesy of the Mississippi Valley Collection
University of Memphis, University Libraries

144

Rufus Thomas, Ann Peebles, and Al Green in 1976
Photo courtesy of the Mississippi Valley Collection
University of Memphis, University Libraries

Chips Moman, C. 1960s
Photo courtesy of the Mississippi Valley Collection
University of Memphis, University Libraries

CHAPTER 8

The 1970s:
Disco Duck Comes to Town

With the success of "Suspicious Minds," the floodgates opened at American. Elvis had been so far removed from making hit records that the consensus was that if Chips Moman could record a hit with him he could record a hit with anyone. From 1969 to 1973, the studios at American, Hi and Stax cranked out hits like there was no tomorrow, making Memphis the undisputed creative center of the American music industry. American alone produced more than 120 hit records during that period.

Chips and Tommy Cogbill, who had joined Chips as a producer/partner, actually had to turn people away. Early in 1970 Columbia Records called to book a session for Bob Dylan at American, but when they insisted on Chips being listed as the engineer and not the producer, they were turned away. Not turned down for sessions at American were Neil Diamond, whose two albums, *Brother Love* and *Touching You*, spawned the hit singles "Sweet Caroline" and "Holly Holy"; Dusty Springfield, whose album *Dusty in Memphis* is viewed by many as one of her best, generated "Son of a Preacher Man" and "Windmills of Your Mind" to the charts; Petula Clark, whose *Memphis* LP gave us "People Get Ready" and "That Old Time Feeling"; B. J. Thomas, who recorded four albums that produced hits such as "Hooked On a Feeling" and "Eyes of a New York Woman"; Paul Revere and the Raiders with their album, *In Memphis*; Herbie Mann with his *Memphis Underground* album; Joe Tex with "Hold On to What You Got" and "Skinny Legs"; Dionne Warwick with "Lost That Lovin' Feeling" and an album, *Soulful*; and Brenda Lee, with her album *Memphis Portrait* and the singles "Sisters In Sorrow" and "I Think I Love You Again."

Of all the above sessions, it would be the ones with Brenda Lee that would have the biggest impact on Chips' personal life. One of the songs chosen for the session was written by a New

York songwriter, Toni Wine. Discovered by producer Don Kirshner at the age of 14, she was a child prodigy who had studied as a classical pianist at Juilliard School of Music for nine years and gave her first concert at the age of 10 at Carnegie Hall. By 1970 she had scored with a number of hits both as a songwriter and a vocalist. She wrote "A Groovy Kind of Love" for the Mindbenders, a No. 6 hit in 1966, "Black Pearl," "Candida," "Tonight You're Going To Fall in Love With Me" by the Shirelles, the theme for the movie *To Sir With Love* and the theme for Dick Clark's American Bandstand. In 1969 Kirshner persuaded Toni to record with another singer under the name, The Archies. It may have been a fictitious group, but the group's first single, "Sugar, Sugar," became a No. 1 hit on the pop charts. Although the Archies sold over 13 million records, the only payment Toni ever received was a dozen roses. It was enough to make her never want to sing again.

"I will always be grateful to Donnie (Kirshner) for putting me in the music business," says Toni. "I love him dearly for that. I hate him dearly for not being honest with me. I never signed anything with him because he was the daddy. That was a very bad thing in my life."

When her publisher called and asked if she would mind going to Memphis, where Brenda Lee was recording one of her songs with Chips Moman, she had no way of knowing that it would be a life-altering journey. "I flew down to Memphis because they had lost the words," says Toni. "I had no plans for the next few days, so I took the song down personally. When Chips and I first met, I had no idea of what to expect in him or in the city of Memphis."

Toni and Chips could not possibly have been more different. Not only was she Jewish, she was New York Jewish, which, to a tattooed Georgia boy brought up to say "yes ma'am" and "no ma'am," was the very worst kind to be, a fact that was proved to his satisfaction by her refusal to submit to his authority, musical or otherwise. Sparks flew. From the outside the studio must have looked like a welders shop. It was love at first sight. Toni had long, black hair and a face that would stop any man dead in his tracks. Chips had never met anyone like her. To her, Chips, with his Gary Cooper good looks and rough-edged cowboy mannerisms, was as exotic as anything she had ever seen in New York.

Chips and Toni turned that three-day visit into a passionate love affair, and eventually into a marriage. "She's aggravating, but she knows exactly what she's doing . . . also what everybody else is doing," laughs Chips. Toni extended her three-day visit to a week, and then left, but Chips had not seen the last of her.

Memphis defined the blues; then reshaped it into rhythm and blues. It invented rock 'n' roll; then refined into it a pop bastardization of jazz. If the genius of the city was that it could create art forms that had never existed before, conjuring them out of thin air, its saving grace was that it could package those inventions in reusable containers. Memphis was never a "band" city. The individual was always supreme. That was the drawing card to both female and male singers in the 1970s. It was where you went to make records that would set you apart from the others.

Petula Clark had a big hit with "Downtown" before she went to American. She was astonished by the laidback atmosphere in the studio. She told reporters that working there was "like having a party." When she was asked if she intended to keep the names of the songs she was working on a secret, she laughed because she had discovered what other artists who worked with Chips discovered: He believed in the rhythm method of sound control. "Yes, it's a secret," says Petuala. "But we're in the dark, too. You see, we won't know until we do them."

There was method to Chips' studio musical madness. "In a way, I aggravate a lot of singers," says Chips. "I let my singers learn a song the same time the band does. To me, there is a freshness when they do it together. Great singers get bored quickly. I keep the songs away from them on purpose."

Chips also had a strategy for song selection. "Going in, I'm a nervous wreck. The artist is a nervous wreck. The band is worrying about whether an amp is going to blow out. You get things going pretty smoothly, and then you pull out your best song. I never use my best songs going in. I'll do a couple of songs before I pull out a song I think is a hit. The ones I'm really counting on, I won't put them in early."

Visualize, if you can, how Gary Cooper would have conducted a recording session at *High Noon* and you will have a fairly accurate picture of what it was like to work with Chips in those days. If it was frustrating for singers because of the uncertainty, it was also comforting in the way in which everyone worked together to make the best record possible. Dionne Warwick was so impressed by her Memphis experience she tried to launch a record label in the city with Marty Lacker, one of Chips' investors at American. They named the label Sonday Records in honor of Dionne's son. Unfortunately, the label fizzled before it could get off the ground and Dionne never returned to Memphis to record.

*　*　*

Willie Mitchell is one of the most consistent figures in the history of Memphis music. Emotionally, he has maintained himself on a straight line, a middle-C, for thirty-five years. I don't know of anyone who knows of instances in which he has ever lost control of himself in public or raised his voice in anger. He has inspired no stories of scandal or intrigue. No stories of drunken binges. As I think of Lil Hardin as one of the grand ladies of American music, I think of Willie Mitchell as one of its true gentlemen. Oh, he can be arrogant at time; but that is more of a defensive weapon than anything else.

Musically, he has a gift for finesse. While his competitors at Stax wrote the book on using horns to accent vocals, he used his more intricate understanding of orchestration to wrap melodies around vocals through a more precise use of horns.

One of the more interesting footnotes of music history is that there were very few musicians involved with the hits that came out of Memphis during the 1960s and 1970s. Willie shared Al Jackson (on drums) with Stax, and Jim shared the Memphis Horns (Wayne Jackson and Andrew Love) with Chips. Even though he was using some of the same players used by the other studios, two things made Willie's sound unique: First, he pulled the drums up so they were more immediate, more hypnotic; secondly, at what at first glance would appear to be a contradiction, he smothered the tracks with a lushness of sound that oozed soul.

Al Green was the perfect singer to complement Willie's vision of music. He wasn't versatile as a vocalist, but what he did, no one could do better. They didn't find each other musically right away.

They had a few false starts. One of their first records was a remake of the Beatles' "I Want to Hold Your Hand." It was a terrible record, and poor sales reflected that, but Willie and Al weren't discouraged. They tried another remake, this time they recorded the Temptations' "I Can't Get Next To You." It wasn't a hit either, but it came close. They were headed in the right direction. What they needed was some good original material.

Willie was feeling the pressure. The last hit to come out of Hi was his own "Soul Serenade" in 1968. In early 1970, Chips had Elvis' "Don't Cry Daddy" and Neil Diamond's "Holly Holy" on the charts. B.B. King was on the charts with "The Thrill is Gone." In early 1971 Ike & Tina Turner scored big with "Proud Mary." Willie believed in Al, so he pushed him to write his own material.

"It wasn't just Al's voice, it was his attitude," says Willie. "He wanted it so bad. That's what I liked about him. He was going to make it one way or another."

Al brought Willie a song he had written titled "Tired of Being Alone." They recorded it and in October 1971 it went to No. 12 on the pop charts. Encouraged, he brought him another song, "Let's Stay Together." Willie, Al Green and Al Jackson worked on the song together, getting it perfect before they released it; then they sat back and watched it climb the charts. In February 1972 it was the No. 1 record in America.

For the next three years, Willie and Al enjoyed unparalleled success with their patented pop-R&B formula—"Look What You Done For Me" (No. 16), "I'm Still In Love With You" (No. 6), "You Ought To Be With Me" (No. 3), "Call Me (Come Back Home)" (No. 15), "Here I Am (Come And Take Me)" (No. 13), "Sha-La-La (Make Me Happy)" (No. 9) and "L-O-V-E" (No. 16). That translated to eight gold singles and six gold albums.

Success in a recording studio is contagious. As Willie and Al were soaring, other Hi acts came into their own. Ann Peebles scored with "I Can't Stand the Rain." Sly Johnson with "Take Me To The River." Otis Clay with "I Die a Little Each Day." The music produced at Hi was becoming "blacker," which is to say fewer and fewer white musicians were participating in the sessions. Among the white, wanna-be singers who hung out at Hi in the late 1960s, before the color bar was raised, was Rita Coolidge. The

Nashville-born daughter of a Baptist minister, she moved to Memphis in 1968 after graduating from Florida State University.

"My parents had moved to Memphis while I was in college," Rita explained to me. "When you get out of college and don't have a job, you go wherever your parents live. When I got to Memphis, it was, to me, the recording center of the world. I had been to Nashville. I had been to New York. I had not been to California, but the music that was being made in Memphis then was the music I had in my collection, the albums that I value and treasure with my life."

Rita was offered an assistantship at FSU to work on her master's degree, but while in Memphis she realized a career in music was what she wanted most. For a while she lived with Don Nix, who by then was one of the major producers at Stax. She became a regular at all the studios, but especially at Willie's. That was scandalous in the late 1960s, of course. That was something nice white girls just didn't do. The scandal became family-wide when her sister, Priscilla, married Booker T., making history with the first interracial marriage in Memphis music history. Booker T. and Pricilla would hold that record for over thirty years, until Lisa Marie Presley married Michael Jackson in 1995.

Willie remembers Rita as a listener."She used to sit up all night with us," says Willie. "Just sit in the studio and watch what we were doing. I knew she was a singer, but we never did anything she wanted to sing at Hi."

For a while Rita did commercial jingles for a while for a local agency; then she recorded a couple of singles at American, one of which was written by Memphian Donna Weiss, who subsequently won a Grammy for "Bette Davis Eyes." Rita left Memphis in 1970 to join the Delaney & Bonnie tour, recorded a string of successful album for A&M and married Kris Kristofferson.

Willie invested a lot of emotional and creative capital in Al Green. That was unfortunate for Willie. Al was skittish, a cat on a hot tin roof, not someone you'd want to put all your hopes on. That sounds negative, and it is not meant to be, but Al—who seems to have spent much of his life imitating a deer caught in the headlights of an oncoming car—was a bad investment, not because he was dishonest but because he was possessed with personal

152

demons only he could exercise.

In 1974 Al was scalded with boiling grits by a former girlfriend, who then committed suicide with Al's own pistol. After that incident, Willie and Al maintained their hit-making relationship in the studio, but it started slipping away and by 1976 Al asked Willie for a musical divorce. Al recorded a couple of albums without Willie; then he abruptly quit music to devote his life to the ministry.

Willie was devastated.

One of the rules of Memphis music is that once something, *anything*, goes wrong in a music-related relationship, you had better hold on for dear life, because disaster is just around the corner. Al Green provided a bridge between pop and R&B at a time when the record buying public was losing interest in black R&B. By 1976 the hits were being recorded by Paul Simon, the Bee Gees and John Sebastian. Al Green was Willie Mitchell's version of Paul Simon and the Bee Gees combined. With Al gone, the reality of the record business set in. Those hit records had been great for morale, but they hadn't translated into money in the bank.

"We had hits with Hi, but they were on London Records," says Willie. "We just leased the masters to London."

" But weren't things jumping back then?" I asked.

"Yes, but who got the money? We got a little bit of the money but the record companies got most of it."

*   *   *

Across town at Stax, the sweet soul upon which the label had been founded was reflecting the times—and the times had become strident. The King assassination had changed everything. Blacks never bought the story that King's assassin acted alone. They had come in enough back doors to know where the trash was piled. No, in their minds James Earl Ray did not kill Martin Luther King. Memphis killed Martin Luther King. Everyone knew that. When it comes to the Devil's work, all roads lead to Memphis.

Fearing the politicization of the music produced at Stax, Jim brought Al Bell in to salve the festering black anger that was lapping at the front door like the advance waves of a hurricane.

If black anger had been the only threat, the situation would have been manageable. But the music industry itself was changing. Organized crime was becoming a factor in New York and Los Angeles. Jim was like a schoolteacher who had been dropped into the middle of a street brawl. When he and Estelle had started up Stax, the atmosphere was one of love and dreams of creating something out of nothing. Now Estelle, the ever present housemother, was gone and the dreams had become nightmares. The music business, as Jim learned, was certainly no place for wimps.

Bell brought a New York record executive, Johnny Baylor, into the fold in 1968. At the time he was operating a small label, Koko, which had one artist on its roster—Luther Ingram. Baylor was black, proud and convinced you never got anything in life you didn't fight for. Luther Ingram gave Stax one of its biggest post-1960s hit, "(If Loving You Is Wrong) I Don't Want To Be Right," but Baylor's new role at Stax was as an enforcer, not as a talent scout. Baylor was Jim's muscle, his protection against the angry hordes chanting outside the door. They were frightening times.

The Stax family was undergoing radical change. Booker T. Jones was the first to leave. In 1969, he took his white wife and his entire extended family, to Los Angeles. He was through with Stax. "There were so many doors that were closed to me there, and at the same time there were doors that were open to me there," explains Jones. "My plan was to take the MGs away from Stax Records and take them to A&M Records, and, of course, that did not work."

Two of the workhorses for Stax during the 1970s were Don Nix and Bobby Manuel. From his start as a sax player in the Mar-Keys, Nix branched out as a songwriter and producer. In the late 1960s and early-to-mid 1970s, he wrote a number of hit songs, including "Goin' Down," and produced albums on Albert King, Leon Russell, Joe Cocker, Delany & Bonnie, Jeff Beck and Freddie King, and he worked on the Bangldesh concert with ex-Beatle George Harrison.

Don had his own way of doing things. Recording sessions at Stax were usually spur-of-the-moment occurrences. That suited Don just fine. Don is a spur-of-the-moment type of guy. Albert King's critically acclaimed *Lovejoy* album offers insight into what Stax was like then.

Don walked into the studio one day and was told it was his turn to produce Albert King. "Everyone else had produced Albert," says Nix. "I was told to do it more than asked to do it, but after we started the album, it was a lot of fun."

Albert didn't have any songs, so Don asked him to do a cover on the Rolling Stones' "Honky Tonk Woman," and Don wrote the other seven songs on the album during the session. "I would get a line, a guitar line—back then they all had one that they repeated—and you just write a song on top of it," says Nix. "When you get that down, you start putting things on top of it. I'd just show the players a couple of simple lines."

Some of the songs that emerged from that session were: "Lovejoy, Ill.," "Like A Road Leading Home," "Bay Area Blues" and "Everybody Wants to Go To Heaven."

Albert didn't mind working that way, according to Nix, and even if he had, it wouldn't have mattered. That was the system. "Albert was an artist," say Nix. "'Just show me what to do. Show me where to stand. Tell me what you want me to do.' He had done that stuff for so long, his attitude was, 'Get me in, get me out.' Albert measured things by the way things sold. He figured it was the record company's job to sell it. If it didn't sell, he didn't blame me, he blamed the record company."

Despite the politics of confrontation that was setting the tone for race relations outside the studio, the mood among the musicians was still friendly. They were there to make music. "The black guys were a lot easier to work with for some reason," says Nix. "Albert might be hard to get along with sometimes. Leon (Russell) always told me to go in there and whether you know or not, act like you know what you're doing. Like I'd do string sessions. I'd have an arranger. I'd go in there. 'Hey, Albert, how you doing?' If he'd say, 'That don't sound right,' then I'd say, 'You're right. Who's doing that?' I did 51 albums. Nobody ever said, 'Do you know what you're doing?' I'd always say, did anyone make any mistakes? then take it from there."

Bobby Manuel was hired in 1968 as an engineer. He was playing guitar with a band at Club Paradise, when he heard that Jim Stewart was looking for someone to help out at the console. The job only paid $75 a week, but it was a chance to get his foot in

155

the door. His first month on the job he was told to help out on a Delany & Bonnie session. "Man, I had no training at that time," says Manuel. "Ronnie (Capone) was cutting someone else. He said, 'Man, you got to do it.' I said, 'I don't know how to do it.' I went in there green. I cut one song out of synch. It was fearsome thinking about trying to get balances. I nearly had a heart attack."

Before Booker left, Manuel sometimes replaced Cropper when the MGs played out on the road. That happened once while Cropper was in Atlanta. They played some dates on the road, and then went into the studio when they returned to Memphis.

"Sometimes it was touch and go," says Manuel. "Cropper was kind of a general, you know, and they were always digging at him. I hadn't been there hardly any time and there I was sitting there playing with the MGs. That was heavy duty to me. Then in through the doors from Atlanta with briefcase in hand came Steve Cropper. I thought, 'Oh, man.' I jumped up. Booker and them didn't say anything. I knew it was going to be horrible. I don't know what they ever did with the tape. I know it was cut."

Before long, Manuel was doing a little bit of everything— writing songs, engineering sessions, playing guitar, producing sessions. When Steve Cropper became the second casualty of the "new" Stax and left in 1971, Manuel's guitar skills became even more in demand.

"I got to do Albert King, Little Milton, the things Cropper had been doing," says Manuel. "In 1973 I started playing with Isaac (Hayes). That was the hottest band happening. Our first job was in Detroit. It killed me to be able to be accepted in those circles by black people. I remember getting a standing ovation for a solo. That meant more to me than anything. I'm not so sure the solo was unique. Maybe it was the uniqueness of one white guy in the band. Regardless, it was a great experience."

David Porter's writing partner, Isaac Hayes scored Stax's second No. 1 record in 1971 with his "Theme From 'Shaft." The song was honored during the 1972 Oscar awards and Isaac set the tone for the remainder of the decade when he rose from the depths of the stage amid whirling clouds of steam, his shirtless, black body bound in glistening chains. The gesture may have been showbiz symbolic, but, for all it shallowness it did represent deeper emotions that were changing America, not just in Memphis, but in New York and Los Angles as well. The music of the 1970s differed from the music of the 1960s. It was all about power and it had an unmistakable edge that intimated chaos.

The revolution had degenerated into a cultural rampage.

American music has undergone many changes since the 1950s, but to understand those changes it is helpful to remember that rock 'n' roll *and* the sweet soul music that came from Stax and American was invented by Southern white boys barely out of their teens. Maybe they weren't card carrying liberals, but neither were they racists. Maybe they didn't go to church every Sunday, but, for the most part, they were super-straight guys who didn't drink on the job (Estelle would have kicked their asses). They were light years behind the rest of the population when it came to drug use.

Don Nix, no stranger to drug use in the 1970s, says drugs weren't a factor at Stax. "I never saw drugs in Stax, never," he says. "In the 1960s I'm sure people took them then, but not in there."

Don laughs with the knowing vibrato of someone who has been there. "I would have seen them. I would have been the guy to know. There was never any drugs in Stax. A lot of people said there was, but there never was. People were having too much fun."

In 1970 Jim Stewart and Al Bell borrowed enough money from an overseas source, Deutsche Grammophon, to repurchase Stax from Gulf & Western. Stax, back home in Memphis where it belonged, forged a distribution agreement with Columbia Records. For two years, Jim and Al operated as equal partners, then, in a mysterious move, Al bought Jim out and stayed on in an executive capacity. By then, the work atmosphere was intolerable. There were guards at the entrance of the studio and a prevailing mood of gangsterism.

Stax Records became the Beale Street of years past.

"When Johnny Baylor and those guys came, that's when things got bad," says Manual. "That's when the ugliness started coming out."

Baylor once fired his pistol in the studio in anger. Polite conversation gave way to intimidation and threats of violence. Jive talk echoed in the old theater night and day. Stax was catching it from both ends. While they were trying to learn to deal with gangsters in New York who wanted kickbacks to distribute their records and payola to put the records on the air, they were being threatened by neighborhood punks who demanded money or they were going to burn the place down. Pistol whippings in the studio were commonplace.

"They pistol whipped a guy in the room next to me in New York once, and I left," says one Stax insider. "There were guns and gangsters and other little punks following them around wanting to be gangsters. The creative forces were breaking down."

Stax got its third No. 1 record in June 1972 when "I'll Take You There" by the Staple Singers topped the charts. The success of the Staple Singers proved that there was still a market for old-time soul, as did a string of hits by Eddie Floyd and Johnnie Taylor, but by then Stax was on a collision course with disaster.

*   *   *

In the early 1960s a preppy, Memphis high school student named John Fry decided to start up a record label in his grandmother's sewing room. He recruited a couple of his high school buddies, John King and Fred Smith. It turned out to be more difficult than they thought and King and Smith went on to other things (Smith started up an air freight company named Federal Express). After high school, Fry explored the various business applications associated with recording equipment. He had about decided the way to go was to record promos for radio stations, when a piano player named Jim Dickinson and several others talked Fry into getting into the record business again. Dickinson, with whom I often have been confused (we got each other's threats), had all the musical talents not possessed by Fry (and none of the business acumen).

In 1966 Fry founded Ardent Recording studio. Unlike most people who open studios, Fry had no ambitions to be a star himself (or if he did he kept them to himself). It was the business side of music that appealed to him. He set out to build the most technically advanced studio in the South. By the early 1970s he had facilities that surpassed those at Stax, American and Hi. Stax often used the studios at Ardent and became one of its best customers.

In 1972 Fry reactivated his record label. The second release was an album by a group named Big Star. His dealings with Stax enabled him to get a distribution deal for the album titled *#1 Record*. Alex Chilton was recruited to front the group. He had been in musical limbo since 1969, when he walked off stage during a Box Tops performance. He never returned and the Box Tops became a footnote in the city's musical history. Chilton had an explosive personality. He hated the media. At times, it seemed he hated his fans. No one ever explained to him that it took both— fans and the support of the media—to have a career in the music business.

#1 Record was progressive for its time. It had Beatles-like harmonies and a hard-edged attitude. Musically, it sounded like it was the verge of something big. Exactly what, no one knew. Unfortunately for Big Star (the name came from a supermarket chain prevalent in Memphis) the release of the album coincided with difficulties Stax was having with Columbia Records. It was a good album and should have produced a hit or two, but it slipped between the cracks at Stax and died a quick death. Encouraged by good reviews of the album, Fry decided to do a second. Titled *Radio City,* it, too, received favorable reviews, but it was totally ignored by the public.

Fry decided to do a third. He had been the engineer/producer for the first two, but he asked Jim Dickinson to produce the third—and final as it turned out—Big Star album. Jim was not the best keyboard man ever to come out of Memphis (he would have competition from Booker T., Memphis Slim, Bobby Woods and Bobby Emmons), but he was perhaps the most versatile and the most passionate about his craft—and he's an excellent producer. By 1974 he had worked as a sideman at Stax and American (he wanted to engineer there but Moman wouldn't let him), had played for six months with the Miami-based Dixie Flyers (but returned to Memphis because he got homesick), and played piano on the Rolling Stones' classic "Wild Horses."

Jim was sort of a walking motion picture. Images flickered on his body like old-fashioned drive-in movie theaters. You could see him coming a half block away because of that iridescent glow. Voices emerge from his coat sleeve, his shoes, his hat. I think Jim had probably absorbed every image, every sound, he had ever come in contact with. I'm not sure, but I think he may have developed that quality while studying drama at Baylor University.

Jim was the perfect person to work with Alex Chilton. Talking to Alex is a little like talking to a barking dog, only without the barking. Jim, the foggy-bottom hippie, and Alex, the mercurial antichrist, shut the studio door to the rest of the world and explored the more creative aspects of musical madness. The resulting album, aptly titled *The Third*, was a masterpiece of organized chaos. As you might expect, it was immediately canned and imprisoned in darkness for six years.

"Most people who make records these days don't understand that you can just walk in and start slogging it out, with people playing all bad chords and out of rhythm and everything, and it can sound great," Chilton told a *Press -Scimitar* reporter shortly after the release of the album on Peabody Records in 1980. Then he added: "But I also like to do conceptual, neatly symmetrical things . . . If you go into the studio with something really disorganized, a lot of the time it's too murky to really hit people right at first as strongly as something that's more arranged."

When the album was re-released in 1995, a reviewer for *Pulse* magazine noted that it was viewed "as alternative pop's flagship album." By then Big Star was being hailed as one of the great rock bands in American history, even though it never had a hit record or sold enough albums to pay studio expenses.

At about the same time that Big Star was self-destructing, a Texas band, ZZ Top, started recording at Ardent. The band had been together since 1969, but after five years of one-nighters, it had nothing to show for its efforts. In 1974 the group performed at the Memphis Blues Show, not exactly a high-paying gig (most of the performers probably paid for the honor), and dropped by Ardent to talk to Fry's chief engineer, Terry Manning. They did some sessions. ZZ Top's royalty checks started getting bigger, so they kept going back to Ardent. Almost all of ZZ Top's post 1974 albums have been recorded in Memphis, a fact the group does not like to publicize (if you don't believe me, just ask them and watch them dash for the horizon, their beards blowing in the wind).

Even Fry is hesitant to talk about it. When he does, he

downplays Ardent's role in the group's success. "I would like to be able to tell you that what we offer them is so unique they could not get it elsewhere," says Fry. "We offer them good facilities and do a good job for them, but there are other people who could do the same thing . . . There is a factor of the chemistry of the people working together, but I cannot paint a picture that would say ZZ Top could not live without Memphis."

In some ways, ZZ Top has a lot in common with Big Star: Neither group has ever had a hit record (Top 20) and both groups are revered by the critics. Unlike Big Star, ZZ Top is one of the most successful touring bands in history. Their fans want to see them perform live. They couldn't care less about their albums. Like their recording sessions, there is an air of mystery about ZZ Top's success. It's all part of that Memphis *thang.*

*   *   *

By 1973 Memphis music was imploding (and exploding at the same time), disintegrating into jagged-edged fragments that were hurling about like debris in a hurricane. Priscilla had left Elvis for a karate instructor and the King was headed for his first—and last--divorce. He had been unable to sustain the success of the hits he recorded in 1969 at American and, once again, the public was viewing him with disdain. Since his contract with RCA Records called for another album, his longtime producer, Felton Jarvis, started putting together a session. But Elvis was tired and depressed. He didn't want to travel to Nashville. He asked if he could record again in Memphis.

Sure, said an associate: "I'll call Chips."

But Elvis, who apparently had not taken direction at the 1969 sessions as well as Chips had imagined, said no. He didn't want to work with Chips again.

Jarvis said he would come to Memphis. He booked studio time in July at Stax and then hired Chips' studio musicians to play on the session: Reggie Young on guitar, Tommy Cogbill on bass, Bobby Emmons on organ and Bobby Woods on piano. It was a strange session. In the other studio that week Isaac Hayes also recorded an album. Jim Stewart posted guards inside and outside the studio. Isaac had his black bodyguards. Elvis had his white bodyguards.

161

When he got to the studio, Elvis was in a foul mood. So were the musicians. CBS was in town to film a segment on Isaac Hayes for the Harry Reasoner Report. They were not interested in talking to Elvis. You can imagine how Elvis felt. He was the King of rock 'n' roll, yet he had been emasculated by Priscilla the love of his life. He was a movie star, but his movies were a joke and he knew it. His entire career since the success of the 1969 album was a joke.

Isaac Hayes, with his shaved head and menacing black glare, had won an Academy Award for "Shaft." Elvis had never come close to winning an Academy Award. By 1973 Isaac had won Grammys for Best Pop Instrumental Performance, Best Instrumental Arrangement and Best Original Score Written for a Motion Picture. By contrast, Elvis had won two Grammys—one for Best Inspirational Performance and one for Best Sacred Performance.

On top of all of the insecurities Elvis felt at that time, he was deathly afraid of something or someone. It went beyond fears of zealous fans jumping his fence. In 1970 he had flown alone to Washington on impulse to see President Richard Nixon and FBI Director J. Edgar Hoover. On the plane he wrote a letter to Nixon in which he pleaded for credentials as a federal agent at large. Drugs were ruining the nation. He wanted to do his part to put a stop to it. He was willing to become an informant against the entertainment community. He would gladly tell the FBI who was using and selling illegal drugs. It was his duty. In his letter, he said he would be staying at the Washington Hotel under the name of John Burrows. "I will be here for as long as it takes to get the credentials of a federal agent."

Nixon met with Elvis, though Hoover did not. He left Washington with a honorary badge that he thought made him an official agent. Some critics have interpreted Elvis' trip as a roundabout means of getting back at the Beatles and other British groups who had knocked him off the charts. Others say he was simply on drugs himself and didn't know what he was doing. Others still say there were rumors organized crime was putting a squeeze play on him and he thought the federal government would protect him if he were a federal agent. Supporting that theory are a number of photos in which Elvis posed wearing a DEA jacket. He was sending a message. But to whom?

The week of his Stax session, Jim Kingsley, a reporter for *The Commercial Appeal*, wrote a brief story about the session. Getting more play in the story was an account of Isaac's session and the Harry Reasoner interview. Kingsley was Elvis's man at the *The Commercial Appeal*. Kingsley had attended the sessions at American in 1969. For Kingsley, his friend, to write a story that gave more space to Isaac Hayes was bad news indeed for an ego as severely bruised as Elvis's. The session fizzled and Elvis went back to Graceland. He returned to Stax in December for another session without the musicians from American, and a number of songs were recorded, but they were all inferior to his 1969 material and Elvis knew it.

By this time, Chips Moman had become fed up with Memphis music. He and his partners at American had produced an incredible string of hits. No studio had ever done more in such a short period of time, yet no one was calling him to accept Grammys or Oscars. Even the local music awards shows ignored his efforts. "For me, it just kept getting more and more aggravating," says Chips. "At the time when Memphis was the hottest thing going, the city didn't seem to really care."

Chips responded in 1973 by shutting down his studio. "We had 80 or 90 Top 20 records that year, and the music business awards came up and a guitar player got nominated and won it who had never played on a hit record. I said, you know this place doesn't seem to like us too much. Why don't we just tear this studio down and leave . . . and we left, every one of us. We pulled the kids out of school and left."

He went to Atlanta for a while, and then moved to Nashville where he set up a new studio. I have spent many hours talking to Chips about his reason for leaving Memphis. My feeling is that he really believes that was the reason. Time has a way of pigeonholing motivations. I think his real reasons for leaving are more complicated. His marriage was falling apart and he wanted to marry Toni Wine. The business of making records had become dangerous, whereas before it had been merely dirty. People started carrying guns. There was talk the Mafia was moving into Memphis. Grand juries were being convened to investigate the music business. The King assassination had made race relations in the city strident. Chips had recorded his share of soul music, but Memphis was more than that to him, it was the birthplace of rock 'n' roll, and he sensed the city's musical identity being subverted by the politics of race relations. The final straw must have been Elvis' refusal to return to American and the decision of his own band, his boys, to sign on for the session with Elvis at Stax. Chips felt betrayed, not just by his band, but by the city itself. Whatever the reason, Chips packed up and left positively overnight. The last record he cut in Memphis was Billy Lee Riley's "I Got a Thing About You Babe."

On the heels of Chips' departure, the entertainment business in Memphis underwent a radical change. In 1974 the first topless clubs opened for business. It had been nearly 35 years since sex had been a part of the Memphis economy. For the past several years, ever since the psychedelic aftershocks of the Vietnam War, drugs, especially cocaine, were again being sold on the streets. The murder rate was again climbing. Memphis was reverting to its old ways. In May 1974, the journalism monthly, *More*, selected *The Commercial Appeal* as one of America's 10 worst daily newspapers.

*   *   *

In its final three years of operation, Stax Records was a runaway train steaming toward a cliff. Under the direction of Al Bell, it engaged in wild financial speculation and became politicized by the strident demands of black activists who saw the company as something other than a record label. Although he had sold his half interest to Bell, Jim Stewart stayed on as president, providing continuity to its musical direction.

Unfortunately, Jim and Al had conflicting visions for the company. Jim saw Stax as a musical entity, a record label that celebrated the black cultural experience. Al saw Stax as an economic entity, a record label that could be used to further black economic and political interests. He saw music as a means to an end. In 1972 Stax invested $176,000 in a Broadway play, an adaptation of Joe McGunnis' best seller, *The Selling of the President*. The idea was to cash in on an album recorded by the cast. But the show closed after five performances, the album was never made and Stax lost its investment. For two years, Stax tried to purchase the Memphis franchise of the American Basketball Association. It signed black comedians Richard Pryor and Moms Mabley to recording contracts, and while Pryor was unmistakably a major talent and record sales soared on his first release, *That Nigger's Crazy*, it was the sort of project that confused the studio staff and did nothing to further the musical direction of the label. Adding to the confusion was an album titled *I Am Somebody* by The Reverend Jesse Jackson. There were even efforts to get in the movie business. Not surprisingly, for a three year period beginning in January 1972, Stax scored Top 20 hits on only three occasions, all with the gospel-based Staple Singers.

Stax financed its ventures during those years with loans from Union Planters Bank of Memphis. Some reports put the loans at $18 million. But if money was pouring into Stax through loans and record sales, it was pouring out into one bad venture after another.

Rumblings from the avalanche that would eventually crush Stax were first heard early in June 1973 when federal prosecutors in Newark, New Jersey, convened a grand jury to hear evidence of possible kickbacks and tax violations in the record industry. The investigation began when federal officials linked a CBS Records official to a heroin ring operating between Canada and New Jersey. Subpoenas were issued to officers in eight record companies, including Atlantic, London and Stax. Associated Press reported that information obtained at a court hearing indicated Stax "lost $406,000 in 1971 because of an alleged scheme in which two vice presidents were involved in kickbacks with Stax distributors." Stax responded by hiring the prestigious law firm of Edward Bennet Williams in Washington to represent its interests.

The nightmare for Stax grew worst by year's end when a federal grand jury in Memphis was convened to inquire into its corporate affairs. Jim and Al were told to turn their records over to the grand jury. That same year the Internal Revenue Service announced it was reviewing the company tax returns for the years 1970 to 1972. As a result the IRS filed a $1.8 million lien against the holdings of Johnny Baylor. In early June of that year, CBS Records fired Columbia Record President Clive Davis and announced it was suing him for $94,000 allegedly misappropriated from company

165

funds. CBS denied that his dismissal had anything to do with the grand jury's probe.

Amid the chaos, Johnny Baylor booked a flight from Memphis to Birmingham. At the Memphis airport, he was asked, as part of the airport security measures, to open his attaché case before boarding the plane. Inside the briefcase, according to a *Press-Scimitar* reporter, was $130,000 in cash and a check for $500,000. Baylor was allowed to board the plane with the money, but when he arrived in Birmingham federal agents were waiting for him. Jim Stewart defended Baylor. He said the money belonged to Baylor and it was his to do with as he pleased. No charges were filed, but the IRS kept the money since it had a lien against Baylor.

The federal probe in New Jersey did not result in indictments against any Stax officials and the company's legal difficulties eased somewhat in 1974, but by then there were problems with CBS distributing Stax products. The federal grand jury in Memphis was still investigating Stax operations, but the company was in dire economic straits and Jim re-invested his money in the company (all of it by some accounts) in an effort to keep it afloat.

In 1975, as the end was drawing near, a group of businessmen from Chicago came to Memphis to discuss moving Stax to Chicago or Gary, Indiana. They were offered a 13-story hotel owned by Holiday Inns of Memphis as an office building. During negotiations with the Chicago businessmen, Barbara Jackson, wife of Al Jackson, allegedly shot him during a domestic argument. The police filed assault charges against Barbara but they were dismissed after she convinced a judge she had shot him in self defense. She testified that he had beaten her and tossed her into a flower bed. She said she shot him to protect herself. Two weeks after the shooting Jim Stewart sent a letter to Shelby County Sheriff Roy Nixon asking that Jackson be considered for a special commission to carry a pistol The letter said Jackson "travels quite extensively and carries large sums of money."

Perhaps spurred by talk of the company's possible relocation, Union Planters Bank pushed for payment of what it said were $10 million in unpaid loans. That put a stop to any talk of relocation.

In September 1975 Al Bell and Joseph Harwell, a loan official at Union Planters, were indicted by the grand jury on charges they conspired to obtain $18 million in fraudulent bank loans. Harwell had already pleaded guilty to embezzling $284,000 from the bank. He was sentenced to five years in prison. The prospect of going on trial with an admitted embezzler being brought to the trial from a prison cell did not paint a rosy picture for Bell. He accused the bank of racism and became the beneficiary of two nationwide defense funds set up by civil rights groups.

On the evening of October 1, Al Jackson went to the Mid-South Coliseum to attend a closed circuit telecast of the celebrated Muhammed Ali-Joe Frazier fight. He had filed for divorce from Barbara and had rented an apartment at 1350 Walnut Hall Court. He planned to move in on Friday. While Al was at the fight, Barbara went for an appointment at a beauty parlor. When she returned home, she was greeted by a young black man who tied her hands behind her back and demanded money. She said she didn't have any. He ransacked the house.

When Al came to the door, the burglar, who Barbara described as a tall black man with an Afro and a mustache, untied her so that she could open the door. Once Al was inside, he tied them both and again demanded money. He told Al to lie face down on the floor. Then he shot him five times in the back. After the shooter left, Barbara got free and dashed form the house to get help. She told police she saw a young white man wearing a white shirt standing near the door. He ran when he saw her. Al's killer was never found. Police attributed the murder to a botched robbery attempt and left it at that.

Two months after the shooting, three creditors filed an involuntary bankruptcy petition against Stax. At the hearing, Jim Stewart spent three hours on the witness stand. He said he couldn't recall a lot of details of Stax' financial transactions. Irvin Bogatin, the lawyer representing the bank, cited the "miserable exhibition" of business savvy demonstrated by Stewart and said it would do little good for the bankruptcy trustee to keep the record company going. He called Stewart an "artist," not a businessman. Stewart's lawyer protested, saying Bogatin was slandering his client, but Bogatin continued, saying Stax's creditors were endangered by the lack of operating capitol in the company. He compared it to a crap game.

"It's just like Las Vegas," he said. "If you continue to roll the dice, you may walk away with $2 million, or you may leave with nothing."

The judge agreed and ordered Stax shut down. Stewart was stunned. Leaving the court room, he told a reporter: "I'm at a loss. One minute you're producing records and the next minute you're shut down. I don't know what to say."

On January 13, 1976, Jim Stewart drove to the studio as usual. He was greeted by federal marshals and a group of Stax employees standing outside the building. The door was sealed by order of the bankruptcy judge. Jim drove back home. The others milled around.

"We didn't know what we were going to do," says Bobby Manuel. "Nobody said much. There wasn't much conversation. I had thought I would retire there. It was security."

Bobby went home and broke the news to his wife.

"We could have made it if they had left us alone," he says. "The majors couldn't deal with us. The local people were running scared. There could have been some racial things involved. Stax was a maverick. It was like a thorn in some people's eyes. You know, 'Look at all those black guys with Cadillacs!'"

The entire Stax family was stunned. Among the artists and musicians there was always a feeling it would be salvaged. "When the crash came, it was a shock,' recalls Carla Thomas. "I always figured that someone, somewhere, would bail Stax out. There were a lot of things happening, the IRS thing, and people felt they didn't want to get involved. But the artists felt, that as important as Stax was, people would not let it go down. There was a lot of resentment and anger about the final crash, including my own."

Watching from a distance, Estelle Axton simply shook her head. Intuitively, she had seen the fall coming. She blamed it on Al Bell. "I wanted (Jim) to get rid of him," says Estelle. "I said, 'Jim, he's going to take the company—and he did. He was going to buy Jim's part after I got out. I think he gave him about $500,000. All he did was make the first payment and the company was going down so he coaxed Jim into getting back in and that's when it went under. Jim lost his house, he lost everything. He trusted Al Bell. I didn't. That was our disagreement."

The crash of Stax affected Estelle deeply. To her, it had always been a people business. "It hurt," she says about the closing. "I just wondered what was going to happen to all those kids. Would they go with other companies?"

Bobby Manuel was among those asking that very question. Like the others, he kept thinking a white knight would ride up and make everything all right again. For two months he stayed on the phone, talking to the others. Surely, Memphis would not allow Stax to die. Then reality set in. The defining moment is emblazed in his memory for all eternity. He had run out of groceries. He loaded his shotgun and his wife into his Mercedes. He drove to the nearest pawn shop. With his wife waiting in the car, he pleaded with the pawn shop owner to give him $50 for the shotgun.

"Think about that," says Bobby, shaking his head. "They felt so sorry for me. That killed me."

*   *   *

In the midst of the insanity at Stax, Estelle Axton's buyout clause that prohibited her from re-entering the record business expired. Once again she was a free woman (in the business sense). You would think the troubles being experienced by Stax—the gangsterism taking place in the studio and the federal grand jury investigations—would have discouraged her from getting in the music business again, but it appeared to have the opposite effect.

In 1974 she decided to start up another label in partnership with her son-in-law, Fred Frederick. They named the label Fretone (again using a hybrid of their names). One of their first acts was to sign Johnny Keyes, a Chicago-born singer who had teamed with Packy Axton in the mid-1960s when Packy had been banished from Stax. Unfortunately, shortly after they began their project, Packy died of liver disease (he had become an alcoholic after leaving Stax). Estelle was devastated. She thought about quitting the music business, but then decided to continue, partly as a way to honor Packy's memory.

When the Keyes project fizzled, she cut demos on some other artists in 1975, but nothing looked really promising. Then in 1976, Rick Dees, a local deejay, came to her with an idea for a record based on the disco craze that was sweeping the country. He had used a duck's voice on his morning radio show with great success and he thought a disco song done in a duck's voice would be a hit.

"I had to think about that for about three weeks before I agreed to produce," says Estelle. "I thought, 'This could be a hit for 10 years and younger. If they can't buy it mama or grandma would have to buy it for them."

She paired Dees with Bobby Manuel, who had started working for her after the shutdown at Stax. She told them that once they had worked up the song, Bobby could produce it. But Bobby was recording another artist for Fretone, Catherine Chase.

"I kept putting (Dees) off because I was doing this Catherine Chase thing," Bobby explained to me. "I said I would finish the Catherine Chase thing, then do the other one. That way I knew I would be able to eat another month. I went month to month then."

Meanwhile, Memphis was desperate for more hits. In 1975 Al Green made the Top 20 with "L-O-V-E" and the Staple Singers grabbed the No. 1 slot with "Let's Do It Again," but the surprise hit of the year came from Chips Moman, who had set up shop in Nashville after a brief stay in Atlanta. He teamed with producer/songwriter Larry Butler to write a few songs. One of the songs they wrote was titled "(Hey Won't You Play) Another Somebody Done Somebody Wrong Song," a title that reflected Chips' amusement at finding himself cutting records in the country music capital of the world. Chips offered the song to B.J. Thomas and by April 1975 they had the No. 1 pop record in the country.

Don Nix left Stax shortly after gunfire became a common occurrence in the studio. He worked with Leon Russell for a while in Los Angles and put together a band named the Alabama State Troopers. They recorded an album or two and were very successful as a touring band. As an added attraction, Nix invited Furry Lewis to be the opening act.

"The reaction was amazing," says Nix. "We had a three hour show. I would come out first and introduce Furry and he would walk out alone and I would watch the peoples' faces as he walked out. Here was an 87-year-old black man with a guitar who they had never heard of. From the first sound of his voice until he got through, they would sit and listen and there would be a lot of applause at the end of every song."

In 1974 Nix moved to France to live and work. He often commuted to England to visit a woman he was dating, George Harrison's secretary. While there, he befriended Harrison and often stayed at his 101-room mansion at Henly-on-Thames.

"When I first met him, it really intimidated me because he was a Beatle," says Nix. "But he was just a good guy. It was real comfortable. Nix said Harrison spoke about the Beatles in the third person, as if he was not a part of the group.

When Stax closed, Nix was in England. "It was on the front page in England," says Nix. By the time Nix returned to America, the dust had settled and everyone had fled the city. Stax was history. I once asked Don about the last time he saw the Stax studios. He did a double-take and looked at me.

"Why, it was with you," he said, recalling a visit we made to the empty building in 1989. "Remember that day we drove down and the ceiling was all falling in? When I think of Stax now, that's how I remember it."

As Bobby Manuel and Rick Dees put together a disco song about a duck, the drama at Stax was being played out to its conclusion. Between January and July of 1975, Union Planters Bank considered the possibility of operating the company itself. The bank already had purchased the assets of East Memphis Music Corporation, the publishing arm of Stax, at a public auction. When it became obvious it could not operate the label as a viable business, Chief U.S. Bankruptcy Judge William B. Leffler declared Stax bankrupt and ordered the sale of the company's assets.

Bobby Manuel remembers the sale of the assets with bitterness. He and Jim Stewart had gone to the courthouse in the hopes of purchasing some of the studio equipment. Atlantic Records had told Jim that it would back him in the purchase of some of the equipment. What they saw nauseated them.

"To see people sitting in the courtroom cutting cocaine and laughing, taking hits in the courtroom—I will never forget that," says Bobby. "They were like wolves."

The equipment was sold for $50,000 in one lot and Bobby and Jim were not allowed to bid on individual pieces. They left empty handed.

171

On the legal front, a jury acquitted Al Bell of all the charges against him, but convicted the bank officer, Joseph Harwell. Two years later Johnny Baylor was convicted of fraud after being charged with diverting $2.5 million from Stax' creditors. Isaac Hayes filed for bankruptcy. Jim Stewart sat in his kitchen and calmly drank a cup of coffee as his home and possessions were auctioned off by the bank.

When Bobby and Rick had "Disco Duck" nailed down, they went into Shoe recording Studio to record it. "We used the same band I was cutting Catherine Chase with," says Bobby. "Everyone's line was 'Well, it's gonna be the worst record ever made or it will sell a million. I don't think it was the worst record ever made. It had a great Memphis groove. It was that old MG thing I learned. It hooked and was in tune with the times. If you were going to be artsy about it, we would say, well it was a parody of disco. But really and truly it wasn't. Some of the guys who worked on it like to say that to people. It was just a fun record."

"Disco Duck" broke the Top 20 in September 1976 and went to No. 1 in October. Estelle had struck again. "She felt vindicated and I think that meant a lot to her," says Manuel. "I'm not sure she was happy the way she left (Stax). She had some money and things had never worked out with her son, as far as records were concerned. But she has an ear for records. I tell you, everyone loves that woman."

In some respects, Estelle Axton is the forgotten woman of American music. No woman has ever had more success in the record business. No woman has ever invested so much of herself. No woman has ever had to fight harder to carve a niche for women in a male-dominated business. She was responsible for the first major hit to come out of Memphis ("Last Night") and she was responsible for the last No. 1 hit ("Disco Duck" was the last hit record to be recorded in Memphis).

There is no shortage of people willing to take responsibility for the hit records and soulful sounds that came out of Stax during its glory years, but it was Estelle Axton who gave the label its most enduring identity. Those teenage musicians and songwriters who found a home at Stax viewed "Miz" Axton as a mother figure.

172

They worked hard to please her. Otis Redding sang "Try a Little Tenderness" for Stax, but Estelle Axton helped keep the tenderness in the music.

* * *

On August 16, 1977, I was driving along a Greenville, Mississippi, boulevard on my way home from the *Delta Democrat-Times*, where I was employed as a newspaper reporter, when I heard on the radio that Elvis Presley was dead.

The deejay was flip. He cracked a couple of "the King is dead" jokes, and then played an Elvis song in tribute. Typical radio schlock. Unknown to me, my mother and step-father were in Baptist Hospital in Memphis at the very moment Elvis was brought into the emergency room. My step-father was there as a patient. The same day my mother learned of Elvis' death she learned my step-father had a tumor on his brain.

The next morning I picked up a copy of *The Commercial Appeal*. Four-fifths of the front page was devoted to coverage of his death. "Death Captures Crown of Rock and Roll" read the banner headline. Inside was another full page of news stories and photographs. Elvis' personal physician, Dr. George Nicholoulos, told reporters that night that a heart attack was the possible cause of death. Elvis had been found face down in his upstairs bathroom at 2:30 p.m. Fire Department medical technicians tried to resuscitate him on the way to the hospital, but got no response. At 3:30 p.m. hospital emergency resuscitation teams pronounced him dead. By 4 p.m. a crowd of 150 people had gathered at the hospital. They all had the same question: "Are you sure there's no mistake?"

T.G. Sheppard had been a Graceland the night before. Elvis was scheduled to leave Memphis the day of his death on his private jet to kick off a tour in Portland, Oregon. Everyone had gathered at Graceland to get ready for the tour.

"I went by and spent about an hour," says Sheppard. "Elvis was playing racquetball and I didn't get a chance to say anything to him."

The next day he left for Nashville and was on the road when Elvis's body was found. When he got to Nashville, the telephone was ringing. It was J.D. Sumner.

"He said, 'Are you sitting down?', recalls T.G. "I knew then what had happened. I said, 'It's Elvis, isn't it?'

"He said, 'Yes.'

"I wasn't surprised. He was huge. I knew something had to give. I could see him deteriorating, with his weight and all that. I knew something was going on inside, but I hadn't spent much time around him in the past few years because of my own career. It was scary (to see him go down), especially when you were there in the lean years and saw him lean, mean and sharp looking. Then, to see him change, it was very depressing."

As Elvis was being rushed to the hospital that day, U.S. Attorney Hickman Ewing was in federal court prosecuting topless kingpin Art Baldwin on cocaine and firearms charges. One of the lead stories in the newspaper that morning had been about the trial. Its sex, guns and drugs theme had generated a lot of public interest. Topless dancers had been fixtures in the courtroom throughout the trial, easily identified by their brightly colored eyes shadow. Memphians seemed incredulous that woman would take their clothes off for money.

"While we were on break, about three in the afternoon, someone came into the courtroom and said they had taken Elvis to the hospital and he had died," says Ewing. "Baldwin, who had never said a word to me in his life, came over to me and said, 'Well, Mr. Ewing I hate to wish ole Elvis any bad luck, but at least it will take the publicity off of me for a few days'—and it did. Then a few days later the jury convicted him."

Otis Redding, publicity photo, c. 1960s
Photo courtesy James L. Dickerson

175

Alex Chilton, lead singer of the Box Tops
Photo courtesy of the Mississippi Valley Collection
University of Memphis, University Libraries

CHAPTER 9

The 1980s:
Memphis Rekindles the Dream

By 1980 the Memphis music industry was fending off extinction. The last hit record, "Disco Duck," had occurred in 1976. There were a few studios still in operation, but, with the exception of the well-financed Ardent Recording, most were subsisting on a meager and musically incestuous diet of nickel-and-dime demo sessions. Ardent flourished because it diversified into corporate video and recording, and attracted a handful of out-of-town recording groups such as ZZ Top by offering them special incentives to record in Memphis.

There were several popular club bands in town, including Fever, Beauty and the Beats, Larry Raspberry and the Highsteppers (a carryover from the Gentrys) and The Breaks, which broke out of the club scene long enough to record two albums for RCA Records. Unfortunately, neither album hit and the group's hopes for success were short lived. Susanne Jerome Taylor, the striking, dark-haired lead singer for The Breaks, emerged from the band's flirtation with success with a cynical attitude toward the business. "I would like to see the record companies get behind the artists they sign," she says. "It's so political. They may not like your manager or something and then you get squashed like a bug."

Taylor's mood was indicative of the despair felt by the entire music community in the 1980s. Despite their best efforts, failure was their constant companion. The record companies wouldn't look once, much less twice, at the talent in Memphis, and local opportunities were confined to the club scene.

Incredibly, the pay scale in the early 1980s was the same as it was in the mid-1960s; bands could expect paychecks of $200 to $400 a night, which for a band of four or five members barely stretched beyond minimum wage.

By 1984, the only Memphian headed for the national charts was Jimi Jamison, who that year became the lead singer for the

Chicago-based band, Survivor. In 1982 the band had scored with a No. 1 single, "Eye of the Tiger," a song Sylvester Stallone used for the movie, "Rocky III." Prior to joining survivor, Jamison had been a member of two Memphis bands, Target and Cobra. Both of those bands were popular in the Mid-South, but neither attracted the attention of a major label. Jamison toured with Survivor for about eight months of the year, but still maintained a home with a big, grassy backyard in Memphis, where his wife, Debbie, and their son, James Michael, lived while Jimi was on the road. His escape from the Memphis doldrums into mainstream music may have encouraged other Memphis musicians, but for the general public his departure from the local music scene was a non-event that passed without notice for the simple reason that Memphians were not all that interested in music.

*   *   *

In 1982 a committee from the National Academy of Recording Arts and Sciences came to Memphis to consider the city for the site of a music hall of fame. NARAS had been talking about building the museum for eight years. Sam Phillips got behind the project. So did John Fry and all the other music survivors left in the city. I wrote editorials in *The Commercial Appeal* putting the support of the newspaper behind the project.

After a brief look at the city, NARAS announced it would build the museum in Atlanta. I wrote an editorial that pointed out the obvious: "Memphis didn't depend on NARAS to carve its music niche in the world and it can't depend on that, or any other, organization to help the city carry on its music tradition. Memphians must do that themselves."

I was baffled by NARAS's decision. Why Atlanta? It didn't make sense. By the time the Rock and Roll Hall of Fame was formed, NARAS scrapped the Atlanta project. Gregg Geller, the former head of A&R for RCA Records, was at the Hall of Fame dinner at which Cleveland, Ohio, was chosen as the site for its hall of fame and museum. He watched with sympathy as Sam Phillips argued that Memphis was where any rock and roll hall of fame belonged.

"There were a great many people, myself among them, who felt that if it could not be built in New York, Memphis was the logical place," says Geller. "There's one major reason why it went to Cleveland. That's because the people there wanted it desperately and they organized themselves to attract it."

In December 1983 *The Commercial Appeal's* "Mid-South Magazine" contained a feature on Beale Street. A Memphis deejay was quoted as saying: "The new is gonna be better than the old. It's gonna be three times as good." That quote caught the eye of newspaper editor Michael Grehl, who asked me to spend some time sampling the nightlife on Beale.

The city was spearheading a project to revitalize the street and the newspaper had expressed mixed feelings about the idea. After spending an evening at Club Handy—the club had just reopened on the east end of the street—I went in the next morning bleary eyed and wrote an editorial that urged the city to get behind the "second chance" history was offering the street. But if Beale Street is going to be "three times as good," I wrote, "It's going to take some second-look thinking among the city's music agnostics, particularly in the financial community."

In the months that followed, Grehl, whose office overlooked a portion of Beale Street, allowed me to write editorials on a regular basis in support of the street's revitalization. Not many people knew that Grehl, crusty, hard-nosed newsman that he was, had a soft spot for the blues. That soft spot was responsible for changing the minds of many Memphians about the city's musical heritage. Many people patted me on the back for standing up for Memphis music. But it was Grehl who really deserved the credit. He was the best newsman I have ever known.

On October 31, 1983, Memphis lost its most dogged foe of organized crime. Scripps Howard announced that it was shutting down the *Memphis Press-Scimitar*. Memphis would henceforth be a one newspaper town. "The 'Press-Scimitar,' like the emblem that emblazons its front page, has been a guiding light during this city's darkest moments," wrote Memphis Mayor Dick Hackett in a letter to the newspaper. "(It) has stood guard through the years for countless thousands of Memphians, sounding the alarm when precious freedoms we as citizens take for granted were threatened."

179

Grehl pledged *The Commercial Appeal* would take up the slack. "The only way to stay ahead is to run scared," he said. Positions for some *Press-Scimitar* employees were found at *The Commercial Appeal*. The others were sent packing. It's too bad Boss Crump wasn't around to comment on the demise of his arch enemy.

With the *Press-Scimitar* gone, Grehel nudged me with greater frequency into local politics. That spring he and his lovely wife, Audrey, invited me and my girlfriend, Laura, to attend a professional football game with them. I wish I had a photograph from that day. Laura was a buxom, 23-year-old woman whose natural hyperactivity stood in sharp contrast to Grehl's bearish reticence, so, of course, I insisted they sit next to each other. I was thinking, *OK Boss, you said you wanted to see some cheering.* The best moment came when the woman directly behind Grehl complained that her feet were cold. Laura volunteered to sit on her feet for the remainder of the game. The following day I wrote an editorial urging support of the football team. I mentioned the incident about the feet in the editorial. Grehl liked a private joke as much as the next fellow.

Shortly after Christmas, 1984, *The Commercial Appeal* editorial board met to discuss ways of focusing attention on Memphis' vanishing music industry. There was a consensus the newspaper should do what it could to help the city's music industry. The *Press-Scimitar* had always been more aggressive in its coverage of music. After some discussion, it was decided I would do a series of Q&A interviews that would run on the editorial pages. It was an unprecedented gesture from a newspaper that, over the years, had kept itself at arm's length from the music industry.

The interviews ran from January 12 to March 17, 1985, and solicited the advice of 27 individuals closely tied to the Memphis or national music scene. They were asked why Memphis had become a musical wasteland. They were asked what could be done to resurrect it. The interview that was to prove pivotal was the one I conducted with record producer Chips Moman. For that interview, I flew to Nashville on a bitterly cold day in January. Moman's studio was located in southeast Nashville, a respectful distance from Music Row, the traditional center of activity for country music. The studio was unpretentious and there was no sign outside to even indicate it was a studio.

I wasn't sure what to expect from Moman. He loathed the press and had done no interviews since leaving Memphis. Two other record producers were scheduled to meet me at the studio for a joint interview with Moman, but they didn't show up. A man wearing jeans, a pullover shirt and a black Greek sailor's cap greeted me at the door. He looked like he might be the janitor. I asked him for directions to Mr. Moman's office. He laughed and said that, well, he was afraid *he* was Mr. Moman.

We conducted the interview in the dimly lighted control room of the studio. The console dials blinked and stared with space-age complexity in the subdued light. To my surprise, Moman was eager to talk about Memphis. He said he left because of the backbiting and the nit-picking. I asked him if he had ever regretted that decision. Moman's eyes glistened. "Let me tell you, that was a mistake," he says "But when you work as much as we did, you sit there in that little building and you get paranoid. We didn't know what we had. I've always considered that a mistake. Not in the sense that we didn't all do better when we left. We did. But if we had done the right thing, and stayed there and tried to help all these people who were doing it wrong and tried to make people understand that Memphis was more than Soul City, who knows, we might have done more there than we did away from there. I think we would have. Every record I've cut since then, I've said, 'Yeah, I cut it in Nashville, but my music is still in Memphis,' because that's there I got it. That's where I learned it, that's where I felt it."

To my surprise, Moman said he would return to Memphis under the right circumstances. "Memphis needs someone to get all those guys there together," he said. "When you pull great songwriters to a place, you're doing more than getting a hit song, you're teaching the would-be songwriters there to do better. If you're around people who are in a rut, you will write in a rut because you don't have to do much to be good. You need competitiveness. Unless you have it, you'll just lie around. What's that old saying? The young fighter fights all the best fighters to learn. It's no different for songwriters. You have to fight all those best songwriters to

181

write great or play great. Something has to set the lead. There has to be a competitive spirit in the city. The only way you can get that is to get it going. Memphis needs very professional help."

Just talking about Memphis had a rejuvenating effect on Moman. The longer we talked, the more energetic he became. At the end of the interview, he invited me to stay for a recording session with Johnny Cash. Moman's wife, Toni Wine, came into the room and we talked more about Memphis. While we were talking, Cash's wife, June Carter, arrived at the studio. She had come to sing background on one of Cash's songs. She bubbled with enthusiasm. As she spoke to Moman and Toni, her bright eyes danced about the studio. Moman introduced us and told her I was from Memphis. With that, June smiled broadly and talked about what a wonderful city Memphis had been in the early days of John's career.

While we were talking, Waylon Jennings appeared in the doorway. He smiled when he saw June, but when he saw me, he paused, hesitant to enter the room, which contained only a sofa and three chairs. June nudged him into the room. Wearing a long coat and a black hat, Waylon warmly greeted Moman and Toni. Then June introduced him to me.

Within a matter of minutes, the sound of heavy footsteps echoed outside in the hallway. Dressed in black, a winter coat falling past his knees, Johnny Cash stuck his head into the control room. He seemed uncomfortable when he spotted me, but June quickly introduced us and Johnny relaxed and fell into an easy banter with Waylon and Moman about the benefits of health food diets and vitamins. Johnny looked at me, his eyes dancing: "See, those are the kinds of drugs you talk about when you get our age."

Everyone laughed. All of them had had some rough years in the pre-health food days. Jack Clement's name came up. He was expected to show up for that day's session, but he had not yet arrived.

"Jack Clement was the silent type, you know," says Johnny. "When he first started he was really shy. A lot of things went on around Sun Records, and later people would sit around and you'd hear people say, 'Who did what, when was that and what happened at that session?' People would argue about it and then they would finally get around to asking Jack Clement. He'd tell them exactly because he was there, all day long every day."

Later, Johnny, June, Waylon and Toni left the control room to do voice-overs on two songs for Cash's album. As they stood at the microphone, Moman spoke to them from inside the control room over the speaker system. He asked Waylon to recite the lyrics of a song for me about Memphis that had been written by Clement.

Waylon said he remembered the lyrics. Before he recited the lyrics, Waylon leaned over to peer into the darkened control room. He looked for me in the shadows. When he saw me, he said: "Be sure you say they are Jack Clement's lyrics."

I nodded.

Waylon smiled and then recited a verse from a song that said there was something about Memphis that was "lost between right and wrong."

After he finished reciting the lyrics, the others nodded approvingly. Everyone, including Moman, suddenly got all warm and toasty about Memphis. That feeling continued throughout the session and into the night, when Clement finally showed up with a bag of food. As Cash sang and Moman gave directions and the engineer, David Cherry, pushed dials, Clement and I sat in the back of the control room and put away an astonishing number of Krystalburgers and icebox lemon pies.

As I flew back to Memphis the next morning, I felt something important had happened in Nashville. It was still bitter cold, but the sky was a brilliant blue and the clouds were a fluffy white. About halfway between Nashville and Memphis, the jetliner jerked—lurching back and forth several times. The passengers all looked wide-eyed about the cabin. We awaited the bad news. Several minutes went by. Then we heard the pilot's voice. He advised the passengers that those ticket holders who had planned to continue past Memphis would be put on another plane for their "convenience." The pilot never told us we had lost an engine. Was someone trying to tell me something?

* * *

My interview with Moman ran on January 31. When I arrived at the newspaper that morning, the phone was ringing off the hook. Moman's comments that he would consider returning to Memphis had energized the music community. At the editorial board meeting that day, we talked about the music interviews. Grehl suggested I interview Ron Terry, the chairman of First Tennessee Bank. He felt it would be a good idea if the business community had an input into the series.

I interviewed Terry in his plush offices in the First Tennessee Bank building. Terry, who said he had read the interview with Moman, recalled with fondness the first time he saw Johnny Cash. Terry, fresh out of the Navy in 1956, had taken a job as a trainee at the bank frequented by Cash. He recalled the day Johnny and June came into the bank to tell everyone goodbye because they were moving to California. Terry acknowledged the impact music had on Memphis' social and economic development and he expressed a hope music would make a comeback in Memphis.

"If you could talk Chips Moman into coming back to Memphis, that would be a major first step," he said. "Maybe Chips Moman would be followed by someone else. But you put a half dozen Chips Momans together with what they do in the music industry, then you have a music industry . . . It's something the banks would love to see. It means good business for us."

After the interview, we chatted some more. Terry suggested that I interview Memphis Mayor Dick Hackett for the series to inject a political viewpoint. As he walked me to the door, he told me to let him know if there was anything he could do personally to help the music industry. Back at the newsroom I asked Grehl what he thought about me doing an interview with Hackett. He said he thought it would be an outstanding idea. Within days, the interview with Hackett was scheduled.

I interviewed Hackett at his office. He had been mayor for little more than one year. At the age of 41, he had shocked everyone by raking in sixty percent of the vote. No one knew much about him. His only other elected position had been as county clerk. We sat in the sitting area away from his massive desk. Hackett said he was willing to put the same emphasis on the development of the music industry that he had put on the development of other areas of the city's economy.

184

Then he said something that astonished me.

"For the right producer or studio, listen, I can make them a bargain on some land, and I'm talking about like one dollar, if they will contribute toward creating that atmosphere or climate in the city," said Hackett. "The city has a lot of land scattered around the city. There is some land on and around Beale Street, and if I can make a contribution on behalf of this community to entice that recording studio to come to Memphis—and I understand from the professionals in the field, that is what we need to get the ball rolling—I will make a substantial contribution by coming up with the land or the buildings we have available. But it will have to be someone with a track record, someone who can produce."

I asked Hackett if he would be willing to go to Nashville to talk to Moman. He said he would. After the interview, as we stood at the door and talked, Hackett said he would make arrangements to go to Nashville as soon as possible.

"Should I take someone with me?" he asked. "Someone in the business?"

"Yes," I said.

"Who should I take?"

"Take Ron Terry," I answered, recalling Terry's comment to me.

"But I don't know Terry that well," Hackett said, looking slightly embarrassed. "He wasn't really one of my supporters. Do you think he would go?"

Yes, I was positive. "Tell him I gave you his name."

"I'll do that," he said, excited. "I'll call him today."

*   *   *

On a cold, windy day in mid-February, with the temperature in the low 30s, Mayor Dick Hackett and Ron Terry de-boarded their jet and walked into Nashville's Berry Field Airport terminal on a secret mission. Hackett carried a red carnation, a signal for a clandestine contact. He had been asked jokingly to carry it in his mouth.

Neither Hackett nor Terry had ever seen the man and women they had come to Nashville to meet. They had seen a picture of the man, but knew nothing about the woman except that she was

185

younger than the man. In the picture, the man wore a Greek sailor's hat and a striped, knit shirt. Across the room they spotted a man wearing such a cap and shirt. With the man was a younger woman. Who else could it be but the couple they were looking for?

Hackett and Terry approached the couple, the red carnation extended as a greeting. "I wasn't about to put this carnation in my mouth," said the mayor, handing the flower to the young woman. He smiled broadly. "My name is Dick Hackett."

The startled woman took the flower hesitantly and looked at him as though he had lost his mind. "Who are you?" she demanded, unsettled by the sudden attention. The woman's companion glared at the two men.

"Aren't you Chips Moman, the record producer?" Hackett asked, looking at the man.

The man and the woman exchanged glances. Then they informed the mayor of the state's largest city and the chairman of the state's largest bank they had made a mistake. With that news, Hackett wilted along with the rose. Hackett and Terry apologized to the couple and tried to blend into the crowd at the busy airport

After what seemed like an eternity, they heard their names on the public address system. They were instructed to go to a car rental booth. There they met Toni, who packed them into a four-wheel-drive Blazer and headed out of town toward Nolansville. The roads were covered with ice, and Toni, only driving the new vehicle for the second time, drove fast, probably a little too fast. Once the Blazer skidded across the ice under a red light in heavy traffic, eliciting a three-part harmony of "shitttt!" by the occupants of the Blazer. By the time they reached the Momans' farm, Hackett and Terry, slightly unnerved by the ride, had loosened their corporate neckties.

"Within five minutes, I felt like I had known Chips and Toni for years," said Hackett. Meeting them, he said, "took a lot of anxiety out of my heart and mind" about making them an offer.

On the same day he went to Nashville to meet with Moman, Hackett offered, in a front page story published in *The Commercial Appeal*, city-owned land or buildings for one dollar to any successful record producers who would move to the city and help rejuvenate the music industry. That story bore my byline. The city desk, fearful that information would make them look bad if it ran first on the editorial pages and not on the news pages, had whined en masse to Grehl about not having a news story. Grehl instructed me to write the story to keep the peace.

On their visit to Moman's farm, Hackett and Terry offered a similar deal to Moman. They offered him an abandoned fire station located just off Beale Street. They also offered him financing to renovate the fire station into a state-of-the art recording studio. They parted company that day convinced something could be worked out. After they left, Moman called me at the newspaper. "Everyone showing the interest they did got me fired up," said Moman. "I was ready to pack and go."

Negotiations continued for several weeks. On several occasions, just when it appeared an agreement was possible, problems arose. Rumors in the Memphis media ran rampant. One day in March, I saw a television report that an agreement had been reached. I called Moman. Not only had an agreement not been reached, but negotiations had broken down altogether. Hackett canceled a flight to Nashville that day to finalize an agreement. Later that night, Hackett and Moman talked by telephone. They reached a verbal understanding, and Hackett came by my office that night so that I could interview him for a news story for the next day. Of course, the sight of the mayor sitting in my office as I wrote another front page story did not increase my popularity with the news editors.

Finally, on April 5, 1995, Chips and Toni came to Memphis to tour the fire station. The next day, with Hackett and Terry at their sides, Chips and Toni signed an agreement to relocate in Memphis. Looking tired and a little bit embarrassed by the publicity, Chips, who had only given a handful of interviews in his life, told a room packed with television cameras and reporters that he was happy about returning to Memphis.

"Chips Moman is going to be the Fred Smith of the music industry," said Hackett. "Right now I don't think anyone realizes what the positive impact of his arrival may be. You are dealing not only with dollars but with an excitement."

Shortly after that, Grehl asked me to invite Moman to the newspaper to meet the editorial board. Despite a disgruntled newsroom that had become annoyed by my "scoops" on the

187

editorial pages, Grehl stood by me and encouraged the newsroom to develop its own news sources. Grehl liked the idea of city government and private enterprise working together to improve the city's economic and social condition. For that reason, he put the full force of the newspaper behind Hackett's and Terry's efforts to rekindle the music industry.

During this time another intrigue was developing at *The Commercial Appeal.* Grehl was having health problems. Scripps Howard sent in an editor from Alabama, David Wayne Brown, to be the newspaper's executive editor. His job was to take some of the pressure off Grehl in overseeing the newsroom. But Brown, who was in his early 30s, was ambitious and had hopes of succeeding Grehl as editor. Nonetheless, he embraced the music series and supported Grehl's efforts on behalf of the music industry.

Moman showed up at the newspaper shortly before noon and was escorted into Grehl's office, where the entire editorial staff was gathered. With Moman was Herbie O. Mell, who had worked with Moman in the early days. Moman had asked him to help him get organized in Memphis.

Mell had been in and out of the music business over the years and most recently had been making a living as an organizer of junkets to Atlantic City and Las Vegas. It was my first time to meet Mell. I was later to discover that Mell had a heart of gold, but his appearance in that meeting created a lot of darting glances between Grehl and the editorial staff. While Moman looked the opposite of the music industry stereotype—affable, bright eyed, sincere—Mell had the dark, bushy-haired look of a worldly music business insider. Grehl gave me one of his, "what have we done" looks, but by the time the meeting was over Mell's true personality had overcome his stereotypical appearance and Grehl was satisfied that Moman had been a good investment of the newspaper's time.

Although the final agreement with the city was still months away from being concluded, Moman, along with Toni and their 8-year-old son, Casey, moved to Memphis. They were offered a suite at The Peabody Hotel by Gary Belz, who at that time was the general manager of the hotel. Belz, whose father, Jack, and grandfather, Philip, owned the hotel along with extensive real

188

estate holdings in the Mid-South, had long dreamed of becoming a player in the music industry. Aside from a business partnership with a Memphis concert promoter, his ambitions had become stalled. He saw Moman as his ticket to the big time.

On June 5, Chips threw a surprise birthday party for Toni at the Four Flames restaurant. I was invited, along with county mayor Bill Morris, Elvis's longtime friend George Klein, restaurant owner John Grisanti and Gary Belz. I sat next to Belz's date, a 21-year-old Memphis State student named Ellen. At one point, Toni and Grisanti cracked a joke about Toni's Jewish heritage.

"Oh," said Ellen. "Some of my best friends are Jewish."

"I'm Jewish," said Belz.

"Oh, I didn't know that," said Ellen, shocked.

A couple of weeks later, Chips called and asked me if I wanted to ride over to Arkansas the next day with him to meet Johnny Cash and Waylon Jennings. The next morning he said we wouldn't be able to go. An emergency had come up. Gary Belz had called him and told him that Jerry Lee Lewis was going to claim Jason Williams, a Jerry Lee look-alike singer managed by Belz, as his illegitimate son. For months Jason had insisted the Killer was his real father. They did look remarkably alike.

Chips said he needed to stay in town to make sure it was on the level. He said he suggested that Lewis and Williams take blood tests. I ended up going over to Jerry Lee's downtown condo with Chips, Belz and Jason. Belz took pictures of Jason and the Killer sitting together and later gave me copies. Eventually, the "lost son" controversy sort of faded away without Jerry Lee ever claiming Jason as his son.

Moman wasted no time putting together his first recording project in Memphis. He had no home, no studio, no office in Memphis, but he did have all his contacts. And he did have a hit album on the charts, *The Highwaymen*, which he had recorded in Nashville with Johnny Cash, Waylon Jennings, Willie Nelson and Kris Kristofferson. Chips decided his first Memphis project would be a homecoming album. He would bring the surviving stars of Sun Records back to Memphis to record a reunion album. The shining star of Sun Records, Elvis Presley, could not make it of course, but the others could—Johnny Cash, Jerry Lee Lewis, Carl Perkins and Roy Orbison.

By the end of the summer Gary Belz had offered office space to Moman in The Peabody. The Momans had not yet been able to find a house in Memphis, partly because of their notoriety. Toni once complained to me that they would see a house advertised at one price, but by the time they arrived to view the house, it would mysteriously experience a sudden jump in price. On August 26, 1985, Moman opened his office. Located on the third floor of the hotel, a location which then was used mainly for hotel business operations, the office was tucked away behind a labyrinth of doors. To get to the office, you had to pass through a double door marked "employees only," then proceed down a long corridor with unpainted walls and dangling electrical wires. Inside the well-furnished office were three desks, a sitting area with leather-like couches and a wet bar.

"That hall suits me," Chips said, laughing. "It's my style."

After a story about the office appeared in *The Commercial Appeal*, every wanna-be and down-on-their-luck musician and singer in the Mid-South made a bee-line to the hotel. Lines formed outside the door, and the telephone rang constantly. Chips wasted no time. In keeping with his theory that songs were always the key to success, that first day he signed two Memphis songwriters to publishing contracts.

*   *   *

Also catching the reunion virus in 1985 were Willie Mitchell and Al Green. Although they had remained friends and kept in touch since recording their last album in 1976, their careers had taken separate directions. Out of the blue one day in April, Green called Mitchell and asked him if he would be interested in doing another album.

Mitchell was ecstatic. Later Mitchell told me he had not slept a day since that telephone call. "Day and night I hear the album over and over," said Mitchell.

In August Mitchell invited me to attend one of the recording sessions. Mitchell's studio is located in a residential area in southwest Memphis not far from downtown. The neighborhood is predominately black and is a curious mix of safety barred windows and screened porches. I had to pound on the steel reinforced door for several minutes before anyone inside the studio could hear me knocking.

Mitchell and Green were like kids that day, laughing and joking like they were in the midst of a school recess. Mitchell played me one of the songs they were working on. The album, *He Is the Light*, was scheduled for release in October by A&M Records. Mitchell cranked the music up loud. With his hands clapping, Green danced back and forth behind the console, singing along with the music. Mitchell raised his arms, punctuating the air with his hands as he kept time with the driving beat of the music. For both Green and Mitchell, it was like the good old days.

When the song ended, Green marveled at the clarity of the tape.

"The album is so clear you can hear every single instrument," Green said. He looked at Mitchell. "I guess that goes to good producing."

Mitchell laughed, displaying the good humor that had always characterized their relationship. "That goes to paying me to be the engineer," he said, grinning. "The more money you've got, the more clearer I can make it."

Green doubled over with laughter. When he regained his composure, he told me that making the album had nothing to do with making money: "This is like Chips Moman, Johnny Cash, Carl Perkins, Jerry Lee Lewis and Roy Orbison getting together."

What he liked about working with his friend Mitchell was his level of professionalism, and his willingness to take charge of the project. "It takes a producer to come up with the right sound, the right voice quality," he said. "It takes a producer with some nerve to tell me to go home to sleep for two days because I've lost the midrange in my voice."

Green looked at Mitchell, the admiration showing in his face.

"I said, 'Come on, let's give it another shot,'" Green said.

"He said, 'You don't have a bottom to your voice. You have only tops.'"

"I said, 'Well, whatever you're talking about, I'm gone.'"

Green and Mitchell exploded into loud, raucous laughter.

"Willie to me is like a counselor," said Green. "But mostly he's a friend. And I take his advice very seriously. I think we're basically trying to prove something to ourselves. I know I am."

I asked Green what he wanted to prove.

"To see if the quality is really there," he said, his voice growing more somber. "We want to see if we really got it. At this age now, I'm in my upper thirties, I want to see if I've really got it."

Mitchell nodded. Amen to that.

*   *   *

By the time the Sun Records reunion project was announced, the music industry—and the national media—had worked itself into a frenzy. Joining in the project was Dick Clark Productions, which decided to tape the entire session for a television special. The session was scheduled to begin on September 15. The day before was my birthday. That night I had dinner at an Italian restaurant with Moman, Toni and Casey, my mother and stepfather, Dick Caldwell. They sang happy birthday to me and presented me with a rubber duck for my bathtub.

The next day a press conference to kick off the recording session was held in the lobby of The Peabody. CNN carried it live. Every major television network was there, as were reporters from most national magazines and newspapers. As Cash, Perkins, Lewis and Orbison walked out to sit at a large table with Moman and Sun Records founder Sam Phillips, the crowd in the packed lobby applauded wildly. People hung over the balcony, tried to climb the pillars in the lobby and stood on chairs to get a glimpse of the music legends, most of whom had not recorded in Memphis in decades.

I sat near the table in the area reserved for the press. I was there to write a news story for *The Commercial Appeal.* By that time, I had left my position on the editorial board and taken a position as music reporter. Sam Phillips was one of the first to speak.

"I would like to say this," said Phillips to a live TV audience. "Jim Dickerson of The Commercial Appeal wrote a series of articles on the editorial page. I think that had a lot to do with this company coming together. Because those articles that Jim wrote were some of the best I have ever read in any magazine, whoever it was written by, I think we are indebted to Jim .   .   . Jim we want to thank you for it."

Amid applause, Phillips waved to me. That recognition both

pleased me and horrified me. I was pleased that the founder of rock 'n' roll had even uttered my name in connection with music, but horrified to think that my anonymity as a journalist had been breached. That recognition, as flattering as it was, made me realize I had come to a crossroads in my career as a journalist.

For about thirty minutes the group fielded questions from the press. Carl Perkins probably spoke for everyone when he said the opportunity to make music history had left him with an "emotional high." The stage was set.

Memphis, always ready to go double or nothing, was about to roll the dice in an attempt to regain its lost fortune.

Al Green
Photofest

Isaac Hayes leaving Stax Records
Photo courtesy of the Mississippi Valley Collection
University of Memphis, University Libraries

Beale Street mid-1970s to early 1980s
Photo courtesy of the Mississippi Valley Collection
University of Memphis, University Libraries

196

CHAPTER 10

Sun Records Homecoming

Johnny Cash, Jerry Lee Lewis, Roy Orbison and Carl Perkins filed into the cramped trailer with the solemnity of pallbearers and the pent-up energy of racehorses being led from the paddock to the starting gate. Waiting for them at the sound board with the quiet patience of a schoolmaster was producer Chips Moman.

In the dimly lit room, the four music legends stood with their backs to the wall as engineer David Cherry pushed the button that sent the reels whirling.

"We remember the King," goes the song, a gospel-blues ballad that celebrates Jesus—or Elvis Presley, depending on your point of reference. As it played, the four stood in stony silence. It had been thirty years since any of them had recorded in Memphis. When the song ended, they stood stock-still. Finally, Perkins spoke.

"Well, fellows, it has taken thirty years for me to look all three of you in the eyes and say this, but I've got to get it out of my soul," says Perkins, his voice low and resonant. "I love all three of you and you won't ever be without a true friend as long as I'm living."

All four men wept.

"If you outlive me," he continues, "I want you to sing a verse of this when I'm gone. If you do, I might just raise up out of the box and help you sing it."

The four men embraced, the tears flowing freely. The recording session had taken its toll, but, then, rock 'n' roll had taken its toll on all four men over the years. Each had his share of problems. Each somehow had survived. No one could have known then the clock was ticking for first Orbison and then Perkins and finally Cash.

"We've got to pull ourselves together," says Moman, his cheeks streaked with tears.

Like smooching teenagers caught in the sudden glare of a porch light, the men broke apart, awkwardly searching the exits. Cash, the most aloof of the four, returned to the hotel. Orbison, the shy one, sought refuge in his bus. Lewis, the wild one, sat on the steps of the trailer with Perkins standing over him.

"Jerry, you know and I know how it hurts to lose someone you love," says Perkins. "I want you to remember these words: When you're running from God, He's crying just like you are now."

Jerry looked up at Perkins, his face expressionless.

"You really do love me, don't you?"

"You'd better believe it. I always have."

*   *   *

In the early years, when the King and the Four Horsemen reigned over American music, Memphis rockabilly was the life-force of teenage rebellion. It influenced clothing styles, created movie idols and eventually changed the politics of a nation unaccustomed to listening to the voices of youth. It helped end a war in Vietnam and revolutionized advertising techniques. In the three decades since that rebellion was hatched in the tiny studio of Sam Phillips' Sun Records studio, popular music has gone through many cycles, as have the artists who invented it, but seldom had the music, or the artists who created it, ever returned to Memphis.

The *Class of '55* session, which took place in September 1985, was unique for a number of reasons. First, Moman had arranged with Dick Clark Productions to tape the session. Gene Weed, vice president of Dick Clark Productions, said that to the best of his knowledge it was the first time a recording session had ever been taped from start to finish. "All this is being done for the first time," he says. "We think the marriage of the two—recording and television—could not only be a revival for the music situation in Memphis, but a revival for music on television."

The second thing that made the session unique was the mass of high-tech equipment brought to the session. Obviously, the equipment that remained in the old studio was outdated. Moman brought in an 18-wheeler with a trailer loaded with the latest digital equipment and parked it outside the studio.

Microphones were set up inside the studio and the wires run outside to the trailer, where Moman sat at the recording board with the sound engineer. Moman communicated with the Four

Horsemen by using a speaker and microphone system. Technically, the music would be created inside the studio, but recorded outside in the trailer. The television crew of seven had a second truck packed with video equipment.

On the first day, when the Four Horsemen walked into the 18-by-29 foot studio, they were surrounded by television and newspaper photographers. The air was electric. The four men seemed to bounce off one another like energized cartoon figures in a video game. When Cash entered with his wife, June Carter, he walked up to Lewis and kissed him on the forehead. Lewis, seated at a microphone, looked stunned. He wasn't used to being kissed by men. He smiled, looking pleased but slightly embarrassed.

After a minimum amount of polite conversation, the four men gathered at the piano and clowned around for the cameras as Lewis pounded the ivories with his customary flare. It was good public relations and that evening CNN and the three major networks all carried footage of the reunion. But the television lights had raised the temperature of the room considerably and, by the time the media left, the four men were exhausted. Moman asked the quartet to rehearse one of the songs. After a few bars, Lewis screwed up and called out for the others to stop.

"What are you trying to do to me?" he says to Cash.

"What do you mean?" Cash asks, puzzled.

"I idolize you and you make me nervous," Lewis says, laughing.

Cash shook his head, speechless and embarrassed by the compliment.

Once the rehearsal was completed, Moman called it a day and sent everyone home. Moman and I retreated to a nearby pancake house for dinner. He ordered an omelet and an order of strawberry blintzes. I ordered a waffle. His eyes sparkled with excitement. What had impressed him most that day was the respect the four men had shown for Sam Phillips. "All four of them still call him Mr. Phillips," he noted with amazement. "That says a lot for these guys."

*　　*　　*

Tuesday got off to a wobbly start. Cash abruptly left town because of a family illness and Orbison stayed shut up in his hotel

199

room all day. Perkins and Lewis returned to the studio, bursting with energy. Lewis began the session with "Keep My Motor Running." At age 49, Lewis was trim and wiry. With Lewis and the band inside the studio, and Moman outside in the truck, the session began. Several times Lewis made mistakes on the piano and the music had to be stopped. Lewis was concerned his playing would not be up to par for the band.

"The guitar is playing lead, but I'll be playing piano—and you know me, if I put a lick in, just call me down on it," Lewis says to Moman.

Moman told him not to worry about it, to just keep playing.

Toward the end of the day, Moman suggested Lewis sing a ballad, "Sixteen Candles." Lewis tried the song while wearing earphones, then complained they got in the way. "I can't cut with earphones," he said, laughing. "That's faking it."

Without the earphones Lewis gave a flawless performance.

Later one of the musicians commented he had never heard Lewis sound better. A string of personal tragedies, including the deaths of two wives and a son—and a serious tear in the lining of his stomach in 1982—may have scared his body and his spirit, but it had left no mark on his art. Lewis was still, well . . . the Killer.

After knocking down "Sixteen Candles," Moman called a break and everyone fled to the back parking lot for a breath of fresh air. After pacing around the parking lot for a few minutes, and throwing pulled punches at friends, the hyperactive Lewis said he thought "Sixteen Candles" had the best feel of any song he had recorded since "Whole Lotta Shakin'."

"I usually do my records in one cut, but Chips wanted three," Lewis says. "It was a blessing for this man to record me. Anything he says to me, Jerry Lee Lewis ain't going to argue with. Playing in there again gave me a great feeling. Nothing could ever hold me back in that studio."

I brought out a small tape recorder, one I had used many times to interview Lewis. Suddenly, Lewis snapped. His eyes glazed and fixed in place, resembling cat's eye marbles. He grabbed the tape recorder and tried to pull it out of my hand. Unfortunately, the tape recorder had a strap that had looped around my finger and I could not have turned it loose if I had wanted to.

For what seemed like an eternity, Lewis and I scuffled elbow to elbow, our feet grating against the gravel of the parking lot as we went round and round in what from a distance must have looked a weird new dance. The spectacle attracted attention from the other side of the parking lot. Within seconds, Lewis' manager ran over, calling out Lewis' name. Lewis never demanded the tape recorder. He just grappled for it, his eyes fierce with determination. Inexplicably, he leaned over and began biting the tape recorder. Sparks seemed to fly from his demonic eyes. Abruptly, the strap broke and the battery cover on the tape recorder pulled off, ending the altercation.

Lewis retreated to the other side of the parking lot with his manager, J.W. Whitten. They spoke for a few moments, and then Whitten came back over to where I stood trying to put the tape recorder back together.

"Jerry wants to apologize, " he says. "He'd like to buy you a new tape recorder."

"That's not necessary. It's not broken."

Whitten reported back to Lewis. After a few minutes of conversation, the manager returned. "Jerry really feels bad," he says. "He'd like to buy you a couple of new recorders. That way you'll have a spare."

I shook my head.

Whitten went back to Lewis. After a few minutes, he returned with a new offer. "Jerry wants to buy you a hundred new recorders," he says. His eyes pleaded, as if screaming out, "Please, for God's sake!"

Again, I shook my head.

Whitten relayed that message to Lewis, who threw up his arms and shook his head. By then it was time to return to the studio. Lewis came over and shook hands with me.

"I'm sorry, man," he says.

It was enough to right the situation.

I told him not to worry about it. Then I changed the subject. I asked how it felt to be back in Sun studios. "I beats playing in the rain," Lewis says, laughing. The joke was his way of getting back on track. "No, it gave me a great feeling. I knew I should have been back in that studio all the time. Chips Moman knew it. These fellows knew it. And you knew it."

Years later, I spoke to a psychologist about Lewis' symptoms. He said it sounded like Lewis might have had an epileptic seizure. That sounded reasonable. Lewis had a history of drug abuse, but I saw no indication of that on that day (although a magazine journalist later reported she had seen pills spill from his shirt pocket). Interestingly, a few weeks later, I saw him do that "eye thing" again. I was seated at a table in a hotel bar in The Peabody Hotel with a small group of people. Lewis entered the room and joined the party. He sat next to me. He was in a good mood and his conversation was animated. We talked a while, then after about 30 minutes he suddenly turned to me and looked me squarely in the face. His eyes fixated, giving off sparks.

"Who are you?" he asks, looking puzzled.

Earlier I had noticed the handle of a snub-nosed .38-caliber pistol protruding from his back pocket. That information, along with the sudden return of his sparkly dancing eyes, convinced me it was time to go home. It wasn't the pistol that bothered me. It was those eyes. Everyone in the music business carried a gun in those days. People felt a little more comfortable if they were packing a piece. Moman carried a palm-sized .25 automatic in his back pocket. Once Moman and I were sitting outside his downtown recording studio, enjoying the celestial fireworks of a summer sky. Moman was on his big Harley, reclining against the handle bars. I sat in a chair a few feet behind him. As we talked, a black youth crossed the street and walked in our direction. He pulled a razor from his pocket and began tossing it into the air, eyeing us with a menacing look. I saw Moman's hand slip into his back pocket. Luckily, the youth stopped tossing the razor and walked on past. I once asked Moman about the pistol.

"I'll take a whipping," he says. "I'm man enough to take a whipping. But I'm not gonna let anybody kill me. That's the only time I would use it—if somebody was gonna kill me."

*   *   *

Carl Perkins was next up in the studio. Like the others, the 53-year-old had his share of personal misfortunes. Drug abuse or the deaths of loved ones were common threads that ran through the

202

lives of all four artists. Like the others, Perkins' career was plagued by periods of public neglect. In 1955 he was on his way to New York for an appearance on the Perry Como Show, where he was to receive a gold record for his hit, "Blue Suede Shoes," when he was almost killed in a car accident near Wilmington, Delaware. After the accident, his career languished and by the early 1960s he was ready to quit show business. Following a European tour with Chuck Berry, the Beatles recorded three of Perkins' songs, which, in turn, led to a series of concerts and new albums by Perkins. Still, despite an active concert schedule in the 1960s, it had been a long time since he had a hit record.

Back in Sun studios again in 1985, he showed none of the scars of thirty years of hard living and neglect. As comfortable as a country preacher at a church picnic, he mixed well with the musicians and the others in the studio, glad-handing his way around the room. He had been born again, and he knew it and he was damned grateful. Before the session began, he walked about the room, almost in a daze, looking at the pictures on the walls. He told me about the first time he walked into the studio.

"I left my two brothers and a drummer sitting out in a 1940 Plymouth," he says. "We had a bass tied on top in a 9-foot cotton sack. When I walked in I guess Marion (the receptionist) could tell I was a hungry picker.

"She said, 'If you came to audition, I'm sorry. Mr. Phillips isn't listening to anyone. We've got this boy called Elvis and he's real hot.'

"I said, 'I know.'

"I looked around. There was a life-size cardboard likeness of him. I said, 'Is that Elvis?'

"She said it was.

"I said, 'God, he's pretty.' And he was. He was a handsome dude."

Perkins is soft-spoken in conversation, but when the picks up his guitar and sings, the language of his music has a raw energy to it that is anything but soft. He sang two songs. The second, "Birth of Rock and Roll," utilized the same hot guitar licks that mesmerized ex-Beatle George Harrison two decades earlier. Of the Four Horsemen, Perkins was still the consummate rocker.

When time came for Orbison to arrive at the studio, the musicians set up, but Orbison did not show. Moman explained to reporters that Orbison had picked up a virus. Actually, he was at the hotel, glued to the toilet seat with a severe case of diarrhea. Orbison had been traumatized the day before, not just by the camera lights and the media commotion, but by the presence of the other Horsemen. He felt out of place. He had never belonged to the same musical club and he felt intimidated by the familiarity shared by the others. His self-esteem had taken a dive.

Eventually, Orbison showed up at the studio, several hours late, looking pale and nervous. He sang the first few bars of a song he had co-written, "Coming Home," then he left for the hotel after spending less than fifteen minutes at the studio, complaining of a sore throat.

*   *   *

Johnny Cash returned to Memphis on Wednesday. He arrived at the studio early, dressed in black. He ambled into the room, engaging in playful banter with the musicians and technicians. He picked up an acoustic guitar and sang a song in which Jack Clement, Sam Phillips' right hand man in the old days, was mentioned. Like everyone else, Clement had moved to Nashville, where he had enjoyed a very successful career as a producer and song publisher. At the precise moment Clement's name was uttered in the song, Clement himself walked into the studio. He had come to play rhythm guitar on Cash's session. Everyone started grinning. Seeing the grins, Cash turned around and stood face to face with Clement. He burst into laughter. Jack had caught him talking about him.

With his sleeves rolled up to his elbows, Cash hammered out the lyrics to a song he had written called "Home of the Blues." Beneath the music, the drumbeat shuffled, a night train without a whistle. As Cash sang, a distant look came over his eyes. It was as if he were singing the song to himself. Perhaps he was.

When he felt he had the song nailed down, he stepped up to the microphone. The tape rolled. Suddenly, the room was quiet but for the unamplified licks of the pickers, and the steady rolling beat of the drummer.

204

When the song was finished, Moman's voice boomed from a speaker: "That sounds good, John."

"Well, let's put it on the radio," jokes Cash.

Cash left the studio, which by that time had become unbearably hot from the camera lights, and walked outside to the truck. He shook hands with everyone inside the cramped space. In the dim light, the interior of the truck resembled a control center for NASA. There were enough blinking lights, dials and levers to put a rocket into orbit. Moman played the song back for Cash. It was a take on the first try, but just to be certain the film crew had enough angles for the television special, he asked Cash to go through it once more. Cash returned to the studio and again sang the song without making a single mistake.

Later, Perkins came into the studio to sing a duet with Cash. The song, "Waymore's Blues," had been written out by Waylon Jennings in longhand on a sheet of notebook paper. Cash and Perkins tried to read the handwriting, but kept stumbling over the words. Finally, Gene Weed volunteered to type the song so it would be easier for them to read. He put a typewriter on a cardboard box and pecked at the keyboard while the band stood around and waited impatiently in the hot studio.

Using the typewritten lyric sheet, Cash and Perkins went through the song again. At the end of the song, Moman's voice broke the silence: "That could use a little more fire in it. It seems to lack energy."

"We'll try it," Cash says.

With his guitar slung high up under his arm, Cash arched his back, then twisted at the waist and spun his face down to the microphone, his voice rumbling like a distant train on the tracks, sparks flying.

"Early one morning it was drizzling rain," he sings. "Around the curve came a Memphis train."

Perkins, hands on hips, twisted and swayed as he sang on background. Occasionally during the song, their eyes met and they smiled. Beneath their voices, the drum shuffled, steady and unrelenting. Moman got his fire and then some.

Playing rhythm guitar on the song was Marty Stuart. Later, he would become a country music star in his own right, but at that

205

time he had just landed his first big record deal. Not only was he a member of Cash's touring band, he was married to his daughter.

"It's like watching two brothers work together," Stuart says, motioning toward Cash and Perkins. "Take the Everly Brothers. They can go fifteen years without singing together, then they can get together and sing like brothers again. John and Carl are the same way. They know each other's limitations and they know what each other is capable of doing."

During the session, Perkins gave Stuart a surprise gift—a Fender Stratocaster guitar. It was the guitar he used in the session. On the back of the guitar, he wrote: "There is a great song in this guitar and you're just the cat to get it out."

Stuart was dumbfounded.

Later, I asked Perkins why he had given the guitar to Stuart. Perkins smiled. "He just had that look in his eye and I wanted him to have it."

Orbison and Lewis stayed away from the studio the entire day. Moman concentrated his efforts on Cash and Perkins. For most of the day, Cash was surprisingly low keyed and kept to himself. By the time the session that day was completed, everyone was exhausted.

Later that night, sitting in the Gridiron Restaurant across the street from The Peabody, Moman and his studio musicians talked about the session over scrambled eggs and grits. Bacon sizzled in the background. At a nearby table, a man wearing a set of plastic eyes attached to 10-inch springs stared at Moman.

"This album is an extremely important part of history," says Moman, ignoring the man with the plastic eyes. "Sun Studio is a monument to music. It's not just history. It's a monument. It's important to me personally because I looked up to these guys for years. Our lives ran parallel but we never got involved. Then down at the crossroads we met."

The man with the plastic eyes dashed from the restaurant and returned moments later flashing a blackjack. Moman's bodyguard, a decorated Vietnam veteran named Frank, was already on edge after a full day of keeping the peace at the studio. When he spotted the man with the blackjack, he watched his every move, ready to pounce into action.

At the end of a full course of eggs and grits, Moman and the band rose to leave the restaurant. As they approached the cash register, the man with the plastic eyes leaped from his chair and hurried over to Moman's plate. There was a moment of uncertainty as everyone watched to see what would happen next. Was he going to attack someone with the blackjack? With his eyes still glued to Moman, the man with the plastic eyes scooped up the food left on Moman's plate, packing his face with the leftovers.

*   *   *

On Thursday the session moved to American Sound Studio, the former location of Moman's American Recording Studios. Dreary and in disrepair, the windowless studio looked old and tired. Nonetheless it brought back warm memories to Moman and the band. "There's something magic about it," says guitarist Reggie Young.

After listening to a practice session from the truck, Moman entered the studio. He was excited. "That old sound is still here," he says, smiling broadly.

For the Four Horsemen it was a new experience.

"I've never recorded here, but I think I'm going to like it," says Cash. "It has a mood more than anything else."

If the walls could have talked, they would have done so with the voices of Elvis, Neil Diamond, Dionne Warwick, Dusty Springfield, the Box Tops, Wilson Pickett, Aretha Franklin, Petula Clark, Brenda Lee, Joe Tex, B.J. Thomas, Paul Revere and the Raiders, the Gentrys and countless others. Between January 1968 and January 1971, twenty-six gold singles and eleven gold LPs were cut in the studio. During those same years, eighty-three singles and twenty-five LPs cut in the studio made their way to the national charts.

Adjacent to the studio was a room filled with Elvis memorabilia When Moman owned the studio, it contained a pool table. The new owners had converted the room into a shrine. Pictures by the hundreds lined the walls. In glass cabinets were Elvis spoons, Elvis cups and Elvis ashtrays. In the corner was a 4-foot high cardboard likeness of Elvis.

Spotting the cardboard Elvis look-alike, Lewis said he wanted to take it home to put in his apartment. Earlier he said Elvis, as a joke, once put Lewis' picture on the toilet in Sun studio.

"I wish he hadn't done that," he murmurs, cracking an uneasy smile.

For Perkins, the persona surrounding Elvis was no myth. Over the years, he had met everyone in the business. "I was in the studio when the Beatles recorded three of my songs. No one has ever had the style Elvis had. I'm never expecting to meet anyone else who is as complete an entertainer as he was."

Perkins, never late for a session, was first to sing that day. The song was "Class of '55," a ballad written by Moman and keyboardist Bobby Emmons. Two nights before Moman had played it for the first time for Perkins in the privacy of his bus. "He's very shy," Perkins says about Moman. "He won't push his own material. Carl Perkins is a million miles from having a hit single but there is a feel on that song that is convincing. It seems like something I wrote myself."

Seated on a stool, wearing jeans and white sneakers, Perkins twisted a pencil in his hand as he sang. "That sure is good," says Moman when Perkins finished. "It makes me feel good just hearing music of mine again in this old building."

For the first time since Monday, all four artists were in the studio together. As Cash sang his part on "We Remember the King," Perkins sat on the floor near the piano, his legs folded beneath him. More than once he gave Cash the high sign, indicating his approval of the way he was doing the song. Later they all would join in on the chorus. Cash, perhaps responding to Orbison's obvious discomfort, put his arm around his shoulder as they sang, holding him close the way you would a brother.

By Thursday everyone but Orbison had recorded a single. Not until late that night did he venture from his bus into the studio. The room was cleared of all but essential personnel and the lights were dimmed. "Coming Home," the song he had co-written for the session, is a ballad that pulls at the heart. Whatever he was feeling that night, he poured himself into the song, living up to his reputation as one of the most durable vocalists in the history of rock 'n' roll.

Hardship was the common thread throughout the careers of all Four Horsemen. Orbison was never linked to drug abuse, but the tragedies in his life were the type that had driven lesser men over the edge. His wife, Claudette, was killed in a motorcycle accident. No sooner had he recovered from that than a fire at his Nashville home killed two of his three children. Somehow he survived.

For most of the Memphis sessions, Orbison looked shaky. His hands shook and his voice trembled. On the first takes of "Coming Home" his voice was embarrassingly tenuous. He was a pitiful sight sitting in that darkened studio with a roomful of musicians.

After several takes, Orbison and Moman, who had stayed in the studio to offer moral support, went out to the sound truck to listen. The technicians in the trucks were unanimous in their verdict. They told him it was a smash. Orbison leaned against the wall and listened to the playback. Once or twice he smiled.

"I think it's great," said Moman, though he seemed to squirm.

Orbison nodded, but said nothing. One can only guess at the emotions that flowed through him while he listened. He had come home to Memphis, but his wife and children, for whom the song seemed directed, had been tragically lost along the way.

For Perkins, the specter of Elvis loomed greater with each passing day. The more he looked to the future, the more he saw the past. "I had been playing that music all my life, but I sure never got a contract," he says. "I sent tapes to record companies, and I would get them back with notes that they didn't know what it was. That's when I set my sights on Sun Records."

*　　*　　*

By Friday everyone was exhausted. For the final song of the session, Moman selected "Big Train (From Memphis)," written and previously recorded by John Fogerty. Shortly before they were to record the song, Fogerty walked into the studio and introduced himself to the Four Horsemen. He flew in that day from Los Angeles after Moman put out word that guests would be welcome to jam on the final song. When Fogerty arrived at the airport, he realized he didn't know where the studio was located. He phoned Duck Dunn, formerly of Booker T. & the MGs and more recently the bassist with Eric Clapton's touring band, to get directions.

Fogerty confessed he felt light-headed in the presence of his heroes. "I was trying to relate back to when I first heard the Sun sound," he says, talking about the genesis of "Big Train." "I was about 10 and used to play on the tracks. You know the old game. You put pennies on the track and a freight train flattens them, all very innocent stuff. Yet that was the sound I loved, and I wanted to write a song about that, with my producer being Sam Phillips. Obviously, it is a tribute to Elvis, but it is more than that. It is a tribute to the whole era."

Also dropping in for the jam were Rick Nelson, who like Fogerty had made a special trip to Memphis, producer Dave Edmunds, saxophonist Ace Cannon and the Judds. Edmunds wandered about the studio speechless. "I'm just overwhelmed by the whole thing," says the Englishman. "Memphis is the home of rock 'n' roll. I'm a bit in shell shock."

Nelson, dressed in black, moved quietly about the room, watching—shyly it seemed—the legends from a distance. I tried to strike up a conversation with him. He politely confessed a loss of words and faded into the background. Later he did talk to me.

"I've always been such a big fan of all these guys," Nelson says, his eyes never leaving the center of the room where the legends were standing. "I wouldn't have missed it for anything."

The next morning, while taking off from the Memphis airport, Nelson's 45-year-old DC-3 developed engine trouble and the take-off was aborted. Nelson left the airplane in Memphis for repairs and returned to Los Angeles aboard a commercial flight.

Marty Stuart, on board the plane when it attempted to take off from Memphis, said it was ironic that he and Nelson were taking about a mutual hero, Buddy Holly, when the plane started down the runway. "We were talking about Buddy Holly's glasses, about how some farmer found his glasses after the plane crash," says Stuart. "Rick was laughing, and he was talking about how the plane used to belong to Jerry Lee Lewis. But I was thinking about how rickety I felt on it." Three months later, on New Year's Eve, Nelson and his band perished in the DC-3 when it crashed under mysterious circumstances in Texas.

On the night of the jam, tragedy was the furthest thing from anyone's' mind. The mood was jubilant. Bassist Mike Leech said he felt like an autograph hound. "I'm taking pictures and getting autographs like people off the street, and I've worked with all these guys at one time or another," he says. "I'll be sitting there talking to someone like Carl Perkins, then I'm thinking, 'Gosh, I'm talking to a legend.' Then the next thing you know I have my camera out taking pictures."

Sam Phillips, who you think would be used to such things by now, told me that he had never seen a group of artists gather under such circumstances. "Invariably, everyone here I have talked to feels the same way," he says. "You can feel it in the air. It's not just, 'Oh, boy, we have us a hit record.' They see a future in a city they know started it all, and believe me, this cycle is going to make itself known again."

The jam itself gave everyone in the room goose bumps. There were seven musicians, fourteen voices—all wailing the words to "Big Train." As the driving bass and guitar licks of the song walked the music downward, the spirits of the singers climbed upward, the collision creating a joyous harmony that filled the room. Even the sound and video technicians, who had kept their thoughts to themselves throughout the session, erupted into spontaneous applause when it ended.

In the early hours of Saturday morning, there was a sudden hush, as if people were thinking *you really can go home again*, then the studio cleared quickly, the Four Horsemen of apocalyptic vision running fastest of all. As everyone filed from the studio, Moman sat on a stool in the center of the room. Tears streaked down his cheeks.

"I can't believe this happened," he says, looking at me with eyes that were bursting with happiness. "I never thought I'd ever see anything like this."

The room emptied, technicians turning out lights as they exited.

We stood beneath the only light remaining in the vast room. I didn't know what to say, so I said nothing. Moman was paralyzed by his emotions. Little did he—or I—know then, but storm clouds were forming over Memphis. Dark, ugly clouds, that would rain on the *Class of 55* session and send Moman's high-flying career into a tailspin. Clouds that would shroud Memphis music in a veil of darkness.

Chips Moman and wife, Toni, protest Memphis newspaper coverage
Photo © James L. Dickerson

CHAPTER 11

Memphis Takes No Prisoners

In the weeks following the Sun Records session, Chips Moman worked feverishly to get the tapes mastered and ready for presentation to major record labels. There were some problems. Upon re-examination, Orbison's shaky vocals made it necessary for Chips to go to California to do some minor overdubs. Horns and strings overdubs were done at Chips' studio in Nashville. By the time Chips got through performing his magic on the album, he had a collection of 10 songs recorded by the pioneers of rock 'n' roll that was unlike anything else on the market.

The album was so unique it quickly became apparent that the miracle Chips had performed in recording it would have to be duplicated in the business arena if the album was ever to see the light of day. To Chips' surprise—and almost everyone else's—the major labels did not jump at the chance to purchase the album, despite a level of publicity unprecedented for an unreleased album. One by one, the rejections mounted. The feeling among most of the record executives was that the album was too special. It wasn't exactly the kind of music being played by rock radio stations. And it wasn't what was played on country radio.

Shortly after the session, Chips purchased a house in Memphis for $420,000 with money borrowed from First Tennessee Bank, along with a $100,000 short-term loan for Toni. In addition, he borrowed $55,000 to purchase a home for his daughter, Monique. The Nashville farm owned by the Momans was paid for and appraised at well over a million dollars. The loans were an attempt to get settled and working as quickly as possible. During this time, Chips took Mell on as his chief assistant and he hired a secretary and continued to work out of the office in the hotel. The strain of working out of a hotel, and the uncertainty of the album's future began to show in Chip's face and demeanor. He looked tired on most days, and he grew more and more irritable. What he needed was a studio to work out of, not a hotel office. He pushed for finalization of the deal Mayor Hackett had been working on since spring.

By the end of November 1985 Hackett was ready to present his proposal to city council for approval. At that time he announced that he was backing down from an earlier proposal to sell city property to successful record producers willing to relocate in Memphis. He didn't admit it publicly, but the reason for that change was that he had been bombarded with complaints from the handful of studios still in operation in Memphis. Their arguments were emotional: You're doing something for Chips Moman, so why aren't you doing something for us? Hackett wasn't about to do that, so he opted to simply stop his efforts to recruit new talent for the city. It was yet another example of how prone the Memphis music community was to self-destruction.

Under the terms of the agreement with Chips, he would be allowed to use an abandoned fire station at Third and Linden for a $1-a-year lease payment and he was given the option to purchase the property at appraised value at the end of five years. In addition, Chips would receive a loan for $750,000 arranged by the Center City Commission. Under that agreement, First Tennessee Bank agreed to purchase the bonds issued by the city. Chips would be required to make his loan payments directly to First Tennessee Bank.

"There's no way we can say we've given Chips a deal," Hackett said in response to critics who didn't want the city involved in promoting the music business. "He's given us a deal." By that, he explained, he meant Chips had brought more to the city than he ever thought possible. "He's exceeded all my expectations."

The internal bickering that had driven Chips from the city in 1970 was beginning to resurface, but in all the excitement no one seemed to notice, or, if they did, they did not think it was very important. Storm clouds were forming, but they seemed so far away as to be inconsequential.

By February 1986, it was apparent the major labels were going to pass on the album. At the urging of Gary Belz and others, who saw not just dollar signs, but stars in their future—show business can be intoxicating—Chips decided to form a record label in Memphis to distribute the album. He tired to start up a label once in Nashville, but the venture was under-capitalized and never got off the ground. Starting a record label had been on his list of things to do from the beginning once he moved to Memphis, but it was not his initial plan to use the homecoming album as the label's first product.

Mell, with his extensive contacts in the financial community, and Gary Belz, who saw a record label as the answer to all his dreams, targeted potential investors. The list of investors they put together, with a few exceptions, read like a who's who of business leaders in the South: Philip and Jack Belz of Belz Investments; financial consultant John Tigrett of Memphis, whose son, Isaac, founded the Hard Rock Cafe chain; Fred Smith, chairman of Federal Express; Benard Blasingame, president of Aqua Glass Corporation; and Buddy Lazar, president of Star Distributors. In all there were 18 investors. They never publicly disclosed how much they invested, but I calculated the total amount to be between $1-2 million. They christened the new label, America Records. That name was chosen to reflect Chips' belief that Memphis was responsible for the creation of much of America's music.

"One of the things we see in the label is the possibility of making Memphis a major music center," Belz told a reporter for *The Commercial Appeal* on the day the announcement was made. "We see more labels, more studios, more live music in Memphis as a result of America Records."

A date of April 11 was set for the new label's first release—the homecoming album. Reaction was enthusiastic. The very thought of having a label in the city again gave hope to a generation of musicians and singers who had only dreamed of the opportunities enjoyed by previous generations of Memphis musicians. Of course, no one was more enthusiastic than Chips. He was smiling again. For the first time since the initial discussions about relocating in Memphis had begun, he was able to visualize the musical pot of gold at the end of the rainbow.

Given the domination enjoyed by the major labels in the marketplace, the biggest obstacle facing any independent label is its ability to secure a strong distribution system. Chips understood that all too well. His solution to that problem was to launch a two-prong attack. First, to secure a retail distribution agreement with a

215

major label. Second, to make an effort to use television to directly market the album to consumers.

"We're trying to set trends, not follow them," he explained. "We're trying to be different. We don" want to use the old-fashioned ways used by the record companies."

To accomplish the former, he contacted Steve Popovich, then the head of PolyGram Records in Nashville. Popovich had made his mark on the music industry with the rock act, Meat Loaf. In 1977, Popovich, who was then with Epic Records, joined with Stan Snyder and Sam Lederman of Columbia Records, to form an independent label called Cleveland International. Their first album release was Meat Loaf's *Bat Out of Hell*, an enormously successful album. Unfortunately, Meat Loaf, the 6'2", 260-pound singer, born Marvin Aday, couldn't stand up to the demands of success and as his career fizzled so did Popovich's.

By the mid-1980s Popovich had relocated in Nashville and taken over the reins of PolyGrams's office there. A big, burly man with an aggressive approach to music, he was just the kind of player Chips wanted on his team. Popovich had himself started an independent label. He knew the ropes. With PolyGram taking on retail distribution, Chips felt confident he could launch a telemarketing effort that would make the album a multi-million seller.

But to have a successful telemarketing effort Chips knew he had to have more than just an album to sell. He needed a package. One evening I got a telephone call from him, which he began with one word, "Busy?"

"No."

"I got something to talk to you about."

Chips picked me up at my apartment and we drove to an all-night waffle house. We ordered eggs and waffles and downed a few cups of coffee; then Chips said he had an offer to make me. If I would write a book to accompany the album for its telemarketing sales, I could retain the copyright and use the book to launch my own magazine. American Records would not pay me to write the book. My compensation would be an opportunity to spin off a business venture from the project.

"How would that enable me to get subscribers for the magazine?" I asked.

216

Chips explained that I could put the name of my magazine on the book and run a full page ad in the book telling people how they could subscribe to the magazine. Although I did not particularly like the idea of writing a book for free, I did see the possibilities it offered. If the album was successful—and everyone just *knew* it would be—so would the magazine. I told him I would think about it. It was a big step for me to take. It would mean resigning from *The Commercial Appeal*, with no certainty of an income. It would be the biggest risk of my life.

The next morning I called Chips and told him I would do it. It hardly seemed possible the homecoming album would not be successful. I knew that a national music magazine based in Memphis would play an important role in the revival of the city's music industry. I notified my editors at the newspaper that I would be working on the book, but they did not feel it was necessary for me to resign until the book was published and I was actually soliciting subscribers for the magazine.

Meanwhile, cracks already were forming in America Records. Almost immediately after getting involved in the project, Federal Express chairman Fred Smith decided he wanted out. The other investors did not think that would be fair, and they balked at releasing him from his commitment. Smith then asked John Fry, owner of Ardent Recording, to represent his interest in the label. Fry, a longtime friend of Smith, would attend the meetings and report to Smith on the operation of the label.

That didn't go over too well with Chips because Fry owned a studio that competed for attention and business with the studio Chips was going to build in the fire station. But to both the credit of Chips and Fry they both tried to make the most of the association. I was at the hotel office one day when Fry and some of the other investors showed up for a meeting. The meeting began and they talked about the album and about new projects Chips wanted to do. I noticed Fry's eyes darted quite a bit during the discussion. He began to squirm. Finally, Fry said he didn't think I should be present at the meeting.

"Why?" Chips asked.

"He might tell people what we're doing," Fry said.

"We've got nothing to hide," Chips said.

I stayed at the meeting.

Later, during that meeting, concerns were expressed about the label's options if the majors decided to play hard ball and block distribution of the album at the retail level. Without pausing, Chips said that would not be a problem because the Hells Angels would be available as enforcers if problems arose. Chips was joking—at least I hoped he was joking—but his comment had the desired effect: the yuppie investors swooned like schoolgirls at the thought of the Hells Angels becoming their partners. Did they envision themselves in a Harley motorcade, with biker chicks at their side and rock music blaring from heavenly speakers? Who knows? But who could blame them if they did? There were probably worse dreams they could have.

Chips' hotel office was always busy. Songwriters, musicians, music publishers, all showed up at all hours of the day and night. Also finding their way to the hotel office were young girls seeking autographs. Because Jerry Lee Lewis and Carl Perkins were often at the office, the girls pursued them for their autographs—and to sing a few bars to Chips. I was in the office once with Carl Perkins when a group of five or six young woman in their late teens or early twenties, came in, saw Perkins and fluttered about the room, taking turns getting his autograph. After they left, Perkins gave me one of the most sensual descriptions of a 20-year-old woman I have ever heard.

"There's just something about those 20-year-old bodies," he said, shaking his head with admiration. Then his voice got low, dropping almost to a purr. "They're so firm—so perfect." He moved his hands through the air, caressing the outline of an imaginary woman.

Once I was sitting in the hotel lobby taking to Chips when a striking former Miss Mississippi came up and sat next to Chips. In between frequent trips to the restroom, from which she always returned with a white powder on her nose, she held Chips' hand and sang to him above the chatter of the busy lobby. Chips took the unusual audition in stride and was polite, although I never heard him make any comment about her singing, which, as might be expected, was not exactly hit record quality.

America Records wasted no time getting the *Class of '55* on the market. The album was released in Memphis in mid-May and sales were brisk at local stores. FM-100 program director Robert John began airing the album immediately. "The reaction has been phenomenal," he told me for one of the last stories I wrote for *The Commercial Appeal*. "There was not one negative call."

By then work was progressing on Chips' new studio, which he planned to name 3 Alarm Studio. It would be a state-of-the art facility with the best digital equipment money could buy.

In May 1986 I handed in my resignation at *The Commercial Appeal* to David Wayne Brown, who had become editor after Grehl's forced retirement. I transferred my life savings to my checking account and prepared to become a magazine magnate. The week I left the newspaper, Grehl called me at home to say he had heard about my resignation. He said he was sorry to see me leave the newspaper and he wished me luck with the magazine. Sadly, that would be our last conversation. He would die of kidney failure before we could speak again.

The summer of 1986 was pivotal for Memphis music. The first major record in over a decade had been released. The national media had discovered the city after neglecting it for years. There were indications other producers would move to the city. A national music magazine based in the city was about to be launched. For the first time in decades, the banks were talking about making loans to music entrepreneurs.

Anxious to try out his new studio, Chips made plans to record an album with Bobby Womack for MCA Records. Perhaps mindful of their first collaboration, he felt the "magic" that would flow from a reunion would make that project as special as the *Class of '55*. Of course, that wasn't what the music community in Memphis wanted him to do. Everyone wanted him to focus on local talent. Chips had signed a local group, Reba and the Portables, to a recording contract and, without fanfare, had worked with them in his studio in Nashville, but his efforts to place them with a major label had been unsuccessful. Chips knew that he would need someone with a track record to help him launch his new studio. Although Womack had been reduced to playing hotel lounges in recent years, the talent was still there and Chips was convinced that they could record a hit record.

It was during that time that I first began to see the obstacles that loomed in the distance like giant pylons. Leaving the newspaper enabled me to become more involved in the music community. I used the sources I had built up as a reporter. I called Michael Barrickman, A&R executive at EMI Records in New York, and he flew to Memphis to sample the talent. I took him by Chips' studio and Chips played him the demos he had recorded on Reba and the Portables. I also invited him to listen to a group called Vienna. It featured a female singer, Claudia Kroboth, who had emigrated to Memphis from Austria and married a Memphis building contractor. Barrickman passed on both groups.

I took another A&R executive from Los Angeles by to hear another group. I still cringe when I think of his brutal, and, I think, incorrect, assessment of the female singer: "The last thing we need is another unattractive female singer." But she has a perfect voice, I argued. "Doesn't matter," he said. I invited Rick Blackburn, head of CBS Records in Nashville, to Memphis. I took him out one evening to listen to about a half dozen acts. He was impressed with Reba, but did not like the band. The visit was not a success.

By May, America Records had moved its offices from The Peabody to a small office complex off Beale Street. The office building offered a nice view of the Mississippi River. Chips had an office there, but he seldom used it.

* * *

By the start of summer the marketing of *Class of '55* hit full stride. "The Birth of Rock 'n' Roll," Carl Perkins' solo effort, was the first single released. Reviews of the album were good. Unfortunately, sales were slow. Television sales especially were disappointing. On a trip to Nashville during that time, I stopped by PolyGram to visit with Popovich. To my surprise and amusement, he was wearing a jogging suit, perhaps symbolic of his desire to make the album a success.

The investors in America Records began to voice concern. Sometimes, on my visits to the office, I would run into some of the investors who had dropped by to help with strategy planning, telephone calls or packaging mail-outs. They were concerned because most of their investment had been spent on up-front payments to Chips, Cash, Orbison, Lewis and Perkins, with each person receiving advances against royalties in the neighborhood of $250,000. It was probably then that they began to wonder how they could tap into Chips' post-*Class of '55* career. It wasn't money they feared losing (they all had plenty), it was the loss of prestige and perhaps most importantly the loss of their dreams to enter the gilded gates of show business.

To help the sales of the single, Popovich decided to do a video. He called Arnold Levine, who had done videos for Bruce Springsteen, Billy Joel and Neil Diamond. Levine flew into Memphis and hired a local film crew to tape the video. The song, which had been written by Perkins and his son the night before the session, was a narrative account of the birth of rock 'n' roll. For the video, Levine got a vintage '55 blue Cadillac. "Basically what I did was take a vintage car and use it as a time machine," said Levine. "I have two kids out on a joyride in the early morning. The two kids happen to be 50-year-olds doing what kids do."

Also included in the video was Jerry Lee Lewis and Rolling Stones guitarist Ron Wood, who made the trip to Memphis out of respect for Perkins and Lewis. Levine said it was important to film the video in Memphis because of the city's claim as the birthplace of rock 'n' roll. I had never watched a video being made, so I went to see how it was done. When I arrived I noticed everyone kept looking at their watches. Lewis had not showed up yet and they had planned to shoot a scene in which he sat in the back seat of the car and danced his feet across the top of the front seat.

Finally, when they felt they could wait no longer, I was asked to be Lewis' stand-in. I changed into his shoes and pants and proceeded to dance my way into video history. At one point in the video, my face is clearly visible. Years later I was amused to discover that a friend, Steve Gardner, a Mississippi-born photojournalist and noted blues performer who worked out of Tokyo, was in the Philippines during one of its frequent revolutions. As the bullets starting flying, he darted into a hotel and hit the floor. A TV set was on in the lobby. To his surprise,

Perkins' video was playing. He looked up, glass shattering all around him, and watched the video as blood flowed outside in the street. He later confided to me that the incident made him lose all respect for revolutions.

Once, while I was viewing the finished video with Perkins, the singer cut his head around during the dancing feet scene and grinned. "You don't keep bad time for writer," he said.

Sales was never Chips' strong point. He was an artist, and he had an artist's temperament. As the weeks went by—and dreams of the album being a major success began to fade—he prepared for his session with Womack. They had worked magic together before. Surely, they could do it again.

Chips confessed he was nervous about the session.

"I'm nervous at the start of every session, but I was extraordinarily nervous about Bobby this time because I didn't know whether the studio was going to go up in smoke," he said, referring to the fact that the new studio, housed in a former fire station, was largely untested. "But you know I couldn't think of anyone I would rather try to get a hit with than Bobby. He's got a distinct style. He's a great singer, writer and guitar player. That's about all you could ask for. He's also one of the best arrangers of horns I've ever heard in my life."

For Womack, the decision to return to Memphis was a tough one. It had been eighteen years since he had last recorded in the city, and he had built a new life in Los Angeles His friends warned him not to go to Memphis.

"I had all the people on my end saying, 'What do you want to go to Memphis for?'" he said. "I told them my music is what Memphis is all about. It's very peaceful, it's loving and caring, and the people there, the musicians, are like that. It's a magical place."

While in Memphis, Womack stayed at The Peabody. One day he ran into Stevie Wonder in the lobby. Wonder was in town to attend an awards show organized to honor black recording artists. Wonder asked why he was in Memphis.

"I said, 'Stevie, this is where it's happening,'" said Womack.

"I called him the next night at the hotel." Womack laughed. "They said Stevie had gone to a studio to do some recording."

Womack said Memphis' magic was partly cultural. "I go where the soul people are, not just for the people in the studio, but for the people who walk the streets," he explained. "This is where you get the raw soul. In L.A. you have to lock the door to get inside your soul, and even then you can get caught up in the electronic slickness of what everyone else is doing." Memphis has a special energy of its own, he said: "This is the capital. You can't cut no bigger than Elvis and Al Green."

Womack's album, *Womagic*, was released in November 1986. The reviews were excellent, but unfortunately sales fizzled and the album stalled on the charts. By the end of the year, nerves were on edge at America Records and tempers were flaring. Chips stopped going to the office, and declined pressure from his partners to record additional artists for the label. In relationships terms, Chips was the spouse who decided to sleep in the guest bedroom.

One night Chips was sitting in his den when he got a telephone call from Gary Belz. One thing led to another and Belz called Chips a motherfucker. Chips calmly hung up the phone, got in his car and drove to Ardent, where Belz was waiting.

Chips strode into the studio and went from room to room looking for Belz. When he found him, he slapped Belz hard across the face, without explanation.

"You call me a name, you do it to my face," he said, and left.

Belz was stunned.

With that gesture, more symbolic than anything else, Memphis music entered a new era. All out war erupted in the Memphis music community—and the dark side, alluded to by record producer Jim Dickinson in such graphic terms, rose from the ashes to bay at the moon.

Record producer Jim Dickinson on Beale Street, 1995   Photo © James L. Dickerson

224

Stevie Ray Vaughan in Memphis
Photo © James L. Dickerson

225

Ringo Starr and Chips Moman at 3 Alarm Studio in Memphis
Photo © James L. Dickerson

CHAPTER 12

The 1980s:
A Beatle Drops the Beat

In October 1987 Gary Hardy, the new owner of Sun Studios (Sam had decided to sell the historic studio several years back) received a telephone call from A&M Records. They wanted to book a full day in the studio. They were after an "authentic" rockabilly sound. They didn't say who the artist was, but that was fine with Hardy.

About a week later Hardy got a call from Jack Clement, who wanted to know if he had heard from U2 yet. Hardy was stunned. That was the first indication Hardy had that he had booked the studio for a U2 session. At that time, U2 was universally regarded as the best rock 'n' roll band in the world. Most of Hardy's clients had been wannabes who booked time at the studio because it was cheap and had a recognizable name. U2 was the big time.

Clement arrived in Memphis on November 1, the day before the session, to check out the studio. He was surprised to hear the studio was back in operation, but not totally surprised to hear from U2. He had worked with them several months before on a Woody Guthrie tribute album.

"We did a song called 'Jesus Christ,'" Jack recalled. "We had a big time and got along real good. A couple of months later they called me back. They said they would only do it (come to Memphis) if I could be there."

Jack agreed to do it on the condition that he could bring his own engineer.

U2 had two reasons for recording in Memphis. The first was to try to capture that old slap back sound for which Sun is famous. The second was to cut a track for an overdub by B.B. King. U2 had met King the year before in Dublin during King's Ireland tour. "They came backstage after the show, like artists sometimes do," recalls King. "When they were getting ready to go, I said,

227

'Sometimes when you're writing a song, why don't you write one for me.' Bono smiled and said yes. I didn't hear from him for over a year and then one day my manager called and said he had just heard from Bono and he's written a song for you."

King's manager told him U2 was kicking off its U.S. tour in Fort Worth, Texas, and wanted to know if he would open the show for them.

"My band and I flew over and got with them and I discovered Bono had written a song, but not just for me, but for us to sing together," says King. "I was real excited about it. But I'm not good with chords. I was teasing him about it. I said I was surprised about some of the lines being done by a young man. They were so strong. That night, according to the Fort Worth papers, when we did the song as a finale, 40,000 people came to their feet. I was really happy."

When Bono, the Edge, Adam Clayton and Larry Muller Jr. arrived at Sun, they did what every tourist does: They gawked at the photos of Elvis, Carl, Johnny, Jerry Lee and all the others that line the walls of the tiny 18 by 32 foot studio. They did overdubs on the "Jesus Christ" song; then they laid down tracks on three other songs that ended up on their *Rattle and Hum* album. For "Angel of Harlem," Clement brought in the Memphis Horns to give the track a taste of the old Stax sound.

What emerged, though, was more a reflection of the work that had been done at American. New York had its wall of sound. In the 1960s and early 1970s, Memphis had what I think of as a briar patch of sound. It was layered more intricately and hit you just above the knees instead of in your face. The second song was "Love Rescue Me," a folk-gospel tune written by Bono and Bob Dylan. The third song was "When Love Comes to Town," the one Bono had written for B.B. King. It was a perfect, back-of-the-beat choice for a duet with King. Once it was released, it peaked at No. 12 on the United Kingdom charts, but only made it to 68 in the United States.

Jack Clement said that U2 was no different than any other four-piece band he had ever worked with. "Of course, they were a lot louder than the bands I worked with in there," he laughed. "But I put the instruments in the same spots in the room. Except I used

228

baffles this time. It does seem to be a magic room. I think that is because there is so much leakage. It sounds better when you play it back than when you hear it in the room. It's magic."

"All they wanted me to do was be a clown and just be what I used to be in that room. So I danced around so they'd pay attention to me and forget the songs. That's what I do. I perform for my artists. I dance for them. It keeps their minds off the songs. People sing their best when they don't know what they're doing. They're not thinking about anything, just watching the dancing figure. They seemed to love it, you know. I danced around with a beer bottle on my head."

When artists get too intense, he deliberately distracts them. "Sometimes if you cut a song more than once you can never go back and cut it like you did. There's times when you have to slow it down so you can start over. I go out and say something to the artists totally out of left field. It shatters their concentration and they get totally out what they were doing and then they're ready to start over."

*　*　*

That year the floodgates seemed to open. Everyone, it seemed, wanted to record an album in Memphis. Between 1987 and 1989, R.E.M. recorded its *Green* album at Ardent; Jim Dickinson produced an album with the Replacements that got rave reviews; Stevie Ray Vaughan recorded his last two albums; the Fabulous Thunderbirds recorded two albums; ZZ Top did another album; and ex-Beatle Ringo Starr came to Memphis to work with Chips Moman on an album.

Sadly, the indigenous talent languished on the vine. Becky Russell sang backup on the U2 album, but her own band, Reba and the Portables, was going nowhere fast. One of the best singer/songwriters in the city, Klaudia Kroboth, seemed close at times, but success always wriggled just out of her grasp. Two Memphians got record deals with major labels, Rob Jungklas and John Kilzer, but their records ran into a brick wall when they got to the charts.

Ever since the Moman-Belz confrontation the music community had taken sides against both Moman and Belz. A local music magazine, the *Memphis Star*, published a readers poll in 1987 in which voters gave Moman and Belz its Captain Oblivion Space Cadet Award for "stupidity." Backbiting and dirty tricks were the predominant activity for local musicians.

One of the most encouraging things to happen for Memphis artists occurred when Bob Pittman, the former head of MTV, created his own record label, QMI Music. Incredibly, he came to Memphis to sign his first two acts. The first was Ella Brooks, a black, R&B singer whose voice seemed ideal for the pop charts. The second was Jimmy Davis and his band Junction. Jimmy was a 23-year-old rocker in the John Melloncamp vein. Pittman made a big deal of the singings and held a party at the rum Boogie Cafe on Beale Street to celebrate his entry into Memphis music.

Pittman had just left MTV and was eager to make a splash as a record executive. As one of the creators of MTV, he certainly had the track record to do great things in music. Whether he had a genius for music remained to be seen, but no one could doubt his genius as a media guru. Memphis was having so much bad luck on the musical front, I was fascinated by his interest in the city's talent pool. I met him at the party and then later talked to him about the signings.

"What I liked about Ella and Jimmy was that they both have a very real sound," he explained. "Originally we cut a deal with Ella. I went to Memphis to work out the deal. While I was there Jimmy performed for us. He was just a natural. He could say stuff that if I said it, they'd say, 'Jez, what's that guy talking about?' But Jimmy says it and you say, 'Yeah, that's right.' Springsteen has that quality."

Pittman said he was determined to do the same thing for QMI that he had done for MTV, though he acknowledged that making a success of an independent label was a tough goal. To date, only David Geffen had managed to pull it off.

"Probably most independent labels that fail are underfinanced and they don't have strong relationships in the business," says Pittman. "They're trying to build their relationships through the label. They also probably get the last look at every piece of music. We have what David Geffen had—key relationships with the players. And we have plenty of money."

Was QMI going to become the Sun Records of the 1980s? Was Memphis talent again destined to rise from the ashes of ignoble defeat and lead the way to a brighter day?

*   *   *

With the *Class of '55* and Bobby Womack projects foundering in shallow water on the charts, Chips Moman decided to return to his pop music roots. That was one area in which American had been unrivaled in the late 1960s. Ironically, for salvation he turned to a former member of the very group that had brought about the demise of the Memphis sound—the Beatles.

When Ringo Starr arrived in Memphis in February 1987 to record at 3 Alarm Studio, the town assumed all the characteristics of a giddy teenager. There was a buzz on the streets wherever people gathered in small groups. TV newscasts contained news of "Ringo sightings." It had been 20 years since a Beatle had been in Memphis. This time there were no Ku Klux Klan protests. No cherry bombs were thrown at the ex-Beatle.

The Beatles had always been my favorite group, so I was delighted when Chips invited me to drop in on the sessions. Chips called in the 827 Thomas Street Band to put down the tracks, so I knew everyone there except Ringo and his beautiful wife, Barbara Bach. When we were introduced by Chips, Ringo was cordial and offered a hearty handshake. Barbara smiled so radiantly with a movie star glow that it nearly made my knees buckle. The sessions lasted throughout March and into April, with Ringo and Barbara going back and forth to Los Angeles for brief periods.

Two things impressed me most about the Ringo session. First, I was surprised at how strong his voice was in its natural state. I had been lead to believe over the years that Ringo's voice required extensive rehabilitation in the studio. Not so. Between takes, Toni Wine spent time with him at the piano, coaching him on specific lines, but his voice was remarkably resonant. Second, I was surprised at how cozy he was with Barbara. Throughout the session, he was extraordinarily relaxed and playful, snuggling during the playbacks with Barbara, who often sat on his lap with her arms around his neck. Never once did I see any indication Ringo was drinking or using drugs.

231

The session was going really well until Ringo and Barbara left town for a few days. While they were gone a columnist for *The Commercial Appeal*, wrote a piece about the session, describing Ringo as an "aging Beatle" who was yesterday's news. I read the column, but thought nothing about it. The columnist was entitled to her opinion.

Later that day, I stopped by 3 Alarm. Chips was livid. He was afraid the column would sabotage the session. His voice was raised. He paced. He called people on the phone. The one thing that he told everyone was, "We've got to do something."

After discussing it most of the afternoon, he decided to picket the newspaper. I tried to talk him out of it. I reminded him that *The Commercial Appeal* had brought him to Memphis. He didn't care, saying simply, "They've turned against me."

I explained to him that the columnist did not represent the newspaper's opinion. He didn't buy that. It must be the newspaper's opinion, he reasoned, or the newspaper would not have printed it. I explained that newspapers print all sorts of opinions. For the first time since meeting Chips, I was totally unable to reason with him. He called for a picket line the following day on the sidewalk in front of *The Commercial Appeal*.

Chips pulled me away from the others in the studio.

"You with me or against me?" he asks.

What could I say? People do silly things for their friends. The next morning I showed up outside the newspaper and walked the picket line with Chips, Toni, their son, Casey, and about two dozen placard carrying marchers. I looked up at the massive glass wall of the third-floor newsroom and saw former colleagues peering out at me. Chips was wrong to picket the newspaper, but it did offer comic relief to a tense situation. Chips really did believe the column would sabotage everything he had worked so hard to build. If carrying a picket sign made him feel better, so be it. Sometimes you do things you know are wrong, but you do them for reasons that you think are right.

Ringo returned for the session. A reporter asked him about the controversy. He said he hadn't read the column.

"Why would I?" he asked the reporter.

Toward the end of the session, Ringo and Barbara gave a party aboard the riverboat Island Queen to show they had no hard feelings toward Memphis. I attended the party, along with Charlie Rich, David Porter and 251 other invited guests. No one was quite sure what to expect when the Island Queen churned out into the massive Mississippi River. It was like any other Memphis party. Lots of barbecue. Lots to drink. Reba and The Portables provided the music.

The highlight of the party occurred later in the evening.

With the river lapping lazily at the bow of the Island Queen, Ringo sat in with the band. The hot, smoke-filled room must have taken him back to the day when the Beatles were playing tiny, people-infested pubs throughout Europe. With a cigarette dangling from his lips, he demonstrated why he is the most celebrated drummer in the world. Within minutes, he had the guests mesmerized.

"I can't believe it," said a girl standing next to me. "I'm really seeing him play."

The girl's amazement was justified. Except for a handful of studio personnel, who actually had ever heard the ex-Beatle play a live set? Not the hundreds of thousands of fans who packed the stadium when the Beatles toured, for they would have been too overwhelmed by the hysteria of the moment to ever hear the music.

A couple of days after the party, I saw Ringo again in the studio and asked him about it. "That was the first time I ever played a riverboat," he said, laughing. He said he was afraid to sample the barbecue. "It's my stomach," he said plaintively, referring to an incident several years ago that almost cost him his life. "Most of the things I eat now have to be broiled. I can't eat spicy food."

Work on the album was drawing to a close. They had sixteen completed songs. Bob Dylan had flown in to sing and play harmony on one of the songs. Chips played me all the songs and I thought it was the best I had ever heard Ringo sing. Chips mixed the album after Ringo left and sent a cassette to his home in Los Angeles.

Ringo telephoned him and told him he had rented a limo so that he and a couple of friends could listen to the tape in style. Unfortunately, there was a problem.

"Wouldn't you know I'd get the only fucking limo in town without a tape deck," he said.

Perhaps it was an omen.

I'm not sure how it happened (I'm not sure *anyone* knows how it happened), but during the next few months the project fell apart. Chips wanted to shop the album. Ringo did not want him to shop the album. John Hartman, a spokesman for Ringo, told reporters Ringo wanted to record tracks with another producer (he tossed out Elton John's name) and wanted to combine the two sessions into one album. I came to the conclusion that Ringo was less concerned about the newspaper column than he was about Chips's reaction to the column. The disaster that Chips feared was becoming a reality.

Ringo's attorneys filed a lawsuit in Atlanta in an effort to stop Chips from selling the album. In the lawsuit, Ringo said he had recorded the album while on alcohol and drugs and considered it an embarrassment. Ringo testified at the trial that he had not signed a formal agreement with Moman. In response, Moman's attorney said Moman would never have agreed to work with Ringo without an agreement. In one light moment, Ringo took the stand and said into the microphone: "Is it on? Are we rolling, Bob?"

During the trial, Toni called me and asked if I would come to Atlanta to testify. I had never seen Ringo drink or use drugs in the studio, so I told her I would be happy to testify about what I had seen. Unfortunately, I could not get a taxi to the airport because of a sudden thunder storm and I missed my flight to Atlanta. I phoned Toni and told her I had rescheduled, but she said they had obtained a continuance and it would not be necessary.

In the end, the court permanently barred the release of the album and ordered Ringo to pay Chips for his time in recording the session. That old Memphis curse, voodoo or otherwise, was again working its black magic. How many sessions could Chips drop and still keep the dream afloat?

*   *   *

Nine-O-One Network's first subscriber was Johnny Cash. The check came in the mail and was signed by John R. Cash himself. Rosanne Cash, his Memphis-born daughter, later told me that Johnny kept a copy of the magazine on his nightstand table. Soon a

234

subscription check arrived in the mail from Jerry Lee Lewis. With supporters like that, how could I go wrong?

From an initial distribution in Memphis and northern Mississippi, circulation expanded to fourteen states by the end of the first year. By the end of 1987, the magazine was sold on newsstands in all 50 states, throughout Canada and in selected cities in Portugal and Japan. Individual distributors reported back that *Nine-O-One* was out-selling *Rolling Stone* in some markets.

Letters arrived daily from Europe, especially from Sweden and Germany. Word filtered in from the Soviet Union that articles from the magazine were being read on the air by the state-owned radio network. Occasionally, tourists from abroad showed up at the door of the *Nine-O-One* offices to pose for pictures with the staff.

As the months went by, it became apparent the Memphis music industry would need more than indigenous talent to re-claim its lost glory. Times had changed. The initial successes at Sun and Stax had been dependent on a symbiotic relationship with radio. But by 1987 radio had changed too much to ever offer that opportunity again. The only way Memphis could duplicate the successes of the past was with a national magazine or television program acting as cheerleader. Since there was no hope of a television program, that left *Nine-O-One* as the sole lifeline to the outside world.

In order to raise money to pay for increased printing costs, I offered 49 percent of the stock I owned in the company to outside investors. Toni Wine was an early investor and supporter, as were a group of Mississippi lawyers, a Memphis physician and a banker, but, by far, the largest investors were my family members. Early returns on newsstand sales were encouraging. The second issue, which featured a photo of Rolling Stone Ron Wood on the cover, sold at an unheard of rate of 60 percent in some markets. Fifteen percent would have been considered excellent.

Ron Wood made the cover after he came to Memphis to appear in a Carl Perkins video. I interviewed him in a bus at the video location. Ron and I sat in the rear of the bus, along with his beautiful wife, Jo. He said the music that came from Memphis had a profound impact on his career.

"It was precious to get good stuff from America," he said. "It was a rare commodity to get a hold of that stuff in England. It was treasured as soon as you got a hold of it, so you did the best with it you could. Whereas the guys over here [U.S.] that were making it and the people who were listening to it, it was right under their nose, so they probably didn't realize it was that precious."

Ron looked at me during the interview as if something was on his mind. You could sense the wheels turning inside his head. Finally, he said, "Don't I know you from somewhere?" Then his face brightened. "I know what it is," he says, looking at Jo. "He's got eyes just like Chuck Leavell."

Jo smiled. "I didn't know you were paying that much attention to Chuck's eyes," she said, laughing.

Deborah Allen, the Memphis-born singer/songwriter who scored a big hit with "Baby, I Lied," was the cover story for the third issue. I had met her before leaving *The Commercial Appeal,* when I wrote a front page story about her efforts to stage a rally in Memphis' Liberty Bowl stadium in support of South African Bishop Tutu. The rally never took place (stadium officials said it would damage the playing field), but one result of the story was that I direct-dialed Bishop Tutu at his home in South Africa and spoke to him about Deborah.

Tutu said he had previously received a "heart-warming" call from Deborah at a time when he was under particularly severe harassment. He said the call meant a lot to him.

Deborah and I became friends after that and I shot the cover photo of her at her home in Nashville. Later she visited me in Memphis, where her parents lived, and we did some interviews for the magazine with the local TV stations and I shot some additional photographs of her on the balcony of my apartment. I used the photos on a subsequent story about Deborah, after she recorded a song called "Telepathy" that Prince wrote and produced for her.

Other cover stories focused on Aimee Mann, who was a real bitch to the reporter that was asked to interview her, Robert Cray, Gregg Allman, who called me from a studio in Miami, thrashed his former wife Cher, then asked me not to use his comments (he just wanted to get it off his chest), David Bowie, Ann and Nancy Wilson, who gave me one of my favorite interviews, the Bangles,

236

who gave me one of my most playful interviews, and Dan Fogelberg, who saw the magazine on a newsstand in New England and called me to do an interview, despite a reputation for disliking the press.

Nine-O-One was unique in a lot of ways. It was one of the first glossy, 4-color magazines to do feature articles on country artists. It was the first to target a Baby Boomer audience with a mixture of musical styles. We ran articles on the O'Kanes and Robert Cray alongside articles on Cinderella and Europe. We were the first publication to take a look at sexual harassment in the music industry. We ran a cover story on the subject in 1988. We did the story after a female employee at a local studio came into our offices complaining of treatment she had received by her employer. One evening after work, she said, the studio owner held her down on the floor and ejaculated on her clothing. The next day she confronted the man, only to have her outrage rejected as unreasonable. After the confrontation, as if to prove his point, the studio owner walked around the studio with his penis exposed when they were alone in the building.

When the woman rejected subsequent advances, she was fired. She filed a complaint with the federal Equal Employment Opportunity Commission. An official there told her they had received similar complaints from fourteen other women, but there was nothing the agency could do since the studio was too small to qualify for intervention.

The world was again taking a look at Memphis music, but, unfortunately, the internecine warfare that had begun after Chips Moman's return escalated. Studio owners and musicians exchanged barbs in the press. Mayor Hackett was besieged with complaints because of his involvement in arranging for the city to lease Chips studio space for one dollar a year. Because I had brought Chips to Memphis, *Nine-O-One* became the subject of an unofficial advertising boycott. Only Graceland, a couple of local studios and a video maker advertised in the magazine. All the other ads came from Nashville and national advertisers. The Memphis music community was once again aiming all its firepower at its musical foot.

Stevie Ray Vaughan stood at the rear entrance of the Peabody, the grand old hotel that serves as Memphis' last link to a more genteel era. He shyly backpedaled into the shadows as fashionably dressed yuppie couples brushed past. Wearing a brightly colored parka with Mexican designs and a black western-style hat, he did anything but blend into his surroundings.

Incredibly no one seemed to notice him.

Stevie was in town to record an album titled *In Step*. Fate would earmark it his last solo effort. A second album, *Family Style*, was recorded in Memphis with his brother Jimmie. I was at the Peabody to pick up Stevie for an interview for Pulsebeat—The Voice of the Heartland, the radio syndication I had begun in 1988. We produced two weekly programs, a 30-minute country show and a 60-minute blues show we did in partnership with radio station KFFA in Helena.

Before heading out for Memphis, Stevie made his publicist, Charles Comer of New York, promise that he would arrange no interviews while he was recording the album; but I had interviewed him on previous occasions and Comer urged him to do the Pulsebeat interview. Stevie, who was registered at the hotel under the name, Ben T. Fender, agreed to do it. It would be the only interview he granted while recording the album. We set the interview up for the afternoon to allow time for him to sleep late after the previous night's session at the studio and to allow him time to attend an Alcoholics Anonymous meeting. Stevie had been drug and alcohol free for four years. He fought a daily battle to keep it that way.

On the way to the studio, Stevie asked if he could smoke. I was a non-smoker and no one had ever smoked in my car, but I told him I didn't mind. He seemed to be enjoying the cigarette until he pulled out the ashtray and saw that it was clean as an unused dinner plate. After that he sort of lost interest in the cigarette and held it at arm's length like it was a sparkler someone had given him at a Fourth of July picnic.

On stage, Stevie had a power-charged presence that made him seem larger than life. Attending a Stevie Ray Vaughan concert was a little like strapping yourself into a roller coaster: It was not a ride during which you chatted and exchanged pleasantries. It was more of a foot-stomping, arm waving, screaming-at-the-top-of-voice descent into fire and brimstone. In person, Stevie was just the opposite. He was soft-spoken and unpretentious. He was polite and laughed easily, sometimes flashing a down-home grin that betrayed his rural Texas roots. At his core, he was a nice guy.

Stevie marveled at the spiritual energy that had made Memphis distinctive in the minds of musicians the world over. He gazed out at the streets as if they were the yellow brick road to Oz.

"This is where it all started," he says, looking in the direction of a shopping mall but seeing, instead, some sweltering primeval pool of musical history. Memphis was a mystery to him. He asked lots of questions. He felt the power, but he couldn't help but wonder what it would be like to be *of the blood*. That was why he recorded in Memphis: To tap into the powerful bloodline of blues and rock 'n' roll. For him the magic was real.

During the interview at the studio, this notion of feeling the music came up often. That was the greatest lesson he had learned from listening to the old masters, he said: "Feel what you play before you play it and then feel it while you play it. I learned early on that if I didn't really care about what I played, it would sound that way. Money pays the bills, but it's not the best thing in life. What we go through inside, that's really it."

Stevie was pleased with the way the album was going. "It's the first record we've ever done sober," he says. "A lot of us (in music) are alcoholics and addicts. But that condition is not just art-related. It's rampant through all parts of society. A lot of artists are under pressure to be larger than life. Thank God some of us have the chance to live through it. Some of us haven't. I'm glad to be among the fortunate ones."

One of Stevie's favorite songs on the new album was one that happened by accident. They were at rehearsal trying to decide what to put on the album. They ran out of ideas. A quietness fell over the room. Stevie drifted over to a corner, his guitar strapped around his neck. Suddenly, the others heard a musical explosion from across the room. "I just felt I had to play this thing," says Stevie, of the song he would name "Travis Walk." "I had never heard it before or thought of it before. It just sort of exploded. It's one of those 'get it' songs."

The interview went so well, we expanded it to a two-hour program. George Hays, who did the on-air interview, subsequently told me that Stevie was one of the nicest celebrities he had ever met. Stevie might have been a badass guitar picker on stage; in person, he was a genuinely nice guy. During one of the breaks in the interview, George and Stevie struck up a conversation about their fathers. George's father has just passed away. Stevie told him how much he missed his own father.

After I dropped Stevie back off at the hotel, I received a call from Comer. He said he had talked to Stevie and he had told him he enjoyed doing the interview.

"Really!" I said, impressed.

"Why wouldn't he?' says Comer. "Don't forget you were involved with the blues, everything he was into." He said Stevie appreciated the work I was doing to boast Memphis music and wanted to do anything he could to help me.

* * *

Like his brother, Jimmie Vaughan was also a fan of Memphis music. In fact, it was his idea for the Fabulous Thunderbirds to record in Memphis. Explained Jimmie: "I had never recorded here, and we had done it in London, in Los Angeles, in New York and in Austin and Dallas, so we just decided to do it here."

Dave Edmunds, who produced the T-Birds' "Hot Number" album in Memphis, said he wanted to work in Memphis because of "the people, the players."

"Amen," said Jimmie. "It's magic here."

While they were recording *Hot Number* at Ardent, I dropped by the studio several times. Once, during a break, Jimmie, lead singer Kim Wilson, Dave Edmunds, their manager, Mark Proctor, and I, piled into a minivan for a trip to Beale Street. The other two members of the T-Birds, Fran Christina and Preston Hubbard, had returned to Austin.

As the heavy-footed driver sped downtown, tossing his passengers about liked loose cabbages, Kim peered out the window. "Man, the people in this town drive like crazy," he says. I pointed out that Memphis, according to insurance company statistics, was the traffic-light accident capital of the country.

240

Kim sighed and eyed the stop-and-go signals with new interest.

We went to a restaurant where we ate barbecue in a back room. Joe Savarin, the founder of the Blues Foundation, presented them with an award, after which a lady in a white dress strolled up to Kim and cooed, "Sing for me." Seconds later, Kim waved good-bye and dashed through the kitchen into the night air.

Back at the studio, Dave said he had been looking forward to solving the mystery of the Memphis Horns. "I always thought the horns on the old Stax records sounded so unique and I wondered how they did it," he says. "Now I've worked with them and I still don't know."

"With a horn player, you can't settle for anything less than the best and those guys just blew me away," says Kim. "It was entertaining to watch them work. I just sat there, drank beer and watched them play. I told myself, 'You'd better keep your mouth shut; anything you can think of, they probably thought of years ago.'"

Before leaving town, Jimmie told me, "Somehow I don't think you're supposed to have as much fun as we're having here."

The T-Birds recorded two albums in Memphis; then they broke up, perhaps a casualty of the "Memphis curse."

* * *

Between the two shows, country and blues, Pulsebeat—The Voice of the Heartland had about 100 radio stations participating in the syndication. According to figures published by *R&R*, that made us a mid-size network. We weren't the biggest, but we weren't the smallest either. Geographically, our stations were spread out from New Jersey to Washington State and up into Canada, where we had a number of stations.

Each week, Kim Spangler, my main announcer, and I wrote two scripts, did two interviews and programmed an hour-and-half of radio time. A tall, leggy blonde, who had worked at both AOR and country stations as a deejay, Kim always made a good impression on the artists we interviewed. Her off-the-wall sense of humor and infectious laughter kept her interviewees on their toes. Working with Kim also kept me on my toes. She was not shy about letting me know if I screwed up. As a result, we became the closest of friends.

241

Most of our interviews for the country show were done in Nashville. For each session, we lined up a half-dozen or so interviews and rented a studio on Music Row to record the shows. Doing it that way actually created a more relaxed atmosphere for the interviews. The artists would wait in an outside office and visit with each other and renew old friendships. By the time they got in the studio, they were so distracted from the reason of the visit they made better interview subjects.

When I heard an album from a new artist I thought had potential, I liked to give them a break. One of those new artists was Garth Brooks. Mark Carter, the head of publicity at Capitol, sent me Garth's debut album with a note that he thought Garth was going to be a star. Garth's publicist, Pam Lewis, also contacted me about having Garth on the show. When he showed up at the studio, he was awkward and self-effacing, sort of in the early Elvis tradition, but he was so sincere during the interview it enabled us to put together a strong show. Unfortunately, when we sent the show out to our stations, I received nasty notes from several program directors who threatened to drop the show if I ever again sent them artists like Garth Brooks. It was obvious to any imbecile, one of the program directors insisted, that Garth Brooks had no talent and was going nowhere in country music.

Over a two year period, we did programs on every major country star in the business. We did some of Kathy Mattea's earliest interviews. Same with Patty Lovelace and Kix Brooks of Brooks & Dunn. We did several shows on Kathy. Once she showed up in a skin-tight aerobics outfit. Doing radio shows with country artists was never dull. Sometimes they performed live in the studio for us. Mary Chapin Carpenter sang and played guitar on one of our shows, as did Skip Ewing.

All of our blues shows were recorded in Memphis. Some we taped at Wilkerson's Sound Studio on Park and others at our own mini studio located in our office. Sunshine Sonny Payne, George Hays and Kim took turns interviewing the artists. I usually escorted the artists to the studio if they were not familiar with Memphis.

Once we scheduled an interview with Canadian bluesman Jeff Healy. When I went to the Radisson Hotel to pick him up, Healy and his manager approached me in the lobby. If you are familiar with Healy's work, you know he is blind. After his manager introduced us, he said, "Well, I'll see you later," and walked off. I couldn't believe it. I had no experience with the visually handicapped. "My car's on the street outside," I said.

"Just show me the way," says Healy. "Let me have your elbow."

With that, I led him out into the street and to the car. I took him to our office, where Kim conducted the interview. When we returned to the car, I reached out and pulled on the door handle. Before I could say anything, he said, "I locked it when I got out."

Our blues network was a mixed bag. We had both black-oriented and AOR stations. That meant one week we might feature B.B. King and the next week we would have Stevie Ray Vaughan. In 1989 a new female singer named Melissa Etheridge came to Memphis for a concert. Her debut album was doing well on AOR stations, so I scheduled her for an interview. No one knew much about her then. Based on her first album, we thought she had a future. As I did for all the others, I showed up at the hotel to give Melissa a lift to the studio.

As Healy had done, she left her manager behind at the hotel, but, unlike Healy and all the others, who to a person had been friendly and talkative, Melissa was standoffish. She insisted on riding in the back seat so I would appear to be her chauffer. At the studio, she warmed up and bantered with the announcer. I asked her if she would sing a song from her album. She did, accompanying herself on a 50-year-old Martin I had brought to the studio for that purpose. It was an outstanding performance.

After I returned Melissa to the hotel, her manager called and invited me to a backstage party after the concert. At that time in her career, there were rumors she was a lesbian, but she had not publicly acknowledged it, as she has since done. I knew she was gay, especially after meeting her and sensing that slight male hostility that sometimes radiates from lesbians.

When I went backstage after the concert, Melissa was friendly and stood and held my hand while she talked to me. That gesture seemed to annoy her traveling companion, who was seated nearby. It is to my discredit that I held Melissa's hand much longer than I should have for the sole purpose of annoying her possessive companion. Oh, how she glared at me. Several years later, when Melissa came out of the closet, I was glad to hear that she had. Looking back, I realize her apparent unfriendliness and desire to ride in the back seat was meant more as a defensive gesture than an expression of any star complex she possessed.

*   *   *

Chips Moman had good days and he had bad days. By 1988 the entire city had turned against him. Projects were sabotaged. Enemies plotted ways to drive him from town. Casey came home from school upset that friends that used to like him now ridiculed him. There were lots of tears. Chips made regular sweeps at the studio to eradicate hidden microphones. The only secure room in the studio, he felt, was the control room. The atmosphere was so tense, I started packing a .380-automatic, a midget known as the bulldog, in my back pocket whenever I visited the studio.

Chips made lots of deals when he returned to Memphis. Deals for a studio. Deals for equipment. Deals for restaurants. Deals for just about anything you could think of. There is no one more savvy than Chips to the twists and turns of deal making in the music business—he is fond of saying the biggest challenge in working with a roomful of music executives is to figure out which one of them is honest—but beyond that sphere he was totally out of his league. Part of it, I think, was social. During the 1960s and early 1970s, he had no existence beyond the studio. He didn't go to parties. He didn't socialize. He was so isolated that he probably had no idea who the mayor was. His marriage to Toni had a lot to do with the change. Toni is gregarious. She has needs of a social nature that Chips does not. To please her, he tried to fit in socially when he returned to Memphis. That was easy when the mayor and the head of the largest bank were wining and dining him at every turn. Unfortunately his newfound social life put him into contact with dangerous people who saw him as just another bag of meat to hoist up on the rack. They couldn't have known how stubborn Chips is, how when told to bend he'd would rather break.

Since his return to the city, Chips had recorded three albums in Memphis—with the Class of '55, Bobby Womack and Ringo Starr—and while all three had been solid creative efforts, none had restored him to his former glory. One of the constant criticisms he received from local musicians was that he was doing nothing for the careers of Reba & the Portables, the only Memphis group he had signed when he moved back. People said he was sitting on the group. Even Becky, the lead singer, expressed doubts to me about Chips commitment to her career. Nothing could have been further from the truth. Chips tried hard to get Becky a deal with a major label. So did I. He probably didn't tell her about all the rejections (and there were plenty) for the same reason I didn't tell her. It would have destroyed her morale. Plus, for Chips, there was some pride involved. He didn't want to admit to Becky that he couldn't get her a record deal.

Somehow Chips kept making music. In 1988 he went to Texas to record an album with Willie Nelson. He liked working with Willie. It was quick (Willie usually nailed a song on the first take), relatively painless (Willie's ego didn't need massaging) and usually profitable (Chip's *Always On My Mind* album with Willie was one of the most successful in country music history).

Chips brought the album back to Memphis and mixed it at 3 Alarm. One day I got a call from Chips. He was at a house he had purchased on Horseshoe Lake across the river in Arkansas. It was summer and he and Toni were having a cook-out for a few friends. A free meal sounded good to me. It was hot that day, pushing 100 degrees, and we spent much of the day on the lake in Chips' boat. Toni and Chips bickered constantly, which, for them, was an indication they were still close. If they ever stopped bickering, and withdrew unto themselves, that would be an indication the relationship was over.

After the other friends left, Chips played me the Willie Nelson album he had just recorded. In a moment of supreme irony, it had been titled *What A Wonderful World.* The album consisted of old standards such as "Spanish Eyes," "Blue Moon" and, of course, the title song. The album had a healing quality about it. Had he recorded it with an unconscious wish to remake the world around him?

When "What A Wonderful World" came up, Toni got up and went into the kitchen (was the irony too painful for her to bear?). Chips and I sat in silence and listened as Willie, as only Willie can, extolled the colors of the rainbow and the cries of newborn babies. The last song on the album was "Ac-cent-tchu-ate The Positive." When the album was over, there was not a dry eye in the house.

Despite all the craziness of 1988-1989, there were plenty of good times. Early one evening I got a call from Chips. Did I want to go on a boat ride?

"Tonight?" I said, looking at my watch.

Well, why not? I drove over to Chips' house and we hooked up a massive pontoon boat to his Blazer. Going with us were songwriter David Porter, whose hits "Soul Man," "Hold On, I'm Coming" and "When Something Is Wrong With My Baby," had influenced an entire generation and another black gentleman, whose name I don't recall. I do remember he owned one of the local Wendy's franchises.

By the time we reached the lake, it was past midnight. It was a small lake located just across the state line in Mississippi. It was just the sort of lake featured in horror movies. The boat ramp was deserted when we arrived, but between the four of us we were able to lower the pontoon boat into the lake and get underway. For several hours we churned up and down the lake, talking about nothing in particular. There were no lights on the boat, but there was a partial moon and we could at least see where we were going.

Things were going great until I decided to tell my snake story. When I was growing up in Mississippi, I went fishing every week with my grandfather during the summer months. This lake we went to was famous for its bream and for its plentiful supply of poisonous cottonmouths. One day this girl was water skiing on the lake when the boat hit a massive bed of cottonmouths. The boat stalled in the water and the girl sank into a swarm of cottonmouths. She died before she reached the hospital. After I told the story, no one said a word. The water lapped at the pontoons.

"Speaking of the devil," says Chips, pointing out across the water.

Ahead of the boat in the moonlight was the black triangular head of a cottonmouth slithering across the surface of the water.

"That's it," says David. "I want to go home."

So we did.

246

*   *   *

One of the first things Chips did when he moved back to Memphis was to put together a joint venture with Chappell and Intersong Music Group, an international song publisher that owned more than 200,000 song titles. It had been twenty years since Memphis had a major song publisher in its midst. Ira Jaffe, a senior vice president with Chappell's office in Los Angeles, told me the venture would enable his company to tap into the Memphis talent pool. He explained: "Chips Moman is a winner. When I first discussed it with him, we both said the Otis Reddings, the Elvises, the Box Tops—they couldn't all have just disappeared."

That was in 1985. By 1987 Chips was forced to release the Memphis songwriters he had signed to the new publishing company underwritten by Chappell/Intersong. No sooner did that happen than he was hit with a phalanx of lawsuits over the construction of the studio. Contractors said he hadn't paid his bills. Chips countersued. He'd pay his bills when they finished the work. Then, when you thought nothing else possibly could go wrong, some of the songwriters filed lawsuits against Chips. Lawyers were thick as thieves. You couldn't walk without tripping over one.

One day we were sitting in the control room of the studio drinking hot chocolate when the telephone rang. Chips' grimaced as he spoke on the phone. His responses were short. The conversation was brief. He hung up the phone and hurried out of the room. Seeing that he was in distress, I followed him out into the kitchen area. He poured himself more hot chocolate. His hands were shaking.

"What's wrong?" I asked.

"My ex-wife is in the hospital," he said, his eyes glistening. "She's dying."

Chips was devastated. He looked desperate.

"I'm going to the hospital," he said.

"You don't need to drive in your condition," I said. "I'll take you."

With the cup of hot chocolate still in his hands, we drove to the hospital. It was located a few blocks west of the old Sun Record studios. Chips' daughter, Monique, was in the waiting room with other family members when we arrived. A few minutes later Toni showed up. The waiting room was small and it quickly filled with

247

family members. Chips left to visit his ex-wife. Toni comforted the other family members in his absence. The prognosis was bleak. She had several heart attacks and had to be resuscitated after the last one. We stayed at the hospital for a few hours, and then I took Chips back to the studio. He kept shaking his head the way people do when bad things happen. Life was closing in on him from every direction. His ex-wife lingered for a while longer, and then gave up the fight. Her body was cremated and her ashes strewn along the banks of the Mississippi River.

I wondered how much more Chips could take without cracking up.

*   *   *

In December 1988, Roy Orbison was visiting his mother in Hendersonville, Tennessee, when he suffered a heart attack. He was taken by ambulance to Hendersonville Hospital, but he could not be revived and he was pronounced dead just before midnight. He was only 52 years of age. Subsequently, his widow, Barbara Orbison, formed her own music publishing company in Nashville, Still Working Music. In 2010 her company was awarded BMI's Song of the Year for Taylor Swift's "You Belong With Me." She died a year later of pancreatic cancer, just one day short of the 23rd anniversary of her husband's death.

*   *   *

By 1989 *Nine-O-One Network* had suspended publication for lack of advertising revenues. The radio syndication, Pulsebeat— The Voice of the Heartland, was holding on by a slender thread. The death of a publication is always a sad affair, whether it is the *Press-Scimitar* or *Nine-O-One Network*, but it was especially so in this instance because with the demise of the magazine went any hopes of a reborn music industry in Memphis.

But I kept fighting.

One day, after spending a half day bemoaning what appeared to be a hopeless situation, Don Nix and I decided to start our own record label. We named it Pulsebeat Records, a spinoff from the radio syndication. We didn't have any money (I cashed in my life insurance policy to put up my share), but we had lots of good ideas. By working on "spec" with studios and session players who believed in Memphis music, we hoped to record albums we could place with the majors for distribution. Stax had done it nearly thirty years ago. Maybe it could happen again.

"The vast majority of the music heard on radio today can trace its roots back to Memphis," I told a newspaper reporter, then brashly added: "That makes Memphis an ideal place for an independent label. Simply put: We're going to pick up where Stax Records left off."

Don's enthusiasm equaled my own. He told a reporter: "When someone sees a record label with the word Pulsebeat on it, I want them to know they have a quality product."

For our first artist, we chose a talented Beale Street bluesman named Don McMinn. He had become a fixture on the street, where his four-piece group appeared nightly as the house band at the Rum Boogie Cafe, a popular restaurant and bar. Over the years he had recorded with an impressive assortment of artists, including John Mayall, Memphis Slim and Jerry Lee Lewis. In 1989 there was a "roots" mentality in country music. We asked him what he would think about recording a country album. He said he had always wanted to do a country album.

For the session, we put together a solid group of local musicians, including Tommy McClure, then playing bass with Kris Kristofferson's band, drummer Greg Morrow, who played on the road with Amy Grant, keyboardist Doyle Newmyer and an unknown steel guitarist named Robby Turner. Chips gave us spec time at 3 Alarm and his daughter, Monique, and Becky Russell came in to sing background.

Nix and I assembled a solid list of songs, one of which, "Black Like Me," we thought could be a hit. Unfortunately, Nashville record executives didn't agree. Something about a 40-something blues singer doing country didn't sit right with them. I met with executives from all the labels. None would pick the album up for distribution. The only thing good that came from the McMinn session was that Chips dropped by to listen to what we were doing. He was so impressed with Robby Turner he hired him to play on the *Highwaymen 2* album. That opened other doors for Robby. He moved to Nashville and became known as one of the best steel guitar players in country music.

Dave Edmunds, left, Kim Wilson in Memphis
Photo © James L. Dickerson

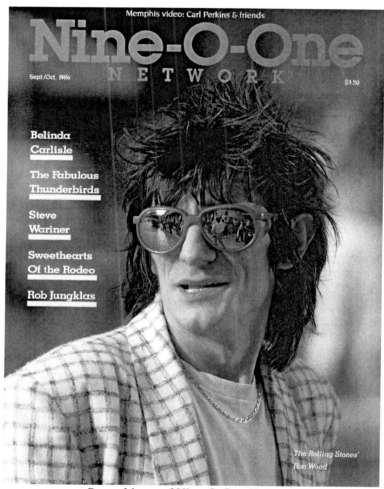

Memphis video: Carl Perkins & friends

Nine-O-One
NETWORK

Sept./Oct. 1986

$3.50

Belinda
Carlisle

The Fabulous
Thunderbirds

Steve
Wariner

Sweethearts
Of the Rodeo

Rob Jungklas

The Rolling Stones'
Ron Wood

Second issue of Nine-O-One Network

ANGRY SONGWRITERS TAKE ON A GIANT

Nine-O-One
NETWORK™

February 1988

$2.50 USA
$3 Canada

SEXUAL HARASSMENT
in the music industry —
How to fight back

OTIS REDDING
Stax survivors
look back 20 years

JACKSON BROWNE
Is Nicaragua
the new Vietnam?

PLATINUM BLONDE
Canada's answer
to white funk

**WHO'S
HIP IN '88**
Julie Brown
Little John Chrisley
The Insiders
John Kilzer
Gary Moore
Vienna

A Hoss
Named
WAYLON

**HEART'S
ANN and NANCY
WILSON**
Broken Heart
until 1992?

February 1988 issue of Nine-O-One Network

Reba Russell, c. mid1980s
Photo © James L. Dickerson

Jimi Jamison, lead singer Survivor
Photo © James L. Dickerson

CHAPTER 13

The 1990s:
Stevie Ray Gets It (Even If No One Else Does)

In the spring of 1990, Shelby County Sheriff Jack Owens's face was blown away by a shotgun blast in the parking lot of a service station. There were no witnesses. Owens was the first law-enforcement officer in Memphis and Shelby County ever to attempt a real war on drugs. He made the apprehension of drug dealers his first priority. A song was written about him. He was on his way to becoming a folk hero.

Then, suddenly and without warning, his face was erased. Oddly, he seemed to know it was coming. In the months preceding his death, he expressed fears of assassination. He started his car each morning with a remote-control device. After an investigation, his death was ruled a suicide.

Murder is one of the biggest causes of suicide in Memphis.

By any measure, 1990 was one of the worst years in Memphis music history. Chips Moman packed up and left town, again. Michael Grehl died of complications from the stroke he suffered in 1985. Forrest "Skip" Wilkerson, owner of the studio where "Pulsebeat" taped its shows, died unexpectedly at his home. Stevie Ray Vaughan was killed in a helicopter crash. *Nine-O-One Network* and Pulsebeat—The Voice of the Heartland went out of business. It was as if a bulldozer had leveled the last vestiges of musical creativity in the city.

No one was surprised when Chips left town. First Tennessee Bank sued him for defaulting on $2 million in bank loans. In the latter part of 1989, Chips sold 3 Alarm to a used-car dealer to raise money for his mounting legal problems, but by 1990 Chips was suing the car dealer to recover missed payments. The used car dealer countersued Chips for removing equipment from the studio. First Tennessee Bank foreclosed on Chips' home. Chips filed for Chapter 11 bankruptcy.

The insanity climaxed in November when Chips wound up in court with the used-car dealer in a dispute over ownership of the studio. During a hearing to determine ownership of certain equipment Chips removed from the studio, Chips jumped to his feet when the presiding judge, Chancellor D. J. Alissandratos, ordered him to return the equipment until a final ruling could be made. Chips protested. Alissandratos ordered Chips jailed for contempt of court. Said the judge, referring to a hit song of the 1960s: "Since we're talking rock music, Mr. Moman, I might borrow from the song to remind you, as you go to jail—"I Fought the Law and the Law Won."'

After 48 hours in jail, Chips returned to the courtroom in handcuffs. He apologized to the court, saying: "I had a bad day . . . I'm trying to learn. I do admit I sometimes lose my temper and I apologize."

By that time, public opinion had turned against Chips with a vengeance. *The Commercial Appeal* continued coverage of events, balanced coverage, I thought, but reporters never looked below the surface to report *why* Chips was fighting for his life. In a story in the *Memphis Flyer*, a weekly tabloid, the front-page headline read: "Good-bye, Mr. Chips: The City Fathers brought him back to save Memphis music. But will Chips Moman just take the money and run?"

"What money?" Chips kept saying to me.

His bafflement over what was happening to him was exceeded only by his frustration at his inability to do anything about it. He was under siege, but couldn't fight back, couldn't even defend his good name, because of fears he would endanger his family's safety. He was fighting a losing battle against an enemy that demanded anonymity.

Finally, by mid-year, worn to a frazzle, with no studio to work in, no house to live in, no friends, a son coming home from school each day in tears, a hostile media, and lawsuits at every turn, his health deteriorating (he had crippling episodes of arthritis), Chips, arguably one of the most successful record producers in American history, packed up his family and returned to his farm in Nashville.

Contacted by a reporter from *The Commercial Appeal*, Chips's Atlanta lawyer said Chips was tired of being a whipping boy: "He's had about all the fun he can take here."

256

Chips left town without a word to me. I got a telephone call from him several months later. He was driving aimlessly around Atlanta. He called me on his car phone. He just wanted to say hello. He didn't know what he was going to do. He was a man without a country. I wanted to tell him I was sorry I had ever encouraged him to move back to Memphis, but some things are better left unsaid.

*   *   *

When I heard the news that Stevie Ray Vaughan had been killed in a helicopter crash, I called Charles Comer. As a publicist, Comer was a heavyweight, working with the Rolling Stones, even the Beatles, but all those years of press savvy were inadequate to deflect the emotion he felt over the loss of Stevie.

There was anguish in his voice when he spoke of the death, or rather when he spoke of a life marked by a constant struggle for sobriety. The tragedy of Vaughan's death was that it came at the moment he had just put his life together. He was sober, in love with the girl of his dreams, and enjoying the first commercial success of his career. He told Comer: "I've been given a second chance in life, and not many people get a second chance." After the accident, *Billboard* called Comer to tell him Vaughan's *In Step* album was going to No. 14 with a bullet.

"We've never been higher than 31 in our lives," Comer told me. "It's selling fantastically."

Driving home that night, I pulled out the ashtray in my car. There it was—Stevie's cigarette butt, just as he had left it, unfinished, a burned out reminder of life's short fuse.

*   *   *

Although *Nine-O-One* and the radio syndication, were no longer in business (the worst thing about losing Pulsebeat was laying off my announcer Kim Spangler, who had become a close friend), I kept the office open to focus on Pulsebeat, the record label. There was a staff of one. Through an unlikely series of events, I was approached by a delegation of Russians who had come to the United States from Moscow to network with music executives.

They wanted to know if I would represent a rockabilly band

named Mister Twister. They had talked to a Los Angeles producer, Richard Podolor, best known for his work with Three Dog Night, Alice Cooper and Black Oak Arkansas, about working with a hard-rock group, Galaxy. I spoke to Podolor and he said he had heard Galaxy perform in Los Angeles and was very interested in working with them.

I was intrigued, so I asked the Russians to send tapes and photos. Visually, Mister Twister was a throwback to the fifties: black leather, tattoos, rebel flags, lots of attitude. Musically, they were right on target. They sent me a videotape of "Blue Suede Shoes." Valery Lysenko, the drummer, played standing up, rockabilly style, and bassist Oleg Usamov, a former English student at Moscow University, sang in decent enough English. I thought they were salable to an American audience.

Their spokesman was Erkin Touzmuhammad, a Moscow-based music journalist. Based on a long series of telephone conversations, Erkin and I became friends. For a Communist turned capitalist, he possessed just the right mix of cynicism and idealism. There was no middle ground for him. By the time the delegation made it back to their American base in Brighton Beach, New York, I agreed to represent them and contracts were signed before they returned to Moscow.

Politically, the situation appealed to me very much. This was before the Second Revolution. The Soviet Union was still in place. Mister Twister and a number of other groups were under the direction of Ovanes Melik-Pashayev, one of the top record producers in the Soviet Union. His production company, Moscow Rock Organization, had created controversy in 1989 when they held a "Rock Fest" at the nuclear test site at Semipolatsinsk to protest nuclear testing. Not only were they playing Memphis music in Moscow nightclubs, they were duplicating American peace marches. Valery, who was nicknamed Hedgehog, was enrolled in KGB Special College when he was given an ultimatum by school officials: He could be a rock 'n' roll drummer or a KGB agent, but not both. Valery chose rock 'n' roll. That took guts in 1989.

The Nashville *Tennessean* ran an item about Mister Twister in June 1990 that credited me with becoming "the first American music mogul to bring a Russian band to the U.S. to record."

While the Russians worked on their English, I put together a "girls" group made up of Becky Russell, Pamela Byrd, a former Miss Memphis who had a girlish upper range to her voice, and Michelle Necaise, a tall, 20-year-old, blue-eyed vocal ringer for Donna Summer. I named the group Heat Wave.

At the time, I was helping Jim Stewart and Bobby Manuel with a fabulous R&B group, The Coolers. They had been around for several years, and Duck Dunn had been one of the group's charter members. When I told them about Heat Wave, they expressed an interest in coproducing the group, using musicians from The Coolers as needed. We used their studio, the Daily Planet, an analog-equipped music factory tucked away on a side street in a black neighborhood. Working with Jim was an experience unto itself. Bobby did the guitar work on the tracks, proving that he is still the best guitarist in Memphis, but he and Jim alternated on the board. Jim has a terrific ear for vocals, and I was amazed at how precise he was at giving direction to the women.

By 1990, Jim's full beard had grayed and he had a professorial look about him. He resembled Sigmund Freud, a stark contrast to his high-rolling, bell-bottomed look in the seventies. Watching him work was a treat. When the music played, his foot tapped and his head bobbed with the beat. It had been fourteen years since the rug had been pulled out from beneath him at Stax and he was still trying, still giving it his best shot.

Nancy Hart, a feature reporter for WMC-TV, the local NBC affiliate, asked if she could do a story on the group. Jim didn't want to do it at first. He had done few interviews over the years. I don't think he had ever done a TV interview. He agreed to do the interview as a favor to me, I suspect, and I arranged for Nancy to bring a camera crew into the studio.

"These guys are great, they can really sing," Jim said during the interview, giving Memphis TV viewers their first small-screen look, ever, at one of the giants of American music. "Nothing like this has ever come out of Memphis."

Jim said music was a "now" kind of business: "You can't live in the past if you want to stay in the business. You have to be mainstream, rather than recreate a Memphis sound."

259

Nancy left knowing she had something, not just for the evening news, but for the archives. The story ran in two parts. We were all optimistic about the group. The time seemed right for another girl group, but when I shopped the demos in New York and L.A., I ran into a brick wall. Girl groups are a thing of the past, they told me. Nine months later, Wilson Phillips, a group very similar to Heat Wave, had the number-one record in the nation.

Undeterred, I went to Nashville to pitch Mister Twister. Russians singing rockabilly! The executives on Music Row, even the ones I had known for years, just didn't get it. Let me get this straight, one label head said—you want me to put out a record of Commies singing rockabilly? No, they're not Communists, I explained, they're just the opposite. In spirit, at least, they're as American as apple pie.

"Interesting," he said. "Commies, huh? Very interesting!"

I shook my head in disbelief.

I kept in touch with Erkin by fax and that Christmas he phoned from Moscow to wish me happy holidays. Muscovites didn't have a long history of phoning Christmas greetings to American friends, so I appreciated the call. I told Erkin the prospects didn't look good for Mister Twister, but I promised to stay on the case.

*   *   *

Can anyone doubt that an ancient curse lurks in the pyramids of the Memphis music pharaohs? Bob Pittman's QMI label ran into trouble before it ever got off the ground. Ella Brooks, its first signee, evaporated before an album could be recorded. Shortly after the release of Jimmy Davis's first single, "Kick the Wall," QMI had a falling out with MCA, their distributor. Davis's album was left dangling in the wind, even as his video was played every three hours on MTV. With no promotion and distribution, sales were zilch. Then Pittman affiliated with Chrysalis Records. Davis recorded a second album for QMI, but Pittman was unable to reach an agreement with Chrysalis on international distribution and Davis's second album was never released.

"We had spent a year making the (first) record and then went through the process of getting it out—and all of a sudden it was over," says Davis. The only money he realized from the two albums, he says, was from the advances, which he describes as small. "Part of me says that's the business, and I know it is, but, yeah, I got a raw deal. Some powerful men over money and pride sacrificed me and my music."

Jimmy Davis wasn't the only one having problems. After years of wrangling with Jerry Lee Lewis over payment of more than $3.7 million in back taxes, the Internal Revenue Service seized his possessions from his Nesbit, Mississippi, home while the singer was touring in Europe. After the seizure, Jerry Lee, his wife, Kerrie, and their six-year-old son, Lee, sought refuge in Dublin, Ireland. While Jerry Lee worked on his autobiography, Kerrie sang at a tavern named Bad Bob's.

When the IRS announced plans to sell Jerry Lee's possessions at auction, Kerrie returned to Memphis. She hired a lawyer, who claimed that many of the possessions taken by the IRS belonged to Kerrie and were not subject to seizure. The lawyer got an injunction to prevent the agency from selling the items until Kerrie could inspect them.

A videotape of the seized items was shown in court. When images of Disney videos and Mickey Mouse bed sheets came into view, Kerrie brushed tears from her eyes.

"Jerry doesn't sleep on Mickey Mouse sheets," she said, her voice breaking.

In addition to items belonging to their son, Kerrie asked for a collection of photographs and trophies. Kerrie told the court the trophies belonged to a park commission team she had organized and named The Killers. The baseball team, she told the court in a halting voice, was organized to counteract negative publicity about her husband. "I wanted something good since all you ever hear is bad." The judge ruled Kerrie was entitled to keep anything she could prove she had purchased.

Jerry Lee's possessions, about 350 items in all, were piled up in the main room of the auction house. I was there when Kerrie arrived to inspect them.

"This is my life," she says, motioning to the enormous pile of household items, all numbered and neatly boxed. There was a look of disbelief on her face. "These are the things I've bought and collected in ten years of marriage. It's everything I've got."

261

A female IRS agent looking through a box of items picked up a tiny automobile and examined it.

"Oh," gasps Kerrie. "Could I have that for Lee to play with on the plane?"

The IRS agent relinquished the toy, but not before contacting IRS headquarters in Washington, D.C. to have a release form faxed to the auction house.

By March 1994, lawyers representing Jerry Lee reached an agreement with the IRS. The Killer ended his exile in Ireland and came home. Kerrie had accepted an award from Irish officials before leaving. They had never received anything like that in America, she said, adding that if they ever did, the IRS would probably impound it. Jerry Lee still owed the IRS money, but the government agreed to return some of his possessions and give him an opportunity to pay off the tab. The IRS was probably influenced by a recording contract offered from Sire/Elektra Records. The resulting album, titled *Young Blood*, was released in May 1995.

The Killer, the most relentless Horseman in the pack, was back, strong as ever. I was glad. For all his excesses, for all his problems and self-inflicted wounds, for all his bravado and arrogance and dancing eyes, he is the best rock 'n' roll piano player the world has ever known.

*   *   *

Memphis In May is the city's showcase festival. It is a month-long affair that celebrates a different country each year. Toward the end of the month, the festival culminates with a concert that features dozens of big-name blues and rock artists. The honored country for 1993 was Russia. Not all Memphians were happy with the choice—there were rumblings of displeasure from the political right—but most Memphians were eager to learn more about Russia.

Memphis In May officials asked if I could book a Russian band for the festival. I considered Mister Twister until I learned from Erkin that Galaxy was recording in New York under a new name, Red Rage. In Moscow, the band had sold an unprecedented 1.2 million albums. Erkin said the earlier deal with Podolor had fallen through and they were working with a New York production

262

company. The band did not have a work visa and could not be compensated for their performance, but they agreed to perform in exchange for transportation and expenses. Erkin told me the band members were getting stir crazy in Brighton Beach and were eager to get out of town.

When they arrived at the Memphis airport, I was there to greet them, along with van drivers for Memphis In May. After two years of telephone conversations, it was my first face-to-face meeting with Erkin. Physically, he was the opposite of what I had envisioned. He had dark hair and a full beard. He didn't look like the Russians you saw in James Bond movies. He more accurately resembled the rugged mountain fighters we came to known in subsequent years during the war in Afghanistan. It was nice to finally match a face to a voice. With him, to my delight, was Ovanes and his lovely wife and their 19-year-old daughter. They had flown in from Moscow to attend the festival. Five band members and a brooding delegation from Ovanes's Brighton Beach organization rounded out the group.

Ovanes fascinated me. He was heavy set, with his dark, thinning hair pulled back into a ponytail; he was probably in his mid-forties. He began as a record producer, at a time when it was a rarity, and through the years had developed a Quincy Jones-type of reputation. After the second revolution, when the walls of communism toppled, Ovanes became an entrepreneur. He took advantage of the changing economics of Russia to become a world-class trader of consumer goods. Erkin told me Ovanes was a millionaire many times over.

Moscow Rock Organization had several bands and solo artists on its roster; I was told I could represent any of them I wished. I considered the possibility of using Memphis as a headquarters for new Russian talent. Red Rage performed on both days of the festival. It was hot and the band members were miserable, but they gave a solid performance and the crowd loved their high-energy act. Because none of the band members spoke English, all communications with the sound crew had to go through Ovanes or Erkin. That created some interesting moments when problems arose and Russian words flew thick as Mississippi mud over the heads of the American crew.

I particularly liked Slava Sintchouk, the lead vocalist. He had given up a career as a boxer for rock 'n' roll. He was well over six-feet tall, weighed about 220, and, on stage, showed the aggressive posturing of a boxer. Before joining Red Rage, Oleg Hovrin, the drummer, played drums in a folk group while serving in the Red Army in East Germany. Guitarist Dmitri Sharayev was a top-ranked session player in Moscow. All the band members had long, shoulder-length hair, like their American counterparts, and they constantly asked me the same question: "Where's the women?"

Everyone in the group was outgoing, with the exception of the Brighton Beach delegation. They remained in the background and complained about the heat. I stayed with the group when they performed and traveled with them in the Memphis in May van from the hotel to the festival grounds. All the van drivers were local volunteers, and, as the trips back and forth increased, I noticed more of the drivers were female.

One perky young driver sent a hormonal tremor through the van when she turned around and asked, in that syrupy voice indigenous to Southern womanhood, "Honey, how do you say fuck in Russian?"

* * *

During the early nineties, a number of hard-rock groups, including Tora Tora and Roxy Blue, were signed in Memphis by major labels. For a while, they benefited from the same level of hype Jimmy Davis had enjoyed a few years earlier.

"There are a lot of people in Memphis getting record deals right now—and that's great they are—but that doesn't mean anything," Jimmy says. "It took us six months to get a deal, and two and a half years to get out of it."

The excitement generated in the early 1990s was short lived. By 1995, Tora Tora and Roxy Blue had faded into obscurity, with neither group ever scoring a hit. When I called Tora Tora's label in 1995 to inquire about new product, they said, who's Tora Tora? Roxy Blue, signed in 1992 by Geffen Records, received the biggest send up of any band in recent memory. With Motley Crue's management and Guns 'N Roses' producer, Mike Clink, backing them, Roxy Blue was on its way to the "Big Time," or so the music critics said. When I called Geffen in 1995 for an update, they said the group was no longer on the roster.

As the century drew to a close, the proud and musically explosive Memphis music dynasty seemed in the final stages of rigor mortis. Thankfully, three heavyweights—Jim Stewart, Bobby Manuel, and Jim Dickinson—were still there trying to breathe new life into the city's music scene. Dickinson almost threw in the towel in 1992, after going to New York to produce the Spin Doctors's second album, *Turn It Upside Down*. He completed the project, returned to Memphis, and then learned the group's label remixed the entire album, erasing all of his work. Jim's reaction was understandable: He went into his room, closed the door, and didn't come out for two years. But Jim had music in his blood. By 1995, he was again poking and prodding Memphis's musical crevices, looking for lost knowledge.

Bobby Manuel is the last Memphis producer to score a No. 1 record, and the fact three decades have elapsed since that hit has not discouraged him from trying for another. My guess is that if he stays healthy, he'll eventually get it. Music is not a part-time job for him. He's at it seven days a week. Same situation with Jim Stewart. On any given day, you can find him working in the studio, usually with a black artist, recording new material for the R&B charts. In 1989, he produced an album for Shirley Brown, *Fire & Ice*, that did well on the R&B charts. Subsequently, he began experimenting with soulful rap variations.

"I have to believe I can make something happen," Stewart says. "This town has been operating on finding a deal for the last ten years. I'm so sick of that word. It's talent . . . it's music. It's not a get rich quick business. It's a get poor business. You can get poor quicker than you can get rich."

Jim doesn't like to look back. When he talks about Stax, he does so as if peering through the reverse end of a telescope. He likes to keep his distance. When he assesses blame, he spreads it around. Still, you get the feeling all is not forgiven.

"Everyone ran for cover and got in some blows of their own to help push it under," he says. "Then they realized later, wait a minute, we've lost something. But it was too late then."

Today the two largest music related industries in Memphis are Graceland and a dozen or so topless nightclubs. Graceland has become one of the most popular tourist attractions in America, so it's not surprising that the biggest music event of the decade was the mammoth Elvis Tribute Concert held at the Pyramid in 1994. Sponsored by Graceland, it attracted scores of artists, from Michael Bolton to Cheap Trick to Tony Bennett. The highlight of the evening was an appearance by Lisa Marie and Michael, an event so bizarre and inappropriate it seemed symbolic not only of the current state of Memphis music, but of its tortured past.

Tax receipts show that the topless clubs are second only to Graceland in tourism dollars generated. Though the clubs do not offer live music, as the clubs did on Beale Street in the early days, they have assumed the same roles. When out-of-town recording artists visit Memphis, they sometimes go by Graceland, but they always go by the topless clubs. They hang out there after their shows and they date the women who work in the clubs. It is one of the main reasons women work in the clubs. Sometimes the bands party at the clubs. Sometimes they invite the girls to late-night parties at their hotels.

Tiffany's was a favorite after-hours hangout for musicians. Guns 'N Roses went by after a concert one night, but Axl Rose left in a huff when a dancer walking down a crowded aisle brushed against him. He had given strict orders that no one could touch him. The other band members stayed. Metallica is another band that frequents the club. Same goes for ZZ Top. One night former Black Oak Arkansas lead singer Jim "Dandy" Mangrum celebrated his birthday on the main stage at Tiffany's.

The clubs are the main drawing card for musicians who come to Memphis, just as the clubs on Beale Street were the main drawing cards in years past. They are the closest thing left to a music scene. The most significant change over the years is that while the female entertainers in the old days were exclusively black, today they are almost exclusively white.

City officials understand the importance of the clubs to tourism, explained Tiffany's owner Steve Cooper, but they won't admit it for fear of voters' wrath. He explained: "It's a good ole dog for the politicians to pick on. I don't blame them from the standpoint it keeps them in office. It helps bring in the votes of the 50-to-60 year olds. The closer you get to meeting God, the closer you come to voting to put (the clubs) out of business."

*   *   *

When the blues were hot, the performers were young and vibrant. With time, they aged—and their music aged—and eventually their music was replaced by rock 'n' roll. Today we are seeing the same phenomenon with rock. The Rolling Stones are in the same situation Louis Armstrong was in the late 1950s: Old men playing a young man's music. Nothing new in rock 'n' roll has been created in American music since the early days at Sun Records. Of course, youth will find a replacement for rock 'n' roll, just as they did for blues and jazz. Maybe they'll find it in Memphis. Maybe not.

As the century drew to a close, Memphis had spun full circle. Once again, it had one of the highest murder rates in the country. Tourists were routinely shot and robbed on Beale Street, as they were in the early 1900s. Drug addiction was soaring. Organized crime in the city was stronger than ever. The crime rate, at times, seemed overwhelming. Within the past few years, a FBI agent and a DEA based in Memphis have been convicted of drug trafficking. A 1995 investigation by *The Commercial Appeal* found 68 convicted felons working in the city school system, with 1,500 other workers with convictions ranging from patronizing prostitution to drug possession.

In July 1995, seven members of a Columbian drug hit team were arrested in Memphis on charges they conspired to murder several of the city's major drug dealers. Federal authorities said the men were sent by way of New York by the Cali cartel to collect up to $5 million in unpaid debts. William Renton, the agent in charge of the DEA office in Memphis, said the arrests proved Memphis had become a market of choice for the Cali cartel. All that was missing in Memphis in the 1990s was another Boss Crump.

*   *   *

As so many had done before me, in 1994 I loaded up a truck with my possessions and headed east to Nashville. I left behind a handful of friends and a pair of burned-out dreams. Looking in my rear-view mirror, I surveyed the skyline one last time. I hoped someone would remember to turn out the lights. *A woman clothed with the sun, the moon beneath her feet.* Yes, I now understood. Even the Four Horsemen knew when to ride with the wind.

Once I got settled in Nashville, I gave Chips a call. We talked about getting together, but it was a year before I actually made it out to his farm. I called in the spring of 1995. Toni answered the phone and said Chips didn't live at the house anymore. They were getting a divorce. He had built a studio out on the farm and was living at the studio. She gave me his number.

Chips told me to come on out. He'd like to see me.

He wasn't there when I arrived, but Monique and her boyfriend, Kim, were at the studio, along with Rivers Catledge, a talented singer/songwriter Chips had discovered in Memphis. Chips had been working with Rivers. I had only been there a few minutes when Chips drove up. It was good to see him again. Though I had talked to him several times over the years, I had only seen him once since he left Memphis. He looked older, somewhat tired, but he still had the old Moman magic about him. It is said actor Robert Duvall, with whom Chips once worked on an album, used Chips as a model for characters he subsequently portrayed in movies. I believe that because I see many of Chips's mannerisms in the character Duvall depicted in *Lonesome Dove*.

Chips played me the material he had been recording on Rivers, plus some things he had recorded with Monique. Other than working with family and friends, he didn't want to make any more records. Music wasn't fun anymore.

Monique went to the store and came back with a mess of ground beef. We cooked out on the grill, talked about the weather and some of the good times we had in Memphis, but we danced around the nightmare part of it.

"I took everything they threw at me," Chips says, shaking his head.

Indeed, he had. Chips was as surely a victim of the Memphis curse, as Elvis and Stax had been—and Lord knows how many innocent passersby—but he was just as much a victim of his own fierce attraction to the musical cauldron that had simmered for nearly a century. It was that witch's brew that has made Memphis unique.

While I was at the farm, Casey came in from school. He had grown into a handsome young man. He has his mother's face and his father's walk. He wants a career in music, but Memphis is a subject he won't discuss. He tossed his school books into a chair, ready for his dad to crank up the studio.

What are we waiting for, his glances asked?

Before I left, Chips and I went for a drive in my Miata. Chips had owned a Triumph in the early days in Memphis. He wanted to see if the Miata drove like his Triumph. We sped up and down the hilly countryside with the top down, Chips pushing the car to the max, zipping past the farms and dirt roads, making the gearbox whine, skating around the curves. The cool, spring wind whipped against our faces. The sun shone brightly. Time stood still. It was a good way to end a day.

I never saw Chips again. He moved to Georgia, where he remarried and found peace of sorts on a farm near where he grew up. He is one of the most interesting people I ever met, and I will always consider him a friend.

*   *   *

In September 1989, Scotty Moore ran into Carl Perkins at a Music Row party honoring Carl for a No. 1 song he had co-written for the Judds. They sat out on the porch for a while, talking mostly about growing up in West Tennessee. Eventually, their conversation turned to music. Carl pointed out that he and Scotty had never recorded together. Scotty acknowledged that oversight, but anticipating Carl's next question he quickly added that it had been so long since he had played guitar that he wasn't sure if he would remember how.

Carl laughed, saying, "It's just like falling off a bicycle—you never forget how."

Scotty said he would think about it, which if you know Scotty, you know that means no. However, shortly after that meeting Carl was diagnosed with throat cancer, the treatment for which made it difficult for him to do vocals. In an effort to encourage him, Scotty told they would record that album as soon as he beat his cancer.

Carl said that if he couldn't sing again he didn't know if he wanted to beat cancer.

Early in 1992, Scotty received a call from Carl. He said his doctors had given him a clean bill of health. That March, Scotty went to Carl's home in Jackson, Tennessee, to discuss their long-planned album. They decided to return to Memphis and record the album at the old Sun Records studio, which had recently reopened for recording sessions.

They did three sessions at the studio, recording remakes of "Blue Suede Shoes," "Mystery Train," and other old favorites. Despite Carl's insistence that he had beat cancer, he had lost a lot of weight and did not appear to be in good health. Nonetheless he hung in there. The album was titled *706 ReUnion: A Sentimental Journey* and released on Scotty's Belle Meade Records.

On July 4, 1995, Carl, D. J. Fontana, and Scotty performed at the third annual "American Roots" concert at the Washington Monument. Organized by the National Park Service and the National Council for the Traditional Arts, the event took place in the pouring rain, creating a challenge for the stage hands who worked valiantly to protect the equipment. It was one of Carl's last performances. Three years later, he succumbed to throat cancer at the age of sixty-six. If there is ever a Mount Rushmore of rock 'n' roll legends, Carl deserves a prime location on the mountain.

Scotty Moore, c. mid-1990s
Photo © James L. Dickerson

271

Justin Timberlake
Photofest

CHAPTER 14

The 2000's:
More of the Same, But Without the Hits

The turn of the century brought even more misery to the Memphis music scene. Rap and hip-hop groups surfaced from time to time with hits of short duration, but the city never again became a Mecca for urban music. Bobby Manuel, despite suffering a heart attack, and Jim Stewart both continued their efforts to mine gold from hi-hop but nothing of substance ever hit big, not so much their fault as a shift in the earth's musical crust.

Memphis's immense talent well finally ran dry.

The only Memphian who could be considered a hit-maker was Justin Timberlake. Born in 1981, during the Death Valley Days of Memphis music, he grew up in a small community between Memphis and Millington, just up the road from American Sound Studio, where so many hits had been recorded. His first instincts were to make a name for himself in country music.

When that effort fizzled, he joined the cast of The Mickey Mouse Club, where he worked during 1993 and 1994 with cast mates Britney Spears, Christina Aguilera, and future actor Ryan Gosling. That led to an invitation to join a pop group named 'N Sync. Not until 2002 did he make a name for himself with a solo album. Titled *Justified,* the album sold more than seven million units worldwide and established him as a major talent in his own right. Of course, by that point he was so removed from Memphis music that the connection was tenuous at best.

In the 2000s, all the news was of the bad variety.

Rufus Thomas died in 2001
Johnny Cash and June Carter Cash both died in 2003
Sam Phillips died in 2003.
Estelle Axton died in 2004.
Atlantic Records founder Ahmet Ertgun died in 2006.
Jim Dickinson died in 2009.
Willie Mitchell died in 2010.

Alex Chilton died in 2010.
Pinetop Perkins died in 2011
Duck Dunn died in 2012.
Andrew Love of the Memphis Horns died in 2012.
CBS Records/Nashville chief Rick Blackburn died in 2012

Of the above deaths, it was the passing of Johnny and June that touched me the most. I hit it off with both of them almost immediately and felt a special kinship with Johnny. I did not understand why until years later, when I discovered that Johnny had been a kindred spirit on the subject of the Vietnam War and was supportive of my position against the war.

But it was Estelle Axton's passing that brought me the most grief. That was because I had unfinished business with her. In 1998 I attended a book signing in Memphis with Scotty Moore, ostensibly to promote our book *That's Alright, Elvis*, but also to draw attention to Memphis music in general. I spoke to her several weeks before the signing and invited her to sit at the table with us and sign autographs, but she said she did not know if she could get away from her job as a cashier at a local restaurant. I never heard back from her and figured that her schedule would not allow her to attend.

When Scotty and I arrived at the signing there were several people gathered off to the side, one of them a nice-looking older lady. She smiled and I smiled back. For some reason, I did not recognize Estelle—it had been a while since I last interviewed her—and by the time it dawned on me that the mystery lady was Estelle, she was gone.

I later telephoned to apologize, but she did not answer. Several additional attempts over the next few months failed to connect. It breaks my heart that I invited her and then did not recognize her. It must have seemed like the ultimate rejection. If I am lucky enough to make it to Heaven, I know she will be there waiting for me, hands on hips, jaw set just so, prepared to have a word or two with me about that unpardonable oversight.

Jim Dickinson's passing also affected me. I first met him in the mid-1980s, when I was writing editorials about the Memphis music industry for *The Commercial Appeal*. From the moment he stepped into my office, Jim impressed me as someone to be reckoned with. He was irreverent, opinionated, and prone to exaggeration, but those are qualities any self-respecting writer reveres in an interviewee.

When I suggested to Jim in the mid-1980s that Memphis music was dead, he quickly objected: "Oh, no, it's not dead. It's alive everywhere on Earth but here. Here it's at home watching television." He went on to say: "The Memphis Sound was produced by a handful of men in a dark studio in the middle of the night. It wasn't produced by committees, bankers or disk jockeys . . . It is a thankless, unrewarding business until you get a hit and then it all changes."

After that first meeting at the newspaper, we became friends and I returned to him whenever I wanted a thoughtful opinion on the disheveled state of music. The running joke that we had with each other was that we each received the other person's death threats because of the similarity of our names. Those threatening conversations usually ended apologetically with, "Sorry, man. Thought you were someone else!"

We laughed. But not without glancing over our shoulders. Memphis had made some beautiful music, but its reputation for most of the 20th Century was as the "murder capital of America." Paraphrasing bluesman Sleepy John Estes, Jim called the city "the center of all evil in the known universe." Maybe that was why he made his home in Mississippi and commuted to Memphis whenever he had a paying gig.

Jim died of complications following heart surgery. About Memphis music, he once said, "I think you can feel [it] when it's there. I'm not sure you can define it, but you can certainly hear it and feel it."

So it is with his own music. Jim is gone, but his work endures.

The Memphis musical dynasty did not end with a bang. It ended with a soulful whimper, the way a soundtrack slowly fades, fainter and fainter, until there is only nothingness, leaving behind regrets, faded memories, promises unfilled, and the sound of footsteps trailing off into the night.

NUMBER ONE POP RECORDS RECORDED IN MEMPHIS
BY MEMPHIS ARTISTS OR FOR MEMPHIS LABELS

SONG	ARTIST	PRODUCER	LABEL	DATE
1) The Letter	The Box Tops	Dan Penn	Mala	1967
2) Dock of the Bay	Otis Redding	Steve Cropper	Volt	1968
3) Suspicious Minds	Elvis Presley	Chips Moman	RCA	1969
4) Theme From Shaft	Isaac Hayes	Isaac Hayes	Enterprise	1971
5) Let's Stay Together	Al Green	Willie Mitchell	Hi	1972
6) I 'll Take You There	Staple Singers	Al Bell	Stax	1972
7) Disco Duck	Rick Dees	Bobby Manuel	Fretone	1976

Source: Billboard Book of Number One Hits

(Note: Contrary to popular belief, Memphis did not
score a No. 1 pop hit until 1967 and there have been no
No. 1 hits since 1976. The No. 1 hits Elvis recorded
prior to 1969 were all done in Nashville with Nashville
musicians. Of course, between 1956 and the present,
hundreds of records recorded in Memphis charted
below No. 1.)

Bibliography

BOOKS

Booth, Stanley. *Rhythm Oil.* New York: Pantheon Books, 1991.

Brown, Peter and Steven Gaines. *The Love You Make: An Insider's Story of the Beatles.* New York: McGraw-Hill, 1983.

Carlin, Richard. *Rock and Roll: 1955-1970.* New York: Facts On File, 1988.

Chase, Gilbert. *America's Music: From the Pilgrams to the Present.* New York: McGraw-Hill, 1955.

Collier, James Lincoln. *Louis Armstrong: An American Genius.* New York: Oxford University Press, 1983.

Dickerson, Jim. *Coming Home: 21 Conversations About Memphis Music.* Memphis: Scripps Howard, 1985.

Garon, Beth and Paul. *Woman With Guitar: Memphis Minnie's Blues.* New York: Da Capo Press, 1992.

Guralnick, Peter. *Sweet Soul Music: Rhythm and Blues and the Southern Dream of Freedom.* New York: Harper & Row, 1986.

Guralnick, Peter. *Last Train To Memphis: The Rise Of Elvis Presley.* Boston: Little Brown, 1994.

Handy, W.C. *Father of the Blues: An Autobiography.* New York: Da Capo Press, 1941.

Harkins, John E. *Metropolis of the American Nile.* Oxford, Mississippi: The Guild Bindery Press, 1991.

Haskins, James. *Voodoo & Hoodoo: Their Tradition and Craft as Revealed by Actual Practitioners* Chelsea, Mich.: Scarborough House, 1990.

Herzhaft, Gerard. *Encyclopedia of the Blues.* Fayetteville, Arkansas: The

University of Arkansas Press, 1992.

Key, Jr., V.O. *Southern Politics*. New York: Random House, 1949.

Lee, George W. *Beale Street: Where the Blues Began*. College Park, Maryland: McGrath Publishing Co., 1969.

McAleer, Dave. *Hit Singles: Top Twenty Charts from 1954 to the Present Day*. San Francisco, Calif.: Miller Freeman Books, 1994.

Miller, William D. *Memphis During the Progressive Era*. Memphis: Memphis State University Press, 1957.

Muirhead, Bert. *The Record Producers File*. Dorset, UK: Blandford Press, 1984.

Murphy, Bruce Allen. *Fortas: The Rise and Ruin of a Supreme Court Justice*. New York: Morrow, 1988.

Panassie, Hugues. *Louis Armstrong*. New York: Da Capo Press, 1979.

Parker, John. *Elvis: The Secret Files*. London: Anaya Publishers, 1993.

President's Commission on Organized Crime. *Organized Crime and Cocaine Trafficking: Record of Hearing IV*. Washington, D.C. 1994.

Schuller, Gunther. *Early Jazz: Its Roots and Musical Development*. New York: Oxford University Press.

Shaw, Arnold. *Dictionary of American Pop/Rock*. New York: Schirmer Books, 1982.

Swados, Harvey. *Standing Up for the People: The Life and Work of Estes Kefauver*. New York: E.P. Dutton, 1972.

Taylor, Frank. C. *Alberta Hunter: A Celebration in Blues*. New York: McGraw-Hill, 1987.

Tucker, David M. *Memphis Since Crump: Bossism, Blacks and Civic Reformers*. Knoxville: University of Tennessee Press, 1980.

Whitburn, Joel. *Billboard Top 1000 Singles (1955-1992)*. Milwaukee:

Hal Leonard Publishing Corp., 1993.

Wilson, Charles Reagan and William Ferris. *Encyclopedia of Southern Culture*. Chapel Hill: The University of North Carolina Press, 1989.

ARTICLES

Baldwin, Dawn. "Memphis Rocker: A Soft Touch for Romance." *Nine-O-One Network*. July/August, 1987.

---------------- "The Main Attraction." *Nine-O-One Network*. Nov./Dec., 1986.

---------------- "Inside the U2/Sun Studio Sessions. *Memphis Star*. Dec., 1987.

Dickerson, James. "901 Interview with Robert Pittman." *Nine-O-One Network*. July/August, 1987.

------------------ "B. B. King." *Nine-O-One Network*. December 1987.

------------------ "Memphis Women Rockers." *Nine-O-One Network*. Jan./Feb., 1987.

------------------ "Perkins & Friends." *Nine-O-One Network*. July/August, 1986.

------------------ "Portraits/Don Nix." *Nine-O-One Network*. December, 1987.

------------------ "The Lady Wants to Rock & Roll, Now!" *Nine-O-One Network*. Nov./Dec., 1986.

------------------ "The Fabulous Thunderbirds Get a Memphis Groove." *Nine-O-One Network*. May/June, 1987.

------------------ "Together Again." *Nine-O-One Network*. Nov./Dec., 1986.

------------------ "901 Interview with Gregg Geller." *Nine-O-One Network*. March/April, 1987.

279

------------------ "901 Interview with Ron Wood." *Nine-O-One Network.* Sept./Oct. 1986.

------------------ 901 Interview with Michael Barackman and Dick Williams." *Nine-O-One Network.* Nov./Dec., 1986.

------------------ "Fabulous Thunderbirds: Texas Band Toughs it Out to the Top." *Nine-O-One Network.* Sept./Oct. 1986.

King, Larry L. "Everybody's Louie." *Harper's.* November, 1967/

Landers, A.L. "Latest Styles, Fall and Winter, 1913-1914." *Ell Jay Garments.* Shelbyville, Tennessee.

Randall, Nancy. "The Men Who Shot Elvis." *Nine-O-One Network.* July/August, 1987.

---------------- "Elvis." *Nine-O-One Network.* July/August, 1987.

---------------- "Where Are They Now?" *Nine-O-One Network.* October, 1987.

---------------- "Survivor's Jimi Jamison." *Nine-O-One Network.* October, 1987.

---------------- "Sexual Harassment." *Nine-O-One Network.* February, 1988.

---------------- "John Kilzer." *Nine-O-One Network.* February, 1988.

---------------- "Elvis -- The Memory Lives ..." *Nine-O-One Network.* December, 1987.

Stuart, Bill. "Otis Redding." *Nine-O-One Network.* February, 1988.

----------- "Wearing the Label." *Nine-O-One Network.* October, 1987.

White, Owen P. "Sinners in Dixie." *Collier's.* January 26, 1935.

CPSIA information can be obtained at www.ICGtesting.com
Printed in the USA
BVOW021407210313

316142BV00008B/140/P

9 780985 885281